Born in 1948 in the Midlands, following a grammar school education, J. R. Hutt followed her passion for horses. Working and travelling as a groom throughout Europe and Canada, culminating in running her own business in the Cotswolds, she moved to Spain and married in 1983 where she continued riding and competing, taught English and had two children. She also lived in Iraq and Turkey, but is currently living in England, with frequent visits to Spain and Canada, to see her family. She came to England to care for her mother, which gave her the opportunity to resume writing and painting, both of which she had enjoyed in her youth.

To my mother and father, with thanks, for allowing me to follow my dream.

J. R. Hutt

EQUINE FEVER

For Lesley
A horse lover like myself!
love
Judy
x

AUSTIN MACAULEY PUBLISHERS™
LONDON * CAMBRIDGE * NEW YORK * SHARJAH

A CIP catalogue record for this title is available from the British Library.

ISBN 9781398408432 (Paperback)
ISBN 9781398408449 (ePub e-book)

www.austinmacauley.com

First Published 2021
Austin Macauley Publishers Ltd®
1 Canada Square
Canary Wharf
London
E14 5AA

Thanks to my family; my mother, Carlos, Ana and Carlitos for their patience, encouragement, and support.

Thanks to Diego Pastor, for his help with the cover image and to Annemarie Wright, for her unfailing enthusiasm.

Thank you too, to friends, Jean Jameson and John Greenaway, for their constructive criticism and helpful suggestions.

Thanks too, to all those mentioned in the book, with apologies for any deviations or errors as it was all recounted from memory.

Synopsis

EQUINE FEVER tells the tale of a small girl who is passionate about horses. I am that small girl and determined to spend my life with them albeit working as a humble girl groom. The work is, at times, arduous and the hours are long, but this does not deter me or diminish my passion for horses. I am neither rich nor famous but have had the good fortune to brush up against, observe at close quarters and learn from some of the world's most talented equine experts.

My work takes me to many parts of England and Ireland, and I travel Europe with a show jumping team. I work in Canada, travelling from East to West, exploring the United States and become involved in the Montreal Olympics. I travel with horses by road, rail and air and work with horses in all climates from 30 degrees below zero to 40 degrees in the shade. I care for horses of all shapes, sizes, abilities and temperaments.

The work is 24/7, a way of life which leads to amazing travel and adventure, but above all, the wonderful relationships I develop with my four-legged friends on the way.

Chapter 1
Early Days

A love of travelling and a passion for horses are innate qualities which prove perfectly compatible and can develop from a very early age. This tale begins in a humble semi-detached house in the pleasant suburb of a not-so-pleasant industrial city.

My mother is a young, attractive, intelligent woman. She wipes her brow, pays the greengrocer and stoops to pick up the heavy bags full of fresh fruit and vegetables. She carries them through the garden gate, down the garden path and into the house. The greengrocer delivers fresh produce every Tuesday with Daisy, his old mare, and their little flat cart. Daisy is a bay cob, she has feathered heels a rather large head with a short neck and scraggy mane and tail, but she is good-natured, has a kind eye and knows her job. Pete the greengrocer doesn't have to pick up reins or whip, with a simple "Come on, old girl" and later "Woah, Daisy" they make their rounds together at a gentle pace.

Having deposited the bags on the kitchen table, my mother looks around and to her consternation, her small daughter is nowhere to be seen. She lets out a gasp and runs back to the road, sure enough, her three-year-old has followed Daisy down the road and is standing between her front legs attempting to reach up and hug her. I am that wayward child and Pete comes to the rescue lifting me up so I can throw my arms round Daisy's neck in sheer delight.

"Don't fret Ma'am, Daisy won't do her no harm," grins Pete, highly amused, but my mother is far from amused, she is terrified of horses and scoops me up torn between thanking Pete and scolding her small daughter who is writhing and protesting at being separated from the beloved Daisy. I fall passionately in love with Daisy from the moment I set eyes on her. Those large, brown, eyes and gentle gaze penetrate my very soul and make my heart thump with joy. I love the feel of her coat, her muzzle is as soft as velvet and I crave that musty, horsey aroma, which my poor mother finds so unpleasant.

We go to Llandudno for our summer holiday, the idea being to explore North Wales and beautiful Snowdonia. However, on leaving our lodgings on the first morning, lo and behold, there are five beautiful donkeys on the beach. I clap my hands and my heart pounds. I grab my father's trouser leg and drag him in the direction of the donkeys. He is amused, being kind and rather soft with his daughter. Thus, he relents allowing me to have a short ride, despite his wife's objections that I am too small. That first ride is sheer bliss until it is time to dismount, which produces wails of protest and tears. How can a family holiday be conditioned by such a small child? I am usually quiet, well-behaved and rather shy, but when there is an equine in sight, I change radically into a passionate, determined little monster to my parents' utter dismay.

Later at school, I daydream about horses, doodle horses in the margins of all my schoolbooks, manage to include horses in artwork, projects and even mathematical problems, biology, history, essays, poetry, in fact, wherever possible. I make a beautiful card-board model of a stable yard, comprising of four loose boxes, tack room, feed room and hay loft. I paint it white with black beams, Elizabethan style. With my horse-mad friends, we form horses with our hands and jump courses made from pencil-cases, books, cups, straws, any available object. School desks and kitchen tables serve as jumping and dressage arenas. Outside in playgrounds, parks, and gardens we create international arenas and become world champions, winning cups and rosettes lovingly made from cardboard. We canter round to show them off in the lap of honour and later hang them proudly in the cardboard tack-room. We are happy and spend hours and hours engrossed in our horse games. This normally keeps us out of mischief, only occasionally we are caught scrumping apples from the neighbour's garden, to feed to the imaginary horses, of course.

Some fortunate friends are allowed riding lessons, and I begin to beg and plead. I am quiet but persistent. Lynne, the daughter of some friends of my parents owns a pony, a sweet chestnut mare called LADY, but Lynne and her sister, Judy, are not remotely interested in horses. How unfair, Lynne has her hair permed and wears jewellery and pretty dresses, which I find boring and even obnoxious, to my mother's chagrin. My poor mother would love to share her love of fashion with her daughter, but it is hopeless, I am a complete tomboy. Finally, when I am seven, my desperate parents relent and we negotiate a deal, one riding lesson per fortnight and no presents for birthday or Christmas. Although I happily agree, when it comes to the crunch the agreement is waivered slightly, although most gifts are inevitably horse-related.

What bliss, my first ride is on a small, albino pony called BISCUIT. He has red eyes, a pink muzzle and a long, wavy mane and tail, it is love at first sight. The riding school is a humble affair belonging to Miss Perkins, a lady who works in the same office as my mother. Miss Perkins owns eleven horses and ponies and takes bookings evenings and weekends. Most of the riding is on the roads and the beginners are taken on a leading rein either from another horse or a bicycle. It is a risky affair and frequently there are accidents when someone falls off and a pony runs loose down the road, or a motor bike or lorry come round a bend too fast, fortunately I am blissfully unaware of the dangers. Miss Perkins asks my mother if I really enjoyed riding, as I rarely speak and make little progress, I simply go into a trance when on the pony. My mother assures her that I live for my riding, which is wonderful for them, as the mere mention of not going riding spurs me into doing my chores and homework with lightning speed and enthusiasm previously unknown. As my sole topic of conversation is the wonderful BISCUIT my grandfather is curious and decides to accompany us and meet this creature that has made such an impression on his granddaughter. Unfortunately, although BISCUIT has all the patience in the world with children, he hates men with a passion. Before Miss Perkins can intervene, BISCUIT rolls his red eyes, menacingly showing the whites. He lays his little ears back flat on his neck opens his mouth and lunges towards my unfortunate grandfather. His teeth contact Grandpa's well-padded tummy, luckily, he is wearing a thick green jumper and more damage is done to the jumper than its owner. My grandfather politely refuses to watch me ride again, furthermore he joins ranks with my mother and they do their utmost to dissuade me from pursuing such a dangerous sport but all in vain.

Having learned the basic aids for steering, stopping, starting, rising trot and changing diagonals at last it is time to canter. Cantering is so much more comfortable than the bouncy trot and with the wind in my face I feel we are flying. We are cantering along a grass verge and all goes well until BISCUIT gives a huge leap over a small drainage channel. I fly ungracefully over his ears and unfortunately land on the hard tarmac. I graze the whole of the side of my face which looks rather spectacular although it is only superficial. BISCUIT stops when the others pull up and shamefacedly, I climb back into the saddle. The next time I canter I hold a good hunk of his curly mane just in case!

Soon I progress to riding GELERT who is 13:2hh a full hand taller than BISCUIT, he is a black Welsh pony who is a little lazy and apt to give small safe bucks, in fact if you place your hand behind the saddle he always obliges. Although it looks fairly impressive, he carefully maintains his head in the air so it would be almost impossible to fall off. GELERT is fun and with me he is not lazy, so everyone accuses me of having an electric bottom.

Following GELERT, I can ride the three moorland mares, they are all bay with black manes and tails, they have the Exmoor mealy muzzles and are very pretty. First HEATHER who is a lovely ride, she is light, obedient, and reliable, she is a little plump but so steady all the children love her. Later BRACKERN who is younger and still tends to shy at anything strange. I ride her on the lead rein the first few times as she has been recently broken-in, horrible expression "breaking-in," I hate it and protest when people use it. Finally, CRYSTAL who is keen and rather fast, a brighter bay than the other two, at least she never bucks or shies but loves to gallop at the slightest opportunity, not canter, gallop as fast as her little legs will carry her.

At this stage I persuade my father to leave me at the stables for an extra hour to clean the tack and muck out the stables in order to earn an extra ride. The only problem being that I arrive home exhausted and covered in hay, horsehair and mud, so am obliged to strip off in the garden shed before going into the house and then straight to the bathroom! By the age of ten I also go for an hour before my ride to groom and tack up and am promoted to the 14:2hh ponies. The beautiful grey CHLOE, who is a bit flighty, and naughty DUSTY who has a reputation for kicking his colleagues so always goes at the back, a great advantage being you can hold him back and canter to catch up so having far more canters than anyone else! My friend Hilary adores him, so all her doodled horses are chestnut with their ears back and their heels flying.

I then have another fall, this time I am riding CHLOE who is rather nervous, and a very noisy lorry doesn't slow down frightening all the horses. They scatter in all directions, and I literally bite the dust, only it isn't dust it is tarmac and I lose my new front teeth. Unfortunately, I lose my top teeth which were perfectly straight whereas my bottom teeth are horribly crooked. My mother is devastated and announces no more riding, enough is enough. With a swollen face and mass of dental work to be done, I still complain bitterly about this drastic decision. I beg and beg to go riding.

I am so unbearable to live with that my parents eventually relent and after what seems to me like an eternity, but is in fact only a few weeks, I can resume riding. They can't fathom from where this obsession has come, my mother is terrified of horses and has a very sensitive sense of smell, so even the aroma of horses is too much for her. During World War 11 my father had in fact joined the Warwickshire Yeomanry and served with horses in Syria and Iraq before abandoning the horses for tanks which must have been appalling for the horses. He took part in the last mounted charge and fought at El Alemein before coming home via Italy and across Europe. However, he denies any love for, or understanding of horses referring to them as "Long faced bastards".

There is, however, a distant link with horses in the family history, there being a town in New Zealand called "Hutt". Rumour has it that the colony was formed by our ancestors of the same name, who had been deported from England for horse stealing.

Soon I am taking small children for rides on a leading rein and helping to take the horses and ponies back to their fields at the end of the day. We ride bareback with just head-collar and rope then race round the field, so I spend more and more time with the horses and earn more and more rides.

In the summer we have day-rides, we all take a packed lunch in a small canvas saddle bag. We ride all morning to a small pub with a field at the back where we untack the ponies, tie them to the fence then water and feed them. We go into the pub for drinks to accompany the squashed cheese and pickle sandwiches and a bruised apple which I share with my pony. On one such occasion a day ride is planned, but Miss Perkins is not well so she asks me to lead the ride saying she will meet us at the pub at lunch time. I can ride her beautiful strawberry roan mare PETRONELLA who is never ridden by anyone except Miss Perkins. I have ridden her once before to take her to the blacksmith and she is divine. She is very sensitive, one has to sit very still, the slightest contact with the leg and she is flying along, but she is so comfortable and what a treat not to be pushing a lazy pony, holding back a puller or dealing with bucks or shies, just floating along in front. I have been on this day ride many times before, although to be honest I have never taken much notice of the way. However, when I mention that I am not sure of the route Miss Perkins scoffs saying that of course I know the way. Stupidly I am far too shy or maybe stupid to argue with her. More by luck than judgement we find our way there, but on the way back I miss a turning. I cut back down the next available bridle path and we come face to face with the hunt, the field Master screaming at us to get out of the way, causing us to divert yet again and consequently we find ourselves completely off track. By the time I get my bearings it is getting dark, so we trot and canter almost all the way. We are eventually met by an irate Miss Perkins, furious that all the horses are sweating, and it is almost dark, apart from which she has had all the frantic parents to deal with!!

Most summers we go on a two-week riding holiday to Wales, all the horses, ponies, tack, feed, luggage and children pile into a huge lorry. We stay on a farm and ride over the Brecon Hills which is glorious as there are no roads, no motor bikes and no lorries. A bonus being that the farmer has two good looking sons, there is lots of hide and seek in the hay barn, for some of the girls this is a real turning point whereby their passion for four-legged friends is replaced for a keen interest in the two-legged species, but not for me, I am a late developer in all senses of the word. One night my friend Hilary and I are checking the horses last thing in the evening and the boys follow us, so we have our first kiss in the hay-barn. I am not impressed; it is wet and unpleasant, so I play avoiding tactics for the rest of the holiday!

Sadly, following more accidents, Hilary's parents move her to another riding school, whereas I stay with Miss Perkins out of my mother's loyalty to her colleague. Well partly loyalty and partly because Miss Perkins, or Hazel as we now called her, has a very strong character.

Hazel also has a little governess cart and two of ponies are broken to harness, SHEILA a little chestnut mare who is rather old and JOEY a little cobby pony with a docked tail. JOEY must be among the last of the equines to have to undergo this barbaric procedure as it is now illegal. HAZEL uses the governess cart to take water, in old milk churns, to the fields where we fill old tin baths tubs so the horses can drink.

Hazel, now Mrs Brown, decides to buy a horse for her new husband John and off they go to Henley Market. I am taking the rides and at lunch time John rushes back to fetch me and takes me to Henley-in-Arden to ride the new acquisition home. As we drive down the High Street there in the middle of the road is Hazel struggling with the most beautiful horse I have ever seen, let alone ridden, a bay gelding rearing and lunging in a state of great excitement, he is already wearing a saddle and a snaffle bridle. No time to waste, Hazel manages to put the reins back over his head and hang on to him while John gives me a leg up almost throwing me over the other side despite the height of the horse. I hastily fumble for the stirrups which are rather long but no time to worry about such details. Hazel loses the horses head shouting "Just head home!" I hear no more we are flying down the middle of the road at a magnificent extended trot the horse snorting with excitement, I hold a hunk of mane with the rein fixed in one hand working hard with the other to prevent my steed from breaking into a canter.

Fortunately, there is a long steep hill leading out of the village and we settle into the rhythm of a spanking trot. The horse is tireless and keeps up an extraordinary pace for the next few miles. I manage to bring him down to a walk for the last mile home as he is in a lather of sweat from the excitement of this new adventure. DAGWOOD, as the new horse is called, is ridden very little by his new owner but proves to be a perfect lead horse being bold and forward, he is extremely handsome with lots of presence and consequently a delight to ride.

I am even allowed to take him to my first ever show where we enter the Working Hunter class. I painstakingly plait his mane although as it has never been pulled the plaits looked more like bananas than rosettes. When we get to the Show Hazel admits she should have trimmed his mane, tail and whiskers because he is a stunning horse and moves like a dream but looks like a bear out of the field whereas the other horses have been stabled, rugged up and trimmed. I am, however, blissfully unaware of all that and just enjoy the ride, considering we have never even ridden in a circle before, apart from happily cantering on the wrong leg we give quite an impressive show with a super trot and gallop and we fly over the fences. Sadly, John is not really interested in riding and DAGWOOD is too good for the riding school, so they decide to sell him. A gentleman comes to try him as a hunter, we make a few jumps from straw bales and poles in the big 40-acre field. I ride him in walk, trot and canter, pop over the jumps and then give him a good gallop up the long side. The gentleman then rides him, he looks fine but comes back saying the horse is far too strong. I don't understand what he is talking about, I have never had any problem with him, probably because I never try to stop him! So luckily DAGWOOD can stay!

Before long I am virtually running the little riding school because Hazel is having a baby. I deliver the weekly takings to her house on Sunday evenings and report on the horses, clients and the week's activities. One Sunday her husband John sends me up to the bedroom, Hazel is sitting up in bed and beside the bed is a crib inside which there is a small baby. I have never seen a new-born baby before and marvel "Isn't he tiny!" to which Hazel retorts "You wouldn't say that if you had given birth to him!"

My obsession for horses shows no sign of waning, on the contrary, so my father decides to take drastic measures. At a Yeomanry reunion he approaches an old colleague who is a professional horseman. Jack Gittins, a successful dealer and showman, says Bill's horse mad daughter is welcome to stay with him and his family for the school holidays. He assures my father that I will have to work hard from 6 a.m. until 10 p.m. even more so on show days, so it will surely cure me of such nonsense, little do they know!

Of course, I am thrilled at the prospect and more so when I arrive and see the horses. They are nearly all thoroughbreds and show horses, they are stabled and wear rugs, even though it isn't winter this keeps their velvet coats fine, shiny and oh so soft, such a contrast to the muddy hairy horses and ponies I am used to looking after.

The house is a rambling old Cotswold farmhouse with inglenook fireplaces and a huge larder that resembles a cellar. Jack's wife Sheelagh is Irish and utterly charming, although not very practical. That doesn't bother Jack who gets up at 5 a.m. every morning to clean the house and take everyone a cup of tea at 6 a.m. sharp. They have three children and Sheelagh has shown ponies and a hack in another yard in the village. She looks after the children and the yard and she is always calm, in her own little world. I am fascinated to watch her making a beautiful flower arrangement and placing it lovingly on a table covered with an inch of dust! In the larder there is a huge side of beef which looks a little green and a whole stilton which is full of maggots, Jack laughingly digs them out and tells them off, then he pours port into the stilton swearing us to secrecy as the experts would not approve, and he carries on serving! Amazingly no one ever seems to have an upset stomach. My mother would have a hard time living there, cleanliness and hygiene are high on her list, whereas in the Gittins household they are somewhat lacking, however, there is an easy-going charm about the whole setup.

Sheelagh buys a baby donkey for her youngest son who is two years old. The donkey goes everywhere with them, in the back of the car like a dog and even to the swimming pool. The little girl who is two years older has a little Jack Russell terrier who also goes everywhere with her and sleeps in her bed. She awakes one morning saying her bed is wet and lo and behold during the night the bitch has had four puppies in the bed.

Saturday night is steak night and Jack uncorks a bottle of French red wine and stands it in the inglenook fireplace where it becomes rather warmer than room temperature. The wine accompanies the candle lit supper. I am only 12 and too shy to refuse anything, having never drunk wine before I gulp it down and sleep rather well that night. There is also a barrel of Guinness in the larder, this is officially "horse food", the horses also have a measure in their feed, "Wonderful tonic" says Jack, "makes their coats shine too" as does the linseed boiled in a huge pot on the AGA in the kitchen for the horses. At 11 a.m. every morning, everyone is given a glass of Guinness, I find it very bitter and unpleasant, I don't like it at all, but when I politely refuse, I am told it will do me good. Jack says I will need all the energy I can get, so I obediently swallow it like medicine, by the end of the holiday I quite like it!

Once Jack went to the United States to compete in a circuit of shows with a string of horses belonging to Mrs Cardiff, a wealthy client, he rang Guinness and said he needed to take a barrel or two with him and that way he could promote their stout in America, they agreed and supplied him with Guinness for his two-month trip.

Every morning I am rudely awoken by a slap on the backside and a raucous "Come on my girl look sharp, down in five minutes and no breakfast until the horses are all mucked out and fed." I throw on my clothes and rush downstairs, there are three others already their sipping tea. I am told to stick with Jack and learn how they muck out then I will be allotted stables to muck out on my own. It is cold and dark; Jack measures the feeds and the team distributes them simultaneously slipping a head-collar onto each horse and tying them up to make it easier to open the doors and muck out whilst they are happily munching breakfast. What beautiful horses, the horses wear traditional yellow woollen blankets with broad red and blue stripes down the sides as in the old prints of racehorses in their exercise rugs. The blanket is thrown over the horse covering his back and most of his neck, then carefully folded up at the shoulders the day rug is place on top and the blanket turned back at the withers to be held in place with a leather roller which of course has to be cleaned every day! Jack believes in deep litter beds as he says the big horses easily cap their hocks and elbows when the bed is loose, and they ended up lying on concrete. It is certainly quicker and easier, Jack shows me how to remove all the droppings and the wet bedding level the bed from the walls which were nearly always dry and put fresh bedding round forming neat walls and levelling off the centre, some are on straw and some on shavings. At e i g h t o'clock we finish, and the yard is swept as clean as a new pin. We line up the wheelbarrows and hang the forks, shovels, and brooms neatly on the wall in the barn then pulling off our boots pile into the house to the welcoming aroma of bacon!

After a very hearty breakfast we all change into our breeches, or jodhpurs in my case, and head for the tack room. I am allowed to ride a steady cob belonging to an elderly client and later the children's ponies whilst the others ride the show horses, young horses recently broken, and horses being prepared to sell as competition horses. I learn the fundamentals of basic schooling, how to canter on the correct leg, collect and extend the trot and the canter and maintain the correct bend. Jack rides show style with long stirrups and the legs forward to accentuate the horse's shoulder, a "good front" being an essential part of the conformation of a show horse.

The saddles are straight cut for the same reason, but none of your nice knee rolls and comfortable padding of a modern dressage or jumping saddle, they are 'pancake saddles'. It is all too easy to fall off, but Jack says it is important to feel your horse and not just to sit in an armchair, he says that way you pick up more messages from your horse because you feel every muscle he tenses!

The morning is taken up riding, three or four horses each, then after lunch I watch and learn the art of lunging and long-reining youngsters, clipping, trimming and strapping (grooming). There is an electric groomer, it consists of a rotating brush which massages the horses, tones their muscles and leaves them gleaming. I learn to pull manes and tails, bandage and poultice and much more. In the evening the tack must be cleaned and organized, often I stay out in the tack room after the others have gone in for a hot bath and to change for supper. I am painfully shy so prefer talking to the cats in the tack-room. After supper two of us go out to check water, give a late-night feed and skip out (remove any droppings). I always volunteer to accompany them so basically, we work from 6 a.m. to 10 p.m. and on show mornings we often start at 4 a.m. to get the show horses plaited and ready as sometimes we have to leave as early as 6 a.m. to go to Shows all over the country. Well, this "cure" has the opposite effect; I go home from my first working holiday more besotted than ever!

I am fortunate to pass the 13 plus and gain a place at Malvern Hall, the best grammar school in the area. I am not an outstanding student but I fortunately I have a bright friend who helps me on many occasions. This includes getting herself into trouble for interfering which really is unfair as she is merely acting on behalf of, and in defence of, her shy friend. Strangely, Jean is not interested in horses, she is already an aunt and adores children, she is intelligent and outgoing, active in theatre, debating, youth club and parties so at least adds some variety to my life. I realise that if it were not for her influence, I would soon resemble a horse! I even go out with her cousin Richard for a while, he is tall, handsome and good fun but alas I am far too immature to appreciate such good fortune!

In part I follow Jean with her choice of subjects, she chooses to study English, Art and History at A level. Art, I love and happily draw and paint horses and animals of all shapes and sizes in all mediums, whilst Jean depicts beautiful, round, cuddly babies. Mrs Christ our lovely Art Mistress creates in us a lifelong love of Art. I choose Maths instead of English as like my father, I love figures. However, I am hopeless at memorizing data, so History is a disaster, I write long essays most of which are my own elaboration on the few facts I manage to recall, hence page after page is crossed out as irrelevant! I have the misconception that success is based on the effort you make, and I make a huge effort which unfortunately is not reflected in the results! I prefer Maths and Science, sadly I gave up science too early for all the wrong reasons. So, with a mixture of Art and Maths I have not a clue what I want to study, except Veterinary Science for which I do not have the right subjects. My tutor Miss Bullock is all too understanding, she is a real lady and kindness personified. She tells my mother I have been born in the wrong era and am too gentle for this modern world.

My wise father observing my lack of motivation for study as opposed to my tremendous enthusiasm for horses takes a brave line. "So young lady, do you propose to go through University and then work with horses?" he queries peering at me over his spectacles, his quiet but headstrong daughter looks him straight in the eye, "Of course." is my reply. He ponders on the matter for some days consults his wife and his friend Jack and confronts me. "Rather than waste everyone's time and money don't you think it would be better to get a decent qualification for working with horses?" You can imagine the reaction! My father had consulted Jack who, although he thought we were mad, recommended another ex-Yeoman John Tilke who runs The Windmill Hill Riding Academy and prepares students for their British Horse Society Exams which involves a residential course for one year which is both intensive and expensive.

My parents have always refused to buy me a pony or horse saying I can buy my own when I am older. However, as I will be moving away from home, they offer to pay for me to have driving lessons, take my driving test and buy me a second-hand car. The car is a shiny black Morris Minor with the indicators which came out of the sides of the car like ears. It also and a handle to start it! I name her Betsy and she is my pride and joy. I discover a new kind of freedom having previously been everywhere on my bicycle.

At School everyone is buzzing with their future plans, Jean will go on to University as will her new boyfriend from the boys boarding school, some friends are planning to be teachers, other nurses. We meet up with the boys after school and one of them asks me what I am going to do, when I tell him his eyes widen... "The British WHORES Society Exams?" Everyone falls about laughing and I will never live it down.

I spend another holiday with Jack when he gives me advice which stands me in good stead for the rest of my life. He tells me to listen, watch and learn from everyone. He says, "Even the poor and humble have their tale to tell" and this especially applies to country life. People living close to nature have a wonderful knowledge passed down from generation to generation, not to be found in university libraries however complete and advanced they may be. He is a great example of humility personified, he deals with Lords, Ladies and Royalty but he addresses them in the same way as he does the road sweeper or the cleaner, everyone he calls "Governor" with great deference and respect and is loved by all.

Jack tells me that there are so many ways to achieve the same result and as every horse is different you can never have enough resources at your fingertips, so to listen to everyone and never think your way is best, it may be in one case but not in another. Regarding horses he always says sit still and try to understand what your horse is feeling, listen to him and use your head, not brute force. A horse is physically stronger than any man and force and fear may get quick results on the surface, but you will never have that magnificent feeling of working together. Once a horse understands what you are asking of him, he or she is amazingly noble, generous and trusting.

Most problems with horses' stem from mishandling or misunderstanding leading to confusion or fear. Horses have memories like elephants, which means it is extremely difficult to overcome problems arising from a negative past experience. Another unfortunate expression in the horse world is "nagsman", nagging has the same effect on horses as on people they become totally numb and unresponsive or angry. Sit still, think what you need to ask for and ask clearly and politely is Jack's advice, and it has certainly worked for him as he has a fine reputation in the horse world and has trained and ridden hundreds of Champions. Typically of Jack, all of his photographs of famous horses and people he hangs in the downstairs loo!

So, I am to embark on a career with horses I can scarcely believe my luck. There is a required list of equipment, the latest riding hat to be worn always with a hairnet of course, beige gloves for everyday and white ones for dressage, breeches and long leather boots, a rat catcher or tweed jacket, a black jacket, white stock, tie and shirts a cross-country helmet. All very different from my jodhpurs, short boots or rubber boots and faded, brown, velvet, second-hand hat with tissues under the lining so it doesn't fall over my eyes.

I arrive with my parents to the induction day for the coming course, there are about twelve students for this course and very mixed, there is another girl similar to myself, not from a horsey background, and we are allotted a mobile home to share, there are five single flats down in the yard where one of the colonel's daughters Celia, two girls from America and two English girls who would bring their own competition horses are to live. The rest of the students shared mobile homes like Wendy and me. We are shown our allotted rooms and then congregate in the living room of the main house where we meet Mr Tilke's formidable wife and friendly elder daughter Judy.

Mr. Tilke explains we will each be assigned a yard of five loose boxes, we will feed and muck out in the morning before breakfast and be responsible for the grooming and presentation, tack, etc. for our charges. We are to be supervised and guided by himself, his two daughters and the Chief Instructor. All meals will be taken in the main house, after breakfast we will change into our riding gear for the daily student lessons. We will have to prepare for dressage, show jumping, cross country and instructing. Initially giving lessons to each other under supervision, later we will all be all given our own clients to teach, these clients have special rates for having student teachers. Many of the horses are liveries at special rates to allow them to be used for classes. Mr Tilke has an excellent business, people paying for their horses, clients paying to ride those horses and students paying to teach them. We will also be given extra duties to include looking after the pigs and chickens, milking the cows by hand, churning the butter and tending the vegetable garden, all of which are deemed essential for "character building"! There are some outraged protests mixed with giggles from the student group, as it transpires soon after the course commences some of the student's rebel. Hilary, one particularly outspoken girl organizes a march on the house and a sit-down protest, although these things really don't bother me. Even looking after the pigs is a delight, I call them Tina and Terence and they follow me around like dogs, until one fine day without warning they are whisked off to market and leave me heartbroken. As for milking the three jersey cows, it proves to be a novel experience and rather relaxing especially as they play music in the little dairy, for the benefit of the cows of course.

There will also be theory and written exams, all lectures to be given in the club room we will have written exams on veterinary, nutrition, breeding, fitness, stable management, shoeing and training and we will all have to take the Red Cross first aid exam. Before being accepted on the course we are required to pass the Pony Club B Test, which I and the American girls haven't done and are duly sent to take. In the section on rugging up I get into an argument with the examiner I rug up as Jack has shown me, placing the blanket up to behind the ears fold back the corners the putting on the rug, folding the blanket back over the rug and securing it with the roller. The horse they give me to rug up was too big and the blanket too small. The examiner wants me to do it with the blanket hanging over his rump, I retort that the blanket will be on the floor in the morning. Never argue with the examiner! I am rescued by Mr. Tilke's younger daughter Celia and pass the exam but with a minimum pass mark, grudgingly given by the irate examiner. Funnily enough at school I never said "boo" to a goose but where horses are concerned equine fever rages. So finally, all is settled and the course is due to begin in September, meanwhile I agree to work in the Ministry of Social Security for two months partly to earn money to buy my new equipment and partly because my mother secretly hopes I will enjoy office work and meet people who may encourage me to stay, alas for Mum no chance!

Chapter 2
Training Near Stratford-Upon-Avon

The course begins in September, I move into the mobile home which I share with Wendy and we are both very excited. Wendy is meticulously tidy and organized whereas I am scattier and untidier regarding domestic affairs. However, I am quite the opposite with the horses, this is quite a common phenomenon among horsey people, immaculate stables and a chaotic house, it is simply a question of priorities I suppose. Despite our differences we complement each other and become firm friends.

The notice board next to the office and the main tack room lists who is responsible for which yard, the student classes with allotted horses, the client classes together with Instructors and the horses to be used. Also, times of lectures and practical demonstrations to be given by professionals such as vets, farriers, and saddlers etc. Everything is run with military precision and woe and behold he or she who is late or behind schedule! There are very few boys on the course John, who is there with his girlfriend Sheila and is a considerably successful point-to-point jockey. Sheila's father runs a riding school near London, and he has received an offer to set up a school in Dubai, so John and Sheila need their B.H.S. exams to run the school in London.

As I express greater interest in training young horses than teaching people, I am lucky enough to be selected to help the chief instructor with the breaking-in of a four-year-old, which had been sent for that purpose. I have helped Jack with this process but following his advice keep quiet as everyone has a different approach. Every spare moment I have I spend with the young horse gaining his confidence. Soon he picks his feet up immediately when I run my hand down his leg, initially I huff and puff and we lean on each other as he simply doesn't know what I am asking him to do. With regular repetition it becomes automatic and effortless as is a simple task like moving over in the stable, and on the lunge, he changes gait to my voice commands.

Lynne, the Chief Instructor, doesn't believe in long reining, but once the horse is lunging quietly with all his tack on, she has me lying across the saddle patting the horse and moving around. Later sitting lightly astride while she leads us round at a walk until eventually, she is lunging the horse with me on top. I am told to sit lightly and still, later gently coordinating the leg and hand aids with the voice aids and the transitions, until I am giving all the commands but still on the lunge. This is a thrilling experience; it is a great honour to be the first person to ride a horse especially when you feel there is communication and real understanding. There are some exciting moments when the horse is startled by something but in general all goes smoothly and I know this is how I want to spend my life.

In theory everything is equal and fair for all, all students work on all yards and ride all the horses, however, within this spectrum there is inevitably some favouritism. For example, Celia's famous dressage mare AZARETTE is ridden by all students. However, whereas the American girl rides her in a dressage lesson to the envy of all, I ride her in a jumping class. We have to jump down a jumping lane without reins or stirrups and to boot on a dressage saddle. The mare has a nasty stop and twice I go flying but I persevere and finally achieve my objective. At least this gains me some respect among my fellow students who thank their lucky stars they were not in my shoes.

The cross country is great fun, the first day I ride a small grey pony SILVER. I am a little disappointed at first, but we prove to be the stars of the day, the pony has been a junior eventer and the great thing about ponies as Jack would say "Ponies have an extra leg so they can take off from anywhere and get out of trouble." This gives one a great sense of freedom you can just push forward whereas with a bigger horse you have to be more careful looking for the stride and measuring each fence and combination accordingly. SHERRY or SHERADON is an ex-racehorse, he is beautiful and gallops like the wind but tends to jump racing style brushing through the tops of the fences. Stephanie who was also a bit wild adores him although everyone is afraid, they will come to grief jumping solid fences at such speed, however, fortunately they survive. JET a black gelding is one of my charges and a super all-rounder such an honest and generous little horse, but I have to admit the best ride cross country and in dressage is RAALTE, not surprising really as he has competed at Badminton.

We also go over to some gallops on the WELCOME hills. They belong to a neighbouring trainer, we circle racehorse style and set off down the gallops one at a time. What a great sensation, when a horse flattens into four-time, especially in a safe place with good going for a long distance. You can just enjoy those rippling, powerful muscles and the sense of speed without worrying about having to stop or steer.

Our group, although very mixed regarding backgrounds, becomes very close and we embark on other activities together, from going to discos, playing darts at the village pub, going to the cinema and we hold séances. This is at the suggestion of one of the American girls, I am sceptical but join in whatever is going. We set up the table with the letters of the alphabet on cards in a circle and a glass in the centre upon which we all place a finger. With our eyes closed we ask if anyone was present, the glass begins to move from letter to letter, one of us writes the letters down and on later scrutiny we discover the messages are in German. Each night we call the spirit back, apparently, so the translation tells us, it is someone from World War II who periodically becomes very scared and tells us all to hide. We discuss the whole thing and decide we must contact the spirit again to tell it that the war is over and there is no need to hide. After several attempts this is achieved, the sense of satisfaction is tremendous, even those convinced it is a trick, with someone pushing the glass find it very entertaining and we decide to continue. The next night when a presence comes the American girl asks if it can hypnotize her, the glass began moving very fast and then repeats "no no no", so she says, "Can you hypnotize anyone at this table?" I really think it is all a trick, but I decide to concentrate to see if anything will happen. The glass begins moving very fast, so fast that apparently everyone removes their fingers because they can't follow. I want to close my eyes but every time I do so, the glass comes really close to my face and is so hot I open my eyes again until I can resist no more and slide to the floor. Everyone is terrified and the glass is full of steam. The next day I can hardly move, every muscle in my body aches, needless to say, we decide not to repeat the exercise. As a result, I am convinced there is more to life than meets the eye but equally convinced it is better not to meddle with such things.

My first client is a lady of sixty who has recently taken up riding and is nervous but within a few weeks I have her cantering with confidence and even enjoying a few small jumps which is extremely satisfying. The worst lessons I have is the group of girls from the local boarding school, talk about St Trinians, what an unruly lot. I discovered that the secret is to keep them moving and not give them a moment to get up to mischief I find getting them to ride to music helps a lot and even manage to put together a quadrille. There are some collisions and completely chaotic moments in the preparation, it is a good way, to stretch them and keep their attention although I find it exhausting.

In my own classes, however, I still have so many bad habits to correct in order to change my old-fashioned hunting and showing seat, with the legs forward, to the modern balanced seat with straight line from ear to shoulder to hip to heel. One day I have to ride a whole dressage class with a stick passing through the crook of my elbows across my back thank goodness I am on a reasonably manageable horse that day.

I complain saying I think my arms are too short to be able to keep my elbows back, absolute rubbish of course!

On another occasion we have to jump without stirrups with coins between our knees and the saddle without losing them, and yet another, ride a dressage test with a book balanced on your head or carrying a glass of water without spilling it. Riding on the lunge without reins or stirrups and wearing a blindfold is the worst, those lunge lessons can be purgatory depending on the horse you are riding and the person giving the lesson. The military influence is evident, and it is more a test of endurance than the art of equitation.

There is a young pony causing problems with the children so they ask me if I would like to try retraining him. His name was BRACKERN, but he is nicknamed HOOVER as he has a habit of plunging his nose to the floor through any transition and there is no way the children can get his head up again. He rushes round like a vacuum cleaner which is very disconcerting for the poor children. I decide to use Jack's breaking tack instead of side-reins. He is very narrow in front so if he wears side reins, he just pulls the saddle over his withers which is even worse for the children than flying round with his nose on the ground.

Jack had his tack specially made from rawhide, there is a crupper which fits under the horse's tail, with two long reins attached and two small buckles, the reins passed under the saddle and separated at the wither to pass each side of the horse's neck through the ring of the bit and back to the crupper. The theory is that when the horse leans or pulls on the reins he pulls on his own tail, this being uncomfortable he establishes a comfortable position with a light contact. Some people use elastic or rubber side reins attached to the saddle or the girth. Sometimes these are passed between the horse's front legs to encourage him to lower his head, these are German, running, or draw reins. The chambon, which passes round the quarters is based on a similar theory to Jack's tack. All of these gadgets are used to encourage or sometimes force the horse into the right outline with the horse's quarters under him and his back relaxed and rounded which brings his head into the correct position perpendicular to the ground. In the end they may get faster results, but better more lasting results are achieved from simply riding the horse correctly. Bringing the hind legs under the horse automatically rounds his back and the head falls naturally into place, then he can move with ease, balance, and natural cadence. However, when there is a problem, gadgets are useful.

I improvise, but Hoover responds well after some initial resistance which I let him sort out by himself on the lunge. He seems much happier when he gets over his horrible habit which he has obviously developed as some sort of defence mechanism.

We also give classes from the gallery which I find particularly difficult. I find it very hard to stand still and am always running round after my students gesticulating madly. Not very professional I am told!

From the gallery we have to use a microphone and control eight horses and riders in a class with other riders also in the school intentionally causing chaos wherever possible. The riders in the class, being our fellow students, are as uncooperative as possible, frequently everyone is totally lost and out of control. For example, when your leading file doesn't know left from right which of course can happen with children. Also, the common concept of keeping half a horse's length distance between horses, some people's concept of half a horse is equivalent to half an elephant and others a rabbit. True it is not easy to keep a good even distance between horses; all have a different length of stride some are too fast and others too slow. There is a lot of merit and training that goes into forming a good quadrille, especially changing rein across the diagonal and interchanging, if just one rider misjudges the distance chaos ensues!

The lectures for the written exams are given in the clubroom and we have some very interesting guest speakers. The Veterinary course is very complete covering anatomy and physiology, together with ailments, injury and disease together with treatment, both topical and medicinal, involving fairly intensive studying. We also have papers on nutrition, breeding, shoeing and training and have to take our Red Cross first aid test. The year flies by, all too soon it is time for the final exams and before long it is time to say goodbye. We are all going in different directions and to different parts of the globe. Jack tells me that once I have the qualification it will open doors for me so I can begin to learn in the real world. He is my mentor and his advice is to move around, work in all sectors and learn as much as I can from everyone, then I will have more resources and criteria to make my own decisions. When people seek his advice, he is always thoughtful and cautious simply making suggestions saying he would try "such and such" and see how the horse reacts, as no two horses are alike and what works with one doesn't necessarily work with another. So, with my qualification I now launch myself into the real horse world.

Chapter 3

Stud Farm in Herefordshire

Foals have always fascinated me with their long wobbly legs they are just adorable, I decide I want to start by learning about stud work. Stephanie one of my fellow students knows the owners of a stud farm and says they are looking for staff so I can probably go there as a working student. Together we make an appointment and I go for an interview. The stud farm is outside the small village of Bosbury which is not far from Ledbury. It is in a rather isolated but in a beautiful setting running the length of a valley surrounded by wooded hills, very picturesque, although the house is a typical working farmhouse the kitchen being the heart of the home and the business. The main yard consists of five enormous loose boxes occupied by the five standing stallions and very impressive they are too. Stallions have great presence and coats that gleam with health covering rippling muscles and emanating power, this is going to be a great experience. The owner is a middle aged, undoubtedly handsome man, but rather serious and in fact quite severe. I am warned he is a 'no-nonsense' kind of person, but I will be able to learn a great deal from him and be involved in every aspect of the business.

I will have my own room, they have three small children, but the house is organized with great precision, his wife, Anne, was the vet's secretary before marrying Don and is still renowned for her efficiency. I will have to clean my room on my day off which is one day per week. I will have my keep plus two pounds per week pocket money. I am to work side by side with the owner with extra theory in the evenings. The pocket money implies if I have my period and need to buy Tampax I can't afford to go home on my day off. However, I am so impressed by the stallions I agree to go for a season. Little do I know I am to learn as much about life and myself as stud work. I realise I have been rather soft and over protected up until now and this experience will certainly "knock the spots off me" in other words I will have to grow up fast!

The concept of a working student is more akin to slave labour, long hours and the worst jobs in return for keep and pocket money. However, sufferers of equine fever are only too happy to accept such conditions in order to be near such beautiful horses. I know I am a late developer and as green as grass so the next nine months are going to be tough and I realise that here I must grow up to survive.

As Jack so rightly told me it is in the real horse world where I will learn the most. I know that my smart new certificate has merely scratched the surface. The first evening I have to study the blood lines of the stallions I am going to look after. Two of the standing stallions were sired by TURTON FAIR a notable thoroughbred, now deceased. TURTON'S SON is similar to his sire a tall, imposing, liver chestnut, thoroughbred whereas WIDDECOMBE FAIR is a smaller, more compact, bright chestnut stallion, very popular with breeders of Polo Ponies and in fact he is the reigning Champion Polo Pony Sire. As far as I can make out everyone loves to trace their horses back to HYPERION and it seems our wonderful English thoroughbreds all have traces of Arab blood.

I move in almost immediately. The first morning at 7 a.m. sharp I accompany my new boss Don to the yard. He is going to show me the routine on my first morning and then I will take over. First the five stallions, the first stable is occupied by WIDDECOMBE FAIR or WIDDY as they call him. He is a champion with an array of trophies and some promising offspring already doing well. His manger is in the far corner of an enormous stable which was more like a barn, Don carefully measures out his feed and gives it to me. The horse is prancing excitedly, determined to be business like I confidently tell him to move back, I slide back the bolt, enter the stable, close the door behind me and walk straight to the manger where I empty and mix the feed. So far so good, as I turn to leave the magnificent stallion plants himself squarely between me and the door and every time I make a move, he goes up on his hind legs, boxing at me with his powerful forelegs and flashing hooves. I try tempting him with the food, but he ignores me and when I move, up he goes again. I try shouting at him, the same reaction, in desperation I actually throw the bucket at him to try to make him move which only makes things worse. I am left bereft of the bucket, my only protection from those flailing hooves.

I become aware that Don is leaning over the door with a wry smile on his face, "Having problems, are we?" he enquires calmly. He opens the door and quietly speaks to the horse, "Get back, old boy, give her a chance." The horse calmly backs off and goes quietly to his manger to tuck into his breakfast. I can't believe my eyes. Lesson number one, know your horse, don't think you know it all! The secret Don tells me is, to go into WIDDY's stable with a broom in your hand, and butter won't melt in his mouth. Undoubtedly at some stage, there must have been a battle with a broom but there is never any need to use it, simply have it handy when handling him, this really is a new dimension!

Behind the five stallions there are two stables with young stallions, these are used as "teasers" to establish which mares are in season and need to be covered. There is another block of stables for visiting mares. Also, several large barnlike stables later used as foaling boxes but currently stabling yearlings. They separated into fillies and colts with sometimes two or three together. All in all, eighteen stables full of horses which I have to feed and water before breakfast.

The little Jack Russel terrier is my shadow throughout these proceedings, his beady eyes upon me at all times. I tease him and asked him if he is a spy later reporting back to headquarters, he is smart enough and even seems to understand my sense of humour. I am extremely grateful to him too as on entering the feed room there are rats scurrying round the tops of the walls and he soon sends them packing.

The home-grown high-quality oats are kept in the loft above the feed store. I have to climb a stepladder into the loft passing the ledge where the rats run. I shudder at the thought of coming face to face with them, so I tuck the little dog under my arm, he gives me courage and luckily, he doesn't seem to mind. I have to fill the hod with oats that are fed into the crusher below, so the horses have freshly rolled oats every day. I then cut chaff, feeding the oat straw into the electric chaff cutter. All rather old fashioned but a very healthy diet for the horses. They have molasses too and I cook linseed and barley for a mash once a week, this adds condition and shine to the coats, for there is no time to spend hours grooming them. Don's trick is to run a piece of damp sacking over their coats when prospective clients came to see them. Stallions nearly always have naturally shiny coats and as Don says they shine with health.

We always have a hearty English breakfast served by Anne; mealtimes are meeting times to plan the day. After breakfast I do the beds, all deep litter otherwise it would have taken all day, then I exercise the stallions. They are loosed in the school one day and lunged the next, that way two go out at a time. Initially I find them rather intimidating, but I soon learn that you just need to concentrate and be serious and they are quite obedient. They just have so much presence, energy, and exuberance and when they start whinnying and prancing around, they are so impressive.

The next task is to take the teaser, the young stallion to see which mares are in season and ready for covering. I have a notebook and log each one, first the mares in the stables and then down to the paddocks where there are more visiting mares plus Don's brood mares. I take the young stallion down a lane which ran between the paddocks and any interested mares come up to the fence and clearly "show" sometimes it all gets a bit exciting and I am glad to get back in one piece. Then I bring all the mares which are in season to the stables and prepare them, plus any which have to be examined by the vet. The mares to be served have their tails bandaged up like polo ponies to allow easier access!

When the mares first arrive, the vet examines them and inserts pessaries to clean them inside so increasing the possibilities of their "catching", a sperm presumably! This process becomes second nature but initially I find it quite alarming. The vet wears a rubber glove which covers his whole arm and his whole arm disappears inside the mare, poor thing, my job is to keep her still and straight. Some vets do this procedure over a half door to avoid being kicked but this vet says he had seen someone break their arm that way. If the mare is nervous, we hobble her to prevent her from kicking or we also use the twitch which I don't particularly like. The twitch is a loop of rope on the end of a pole which is slipped over the horse's top lip and twisted until it is tight. As with everything it is not what you do but the way that you do it. If the twitch is tight enough not to slip off but not so tight as to distress the horse it simply serves as a distraction from the real matter in hand.

The vet seeing that I am really keen to learn one day allows me to examine a quiet mare guiding me round the inside of the mare until I feel her ovaries. Hard though life is at the stud, I learn more in a day here than I learned in a whole month on the B.H.S course. At lunch time we go through the list of mares to be served by which stallion and after lunch the covering takes place. Don handles the stallions and I prepare and hold the mares, walking them up the drive immediately afterwards to help them to retain the semen. Sometimes the whole process is tricky if the horse is not interested in the mare, it is my fault because he isn't having enough oats or has had too much exercise and is tired. Sometimes on the other hand they get so over excited the whole operation is impossible, this is due to too many oats and not enough exercise, a no-win situation! I think that horses like people must be more attracted to one female than another, one of the stallions for example cannot abide grey mares. The sex drive in a horse is many times greater than that of a man according to Don, they get so excited and are so strong. I have to take care to avoid those flailing front hooves and teeth especially when I am having trouble keeping the mare straight and sometimes Don helps the stallion find his way into the mare. My eyes nearly fall out of my head and I go red as beetroot the first time I witness this, hoping I won't be expected to perform this operation. It requires speed and dexterity too, but fortunately allowing the horses to follow their natural instincts means that in most cases all goes smoothly without intervention.

A horse's age goes from the year he is born, so the objective is for the foals to be born as early in the year as possible. There is a vast difference in the development of a two-year-old born in January and one born in September of the same year for. So as the gestation period is eleven months February is a busy time for covering mares. The main problem being the weather, often the mares don't come into season in the cold weather. They come into season every three weeks, so it is quite normal for visiting mares to stay for a month or so. If they don't "catch" the first time the process is repeated with the following season. They come in season for approximately six days and are covered daily or alternate days during this period.

Foaling time is really what I have been waiting for, when the mares are close to foaling, they come into the big foaling boxes and I get up every two hours during the night and go round quietly with a torch to check on them as they often foal at night when all is quiet. The first foaling I witness is not straightforward. The mare is twenty-six years old, but she has bred foals for most of her life. She is a lovely chest thoroughbred with a wise kind look in her eye, she must have been magnificent in her youth.

During the torch round at 5 a.m. I find her distressed and sweating, pacing round and groaning. I rush back to the house and tap on Don's bedroom door; he is out in a flash together we go back to the mare. She has always foaled quickly and easily, if not he wouldn't have considered putting her in foal again. He decided to leave things to the wisdom of nature believing that if she wasn't in condition to carry a foal she wouldn't take. She has had a smooth ride so far with lots of extra care, minerals and vitamins, so he is really concerned. Don decides to call the vet, despite the unsociable hour. I stay with the mare; she is now lying down and moaning. I try to calm her and prevent her from rolling. It seems like an eternity before the vet arrives, quickly he dons his long rubber gloves and soon discovers the problem. The foal which should be born with its two front feet first has one foreleg back, making the birth impossible, the poor mare has been pushing in vain and is exhausted. He has to push the foal back into the mare and find the missing foreleg this was quite a tussle but once he has both tiny hooves in his hand the foal slips out relatively easily. He is incredible, he has a short little body, a short little neck, giraffe like legs, large floppy ears, a velvet muzzle that fits into the palm of your hand and tiny hooves that are like egg cups. He is perfect, just gorgeous, and a total mystery how those long legs had folded to fit inside his mother.

Animals learn so much more quickly than humans. We are dependent on our mothers for such a long time. Within twenty minutes the wobbly little foal, after several attempts to get to his feet with his legs spread eagled, is up and suckling from his mother. She is an old hand and gently nuzzles him, positioning herself to help him find where to suckle, what a magical night. We give the mare a lovely warm mash, fill her hay-net, give them fresh bedding and go to the kitchen for a much appreciated, hearty, breakfast. On the way Don tells me the placenta, or after-birth, should come away soon and I will have to remove it. When I enquire as to what I should do with it he says it should be buried quite deeply to prevent the dogs from digging it up. He adds that alternatively I could take it up to the woods for the foxes to eat.

Being a "towny" and ignorant of country ways I think that if the foxes could benefit from the placenta this is by far the best option. Later I duly find the afterbirth, which is far larger and heavier than I imagined, it is slippery too, after several attempts I manage to get it into the wheelbarrow. The woods are at the top of the hill across the far side of the forty-acre field it is really hard work to push the loaded barrow up there. I persevere and heaving and straining finally make it, feeling satisfied I trundle happily down the hill with my empty barrow. At lunch time they ask me where I have buried the after-birth, I proudly say I have taken it up to the woods for the foxes. This is greeted first of all, by disbelief and then by hoots of laughter. Don says, "Well let's just hope the foxes find it before the neighbour's dogs or we will be in trouble!" I have a problem; I never know when he is serious or when he is pulling my leg, consequently he takes great delight in doing the latter.

The foals are adorable without exception, I love catching them for the vet and holding them in my arms for him to examine or vaccinate. I love putting on little foal slips and teaching them to be led, behind their mums of course. When the weather improves, we turn them out on fresh green pasture then watch them playing, running, and cavorting with their long gangly legs. There is one particularly cheeky colt foal who performs circus tricks and keeps everyone amused. His favourite trick is to rear up and put both his forelegs over the back of his playmate and as his friend canters off to escape, he does the polka on his hind legs. Surprisingly enough they don't seem to hurt each other, they also love to have boxing matches standing on their hind legs.

Don has a way of making me feel guilty regarding the care of the animals, one day he comments on the appalling state of a mare's feet. She is not shod and her hooves are rather long and splitting. He expresses shock that with my qualifications I am not capable of trimming a horse's feet. I know the theory and the instruments but have had very little practice. So, with one lesson in trimming feet, I have to take over this small additional task of checking and trimming all the horse's feet!

When the foaling and the covering of mares eases up and we are well into spring Don decides it is time to bring in the three-year-old colts. They have been turned out at the far end of the farm running wild for the past two years only to be fed and checked daily. I have a nice home bred gelding to school and to sell on, so I ride him down to see if the colts will follow. Several people come behind on foot with the dogs to help. With some difficulty we herd them into a lane leading back to the stables, from there into the indoor school.

There are five in total and they are very excited, as is the horse I am riding. I put him back in the stable and take off his tack. As I make my way back towards the school the vet draws up and we go towards the school together, he asks me if I have ever seen castration before, I blush and say "No" at which he chuckles. Luckily with three strong men one by one they corner the colts; the vet injects them, and they sink to the ground in a peaceful slumber. I make sure they keep their heads down and Don pulls up a hind leg while the vet examines them to check that the testicles were low enough for the operation. The vet's assistant brings over the equipment and he makes an incision, pulls out the testicles one at a time and unceremoniously cuts them off. Some vets use the same method as is used for sheep, placing a tight rubber ring above the testicle so strangling it and it eventually drops off, I imagine this must be most painful. It is something

I had never really considered before that we castrate most of our domestic animals, except the minority especially selected for breeding. Working with the stallions and appreciating their terrific presence, elegance, and power, oozing with pride and character, I can't help feeling a pang of sadness for these young colts. There are very few stallions in top competition as they are easily distracted, if there happens to be a mare around forget the dressage test. There are some exceptions and they do have that lovely distinguishing presence.

As we are leaving the school Don turns to me and casually comments "I'd pop head collars on them if I were you, while they are still sleeping, I want them all ridden in six weeks." What a bombshell!! I fly to the tack room to rummage round for five suitable head collars rush back to the school quickly fitting the head collars on the still groggy boys.

Back in the house over tea Don calmly states that as he has heard that I love training young horses he thinks I deserve a treat so decided to give me five! Still with the eighteen boxes to look after and the stallions to exercise, I have to plan the work with the five new boys who were totally unhandled. Don helps me to catch them and get them into stables, then I am left to it and I frankly prefer it that way. I have discovered it is much easier to deal with young horses that have never been handled than those that had been messed about and learned a trick or two.

First to gain their confidence, so I get up half an hour earlier and feed the young horses last. I spend five minutes in the stable with each one while they eat their breakfast. In the beginning they back away nervously but soon their hunger overtakes their fear and after a few sessions they come towards me when I go in. I hold the head collar with one hand and place the other on the neck little by little running my hand down the neck and the shoulder and then gradually all over the body. Often when I run my hand down their legs, they get nervous but soon get used to it. I teach them to be led by gently pulling them off balance and praising them when they take a step, in response. This is easy in a stable and always using the same voice commands of "Walk on" and "Woah" until they respond to the voice with the slightest physical contact. I teach them to be tied up using a piece of string which if they ran back will break so they did not injure themselves, but I can catch them straight away and they don't realise they have escaped. They all respond well, with the exception of one rebellious chestnut SOLO who repeatedly pulls back. Don observes with an amused expression and says: "If you chain him to the tree with two strong head collars he'll soon learn" to which I retort "Sure if he doesn't break his neck or a leg in the process". I carry on in my own way and ran a lunge rein through the ring on the wall and when he does it again, I run the rein behind my back and lean my weight against him the stable wall does the rest and he soon gets the message, fortunately for him if not he would probably end up chained to a tree!

So, I handle them all over, teach them to pick up their feet and the principles of lunging, all in the stable, to walk on and halt to command then to repeat the operation outside and in the school where in an enclosed area I introduce trot and canter. Back in the stable I put an elastic bandage round the girth, also around the chest to act as a breast plate and stop it from slipping back. Every time I go into the stable, I tighten the bandage a little, so they became accustomed to the feel without being afraid and fighting. Unlike what happens in the wild-west where the expression "Break" comes from, the animal is brutally tacked up and fights until he is exhausted and his spirit is broken, so sad and unnecessary. The bandage is replaced by a surcingle which is in turn replaced by a roller followed by a saddle without stirrups, then a saddle with stirrups and if a young horse is not frightened, he accepts it all with no problem.

The same with the bridle undoing the cheek piece and gently slipping the bit into his mouth, using a little of honey helps. Then I leave it on in the stable so he can mouth and get used to it sitting comfortably on the bars of his mouth, a gap in the teeth which seemed to have been made for that purpose. Now for the long reins again starting in the stable passing a lunge rein from the outside rein behind his quarters and applying light pressure accompanied by the now familiar commands so they understand the aids for turning and halting, then outside I drive them everywhere so they learn to go wherever I asked them so becoming used to traffic and people, bicycles, dogs and all of the frightening hazards of life.

Finally, they are ready to be mounted and again I do this alone in the stable. Jack always says a horse will not buck against a brick wall! First, I lay my body across their backs to get them used to the weight, patting them and making noises. When they seem comfortable with this procedure, I pass my leg over their rump, so I am sitting astride and slowly I sit up. Some horses are startled by suddenly seeing a person above them, I pat them and talk to them continuously. Finally walking, halting, and turning in the stable.

Now we are ready to go into the big wide world. Most horses are reluctant to leave home and anxious to return so taking advantage of this I long rein them down the lane, take off the long reins and stuff them in the hedge to be collected later, climb onto their backs, and ride them home. Each time I add a little more, riding into the school, first circling at walk, followed by trotting with plenty of transitions and eventually cantering round always encouraging them to go forward and praising them. If they seem too enthusiastic, I use circles to slow the pace. A very humbling experience and a special relationship evolves with each one, sadly they are all to be sold and I just hope they will have kind homes. Each one has his own personality, they are all different, just like people, but all have endearing characteristics.

Don does not praise me because it is not his style but the odd sarcastic comment tells me he is not displeased with my work, as I ride back one day he says, "You almost look like a professional," this is praise indeed! However, he is still able to reduce me to tears which he seems to find amusing. A classic example is when one of the colts becomes swollen after the castration, I notice immediately and report the fact at breakfast when plans for the day are being discussed. Don grunts and says that this is not uncommon. I repeatedly report the situation of the colt and on the third day I get quite upset because his hind legs are also swollen so Don goes to inspect. When he sees the colt he fumes with anger, calls the vet immediately, then turns to me shouting offensively, "Your problem is you don't care a damn, the bugger could die for all you care, as it is not your horse!" I am devastated and the tears of dismay run down my cheeks. Don's wife Anne who witnesses the scene gently reproaches him with "Oh Don, really", but she cannot conceal an amused smile. I run to my room and sob my heart out. My reaction is also partly due to exhaustion as I have been working long hours, day and night seven days a week, to the point I have lost two stone in a month and my periods have stopped.

When I go home for a long overdue weekend my mother is horrified and calls the Doctor who duly examines me. First asking my mother to leave the room he then asks me if there is any possibility that I am pregnant. "No!" is my emphatic reply and I ponder that chance would be a fine thing!!! My mother is loath to allow me to return but I have promised to stay at Kynance Stud for a whole season and I intend to fulfil my promise. Jack has been in touch with me and told me some very good clients of his are looking for someone to ride second horse to the Field Master of the Fernie Hunt in Leicestershire. I know nothing about Fox hunting, and it appears to be a unique opportunity to learn. When I mention this to Don, he says he will build another five stables and buy five young horses for me to hunt and sell on. Although I insist that I know nothing about hunting he dismisses my objections as invalid. I thank him for his offer and decline politely. However, I agree to stay on while the family go for a much-needed holiday and then find someone to replace me.

The visiting mares and foals have all gone the young horses sold and the stallions turned out for a holiday in their respective paddocks, so Don asks me if I can do some muck spreading while they are away. The stables are all large and on deep litter, if not no way I could have managed everything alone. Being the gullible soul I am, plus the fact I feel somewhat guilty about leaving I am determined to clean all the stables out and disinfect them while they are away.

I start at 7 a.m. every morning. I have to fork the muck into the muck spreader by hand and then spread it on the fields set aside for growing oats and hay. I manage two loads before breakfast, then a round of the livestock to check fences and water and continue muck spreading until dark. I am really quite happy with the little grey Fergie tractor and the muck spreader. A neighbouring farmer pays me a visit, he has seen me out with the tractor from dawn to dusk and can't believe it. Even Don is amazed when they come back to find it all done and dusted, but his only comment to me is "Well that sort of simple task would suit you as at least you can't make too many mistakes." I am at last getting used to his caustic comments and merely raise my eyebrows and decline to comment, smiling to myself that I am now confident enough not to be affected by other people's opinions, satisfied that I have done my very best even if it is not up to some people's expectations.

One day, whilst driving with Don and his four-year-old son Michael, he asks me the names of some trees as we pass. I am ashamed to say apart from oak, horse chestnut and poplar I fail miserably. The four-year-old knows the names of all the trees, most embarrassing! Strange as it may seem I have become fond of this blunt man, he has taught me a great deal about breeding horses and even more about life and myself, so we part on good terms.

Chapter 4

Hunting in Leicestershire

I have a month before embarking on my new venture in Leicestershire. I spend two weeks with Jack and accompany him to a couple of shows while he fills me in on my new employers. I go home for a week and am amused by my mother's delight that I have left "Wuthering Heights" as she calls the Stud Farm. Finally, I go to see my old school friend Jean at her University and coincide with the Ball, cheating really taking advantage of the social life without the studying. Jean is doing well at University and she has a slightly hippy air about her. She has become vegetarian, so she frowns at me saying, "I really don't understand you! You say you love animals and you eat them, now to cap it all, you are going to hunt them!! I don't particularly like animals, but I would never harm them!"

Finally, the day comes to move to Leicestershire and into a completely new world. I have lodgings in the village with the Edwards family. Their house is within walking distance of the stables and Mr Edwards is my new boss's accountant. They have three children but only the youngest daughter remains at home hence they have room for a lodger. They are welcoming and live in a comfortable detached house. I have a spacious room and am to have all meals with them living as one of the family. My parents accompany me and we leave my belongings there before making our way to the stables.

Major Cowan, my new employer, is a tall, distinguished gentleman. He shakes hands with all of us but seems a little shy of female company and more comfortable addressing himself to my father. He leads us to the tack room in the corner of the immaculate yard where we are introduced to the rest of the staff. They are all men as I am the first girl to join the team, they are polite but quite obviously sceptical.

The head groom is a wiry man in his fifties of a slightly nervous disposition doubtless quick and efficient and sure not miss a trick. Percy is older in his late sixties; he is a gentle slow soul with kind eyes. I am to replace Percy riding second horse to the Major as it is now too much for him. The men have four horses each to look after on the main yard and I have only two in my own little yard at the back. These are the horses we have to muck out feed, groom rug up and bandage on a daily basis, I only have two as my main job is riding.

What a contrast, I am not even allowed to pick up a straw bale. When I think of the gruelling physical work I did at the Stud Farm, where I carried tons of oats in sacks on my back up steps into the loft and stacked the barn with haybales single handed. Here Percy carries the bales to my boxes every morning and fills the heavy water buckets. This is before the days of automatic water and the buckets, like everything else, are exquisite, large wooden pails with steel rims and freshly painted with the Major's initials painted on each one. The stables are also freshly painted this is what the men do during the summer when the horses go out to rest. I am just employed for the Season, the arrangement being that I will go back to work for Jack for the summer showing season.

Here the timetable is very strict, for the first time ever I find I have time on my hands, I am unused to this and prefer to be with the horses all day, whereas here there is a long break for lunch. One lunch time I venture back with the intention of pulling the mane of Pilgrim the chestnut mare in my charge. The head groom sees me from his living room window and comes storming across the yard forbidding me to interrupt the horses' and his siesta time.

Sometimes I exercise my landlord's daughter Joy's horse during the lunch break, Della is a little bay mare and she is plucky and adventurous like her owner. Joy also takes me along to Young Farmers, so I start to have some social life. I have time to read an activity I have sorely missed my father being a great reader I had acquired the habit from an early age. I still find I have time to spare so decide to take on a correspondence course.

In the morning once I have attended to my two charges, I school one horse before breakfast. The horses are big quality horses as all the family are tall. The Major and his two sons hunt in "pink" (red coats) with top hats and the mother and daughter hunt side-saddle, so elegant in their habits with an apron, they also wear top hats with face and stylish bun covered with a net. I have ridden a little side-saddle at Jack's because Sheelagh sometimes shows side-saddle, but I am far from being an expert. True it is practically impossible to fall off, but perched on the top and only using one leg I feel like a passenger not a rider. Plus the fact it is difficult to keep even weight on both seat bones and jumping it is almost impossible to lean forward over the fence to take the weight off the horse's back. I far prefer to wrap my legs round the horse and feel close to him, to be aware of his breathing, the tensing of his muscles and feel the power beneath me.

Despite the size and strength of a horse they are so very sensitive. There are moments when they respond to your thoughts or the slightest alteration of weight or movement of the fingers. One of the top dressage riders says that she only has to move her head from side to side to execute flying changes in canter. The head is heavy she explains, so simply the alteration of weight is sufficient aid and signal for the horse to understand and change legs. Surely this is the art of riding! There are times of course when it is like trying to control an express train with a piece of ribbon!

The schooling consists of flat work for flexibility and obedience, jumping and later fast work for which I take them into a huge grass field. After breakfast we do the road work, riding one horse and leading another we go out in convoy. This is a long slow process to get the horses fit and harden their tendons, walking then slow sitting trot, or hound jog as they called it, building up to two hours and including hill work. We go out in two lots and this also helps me to get to know layout of the country.

The afternoons are dedicated to strapping, which is thorough grooming, leaving the horses gleaming, complete with leg and tail bandages and their smart initialled day rugs. They have leather head-collars with shiny brass buckles with name plates, all fit for a queen, it is such a treat to have time to do things properly. The stud groom does the clipping and trimming and then we all clean the tack on a daily basis. Thanks to these hours spent in the tack room I not only learn a lot of the old tricks regarding the care of horses, but also marvel at the older men's tales of their lives in the horse and essentially the hunting world. They have both worked in kennels for years and know the "ins and outs" of the hunting.

They also defend their Master vehemently. Percy tells the tale of when he applied for the job with the Major, the conditions of work and the wages were far better than anything he had ever dreamed of and also included a house. Percy hastily accepted the offer but the Master said "No Percy you cannot accept, not until your wife and son have seen the house, if they are not happy you will not be happy and if you are not happy you cannot work well." This detail on the part of the Major gave Percy the greatest love and respect for him and he cannot speak highly enough of his employer.

About this time V.A.T is brought in and the indignation in the tack room is heated, "More taxes!!!" bellows The Head Groom, and Percy snorts that the government are robbers and short sighted. If they tax their poor Master any more what will happen to them the workers? Little do they realise that they too will be subject to V.A.T. Such is their loyalty and love for their employer and their work, if a touch naïve it is also a real breath of fresh air when you consider the all too frequent attitude we encounter in other sectors, so often rife with complaints, strikes and protests. The modern working environment seems to have become excessively competitive and stressful.

Fox hunting is an integral part of English country life, the breeding and training of horses and hounds creates many jobs especially in this part of the country. Due to human intervention foxes have no natural predators and unfortunately cause havoc to the farmers. A fox will not just kill one chicken for food, he kills them all leaving devastation in his wake. The new-born lambs are another key target for the foxes, not only the killing of the baby lambs but causing the terrified ewes to abort as they try to flee from their predators. This is a real problem for the farmers hence culling is a necessary evil. These days we also have urban or dustbin foxes creating a threat for domestic animals and some health concerns, on the other hand some people feed them and even make pets of them.

Killing any animal is undesirable but if it is paramount to maintain the balance of nature, hunting with hounds is by far the most natural, accurate and humane method. The farmers can often identify the fox that has done the damage on their farm, the one with the white foot, the bent ear or the big light coloured one who causes his ewes to abort or kills his chickens. The earth stoppers know where all the foxes live, the hounds go into the covert, often a small wood, and when a fox breaks covert they follow the scent. If the huntsman doesn't want to hunt that particular fox, maybe a vixen for example, he calls the hounds off with the help of the whippers-in and sends them back into the covert. Once they are onto the fox they want, if they catch him, he dies in an instant, although it is not a pleasant sight. If, however, he is clever enough to escapes he has had a fright but is unscathed, and even gains some respect from the hunting fraternity it implies he is healthy and astute.

The alternatives, as proposed by the anti-hunting supporters, mean that foxes will still be culled, they propose sending people, who don't know the country or the habitat, with guns ostensibly to shoot them. This means there is a danger of leaving animals maimed, also terrifying the birds and other wildlife. Not to mention the fact they don't distinguish between the foxes; they shoot at anything that moves. Gassing is another option, but it is as bad as they kill whole families and other creatures too. Whereas trapping is equally horrible incurring a slow, painful, death or leaving the foxes maimed for life, apart from which other animals can be trapped by mistake including domestic dogs. In conclusion fox hunting with hounds seems the most natural way and least devastating to the rest of the wildlife.

I am no expert, but this is, more or less what I understand after listening to these wise old country folks. I remember Jean's comments somewhat shamefully and hope I will never have to be present at the kill, in fact few people are. I also remember somewhat ruefully winning a poetry reading prize for reciting "Reynard the Fox". In England and Ireland, I have to admit that hunting young horses in preparation for competition is invaluable. Galloping and jumping with other horses gives a young horse great confidence and develops their skills for dealing with the unexpected like a huge ditch or a drop on the other side of a thick hedge so learning to get out of trouble. Most horses love the excitement and after hunting a few times come out of the stable with ears pricked as if to say, "Where are we going today?" Well for the moment I am committed for a season and still have a lot to learn.

We work steadily to get the horses fit and begin cubbing in October, essentially a training period for young hounds and horses, also to establish where the new young foxes live. There is no galloping and jumping as in the open season which starts in November, but the horses learn to be quiet and patient among a crowd and get used to the hounds and the horn. Everyone wears "rat catcher" or tweed jackets, instead of pink and or black, and bowler or riding hat instead of top hat. During this period the Major does not require a second horse, but I accompany him usually on the younger horses. Major Cowan is the Field Master, his task being to control the mounted followers. I learn a little of the protocol for example one must always stay behind the Field Master and follow his instructions. On other occasions I follow in the huge horsebox with Edwards and Percy and learn about the country we will be covering.

How we manage to locate each other is a mystery, by instinct and experience together with a little trial and error, somehow, we always manage to find which way the hounds have run. Percy tells me that my job will be to follow the hunt on the second horse and keep him clean and fresh and be there when the Major wants to change horses, then I am to take the tired horse and find the Horsebox by locating the car followers. I am more than a little dubious about my capabilities in this direction, ruefully remembering the time when I got lost on the day ride! Percy reassures me "You have a tongue in your head my girl and there will be people around watching who know this country like the back of their hand!"

Sometimes if they have a quiet morning and especially if the Major is riding his old favourite DERWENT, he will ask me to hunt with them until the younger horse has settled. This I normally enjoy, except for the first time when I am caught unawares as MURPHY who I have galloped and jumped at home quite happily, is much stronger when taking off at a gallop with a crowd of other horses. He is a big strong Irish horse and he nearly runs away with me! I almost overtake the Field Master and have to make a huge circle to get him back under control so my debut is rather embarrassing. Fortunately, the Major just laughs in a good-natured fashion.

People with difficult horses sometimes lend them to the hunt in the hopes they will settle with the long days and hard work. Sometimes it works and sometimes it doesn't. Mostly the huntsman and whippers-in (his assistants) will ride anything on four legs as they are focused on the hounds and their job. The horse being just a means to get them from A to B as fast as possible over whatever obstacle may be in the way. However, there is one horse they don't want to ride, he has thrown all of them and they are fed up with him.

Unfortunately, the Major's older son Gavin takes a shine to him and begs his father to buy him. The horse in question is a flashy chestnut, very good looking and with a lot of presence and character but cold backed which means when first mounted he bucks and bucks in real bronco style but who has to ride him? Me of course! They take me to the Kennels to collect him and ride him home, the whole yard is gathered to see the exhibition and see if I will survive! I have insisted on a martingale if only to provide a neck-strap for me to hang on to. I mount as lightly as I can, careful to keep my weight in the stirrups, but although I am gentle, I feel him tighten and he plunges off in a series of enormous bucks as the men jump back to safety. I stand up in my stirrups leaning back on the neck-strap trying to keep his head up and straight. I encourage him to go forward and let him buck beneath me, if I sit on the saddle it will be like an ejector seat. The bucks finally give way to plunges and then settle into a spanking trot down the road. Following the initial display, he is a lovely ride and doesn't put a foot wrong.

Every day I have to go through this rather hair-raising ritual. I would love to do things my way, which would be to look after him in the stable and work with him on my own but that is impossible. Furthermore, the Head groom insists on preparing him for me and holds him whilst I mount. This is disastrous as he holds the horse tightly and shouts at him to behave, which has the opposite effect.

On one such occasion, after a rather unseating buck, I hit the side of my hand on the hard muscle on his neck as he throws his head up on landing, the pain is excruciating but I can't stop. I have to concentrate and ride on, once he settles, I hold both reins in the other hand. By the time I finish riding my hand is swollen and my fingers don't work. I have extreme difficulty untacking him finally resorting to using one hand and my elbow and my teeth. Edwards dismisses my complaining and tells me to put some ice on it. Fortunately, it is lunch time, there is no one in at my digs so I decide to catch the bus to the nearest hospital, which is half an hour away in Kettering. The Emergency is packed so I have to wait, realizing I will be late back to work I ring the head groom to inform him. Finally, it is my turn and after having an x-ray it is clear that I have a broken bone which they think they can get back into position without operating by almost pulling my fingers out of their sockets, it is excruciating, then they put on a plaster cast which seems to take an age. When I emerge into the waiting-room I am astounded to see the Major's wife. Apparently, she called in at the yard after lunch and was furious with them for not taking me to the hospital, and also with her son for buying such a difficult horse and expecting someone else to ride it. She is thoroughly charming and takes me back to my lodgings telling me to take the rest of the day off. I am dubious about the reception I will have from the Head Groom the next day, he is sure to be angry and even more so because I am now hampered by having my right arm in plaster. However, to my surprise, he is more than a little contrite, apologizing and saying if I had rung him earlier, he would have come to the hospital.

It is amazing how we can adapt to our circumstances. Initially I am so slow even dressing and writing is a joke. Eventually I manage to do most things left-handed, riding is the easiest activity once I am on top of the horse. I don't have to ride the bucker, he is to be lunged until I have my plaster off. The most difficult thing is putting on the bridle and doing up the buckles with one hand, I have to use my teeth. The other problem is my correspondence course as writing with my left hand is laboriously slow apart from which the end result resembles the efforts of a five-year old! As anyone who has had their arm in plaster knows well, dressing takes twice as long, also cleaning your teeth and combing your hair is weird with the left hand if you are right-handed. Ironically by the time the six weeks are up I am quite dexterous, even my writing is more or less presentable, but I am desperately behind with the course.

Another factor which hampers my good intentions of studying is the sudden increase in social life thanks to Joy who is studying to be a nurse. She and her little mare DELLA are well suited and they hunt too, they are a brave pair and jump everything in sight. Joy takes me along to the Young Farmers and apart from their weekly meetings, where they often have interesting speakers there are various projects plus additional activities and outings. Most of the young farmers are in fact farmers, or from farming families and the majority are boys, it is wonderful to get to know the farmers and their land. They are a bit wild, most of them have minis or mini pick-ups. I have my dear old Morris Minor Betsy and she is not as fast as a mini. They like to race between villages where there are no speed restrictions, no seat belts and no drink and drive regulations. This is a risky combination especially in conjunction with the imprudence of youth, when we are young, we see no danger. The only way I can keep up is by going as fast round the bends as I do on the straight and the Morris is so heavy, she holds the road well. I wouldn't swop my BETSY for a racy mini for all the tea in China. Joy once lost control on a bend and her minivan, left the road and rolled down a steep bank. The minivan rolled over three times and landed on the roof which caved in and there isn't much headroom in a mini to start with. Joys only comment when telling the tale is "Blimey it was a close one!" she was miraculously unharmed except for a few bruises. On the first spin the door flew open and Joy was ejected onto the soft grass, mercifully she wasn't wearing a seat belt. This kind of close shave has a sobering effect at least for a while.

Joy's mother and older sister are also called Judith so to avoid confusion they decided to call me by my second name which was Rosemary. I have a fair complexion and when I am out riding in all weathers my face goes bright red. I am riding home at a spanking trot one cold windy day when one of the young farmers draws up alongside me and roars with laughter "Now I know why they call you Rosie!!" I grin, I don't care a hoot and retort "You should see my knees!" to which he replies, "Don't mind if I do!" with a cheeky wink drives off, it is all good clean fun. Having grown up as a "townie", I realise that people who have

48

to wear suits for work like to dress down in their free time whereas in the country the opposite applies, the farming folk love dressing up, in fact they wear long dresses to all the dances and all the boys wear their dinner jackets, bow-ties, waistcoats and cummerbunds. I am not very interested in such things, but Joy and her mother are talented seamstresses and make lovely dresses, very reasonably and quickly. Under their guidance I make a couple, but it really isn't my forte, apart from which I am more at home in jeans and trainers.

The Young Farmers also plan a holiday to Spain, Joy and I are the only girls who sign up, so off we go with 14 boys. They say there is safety in numbers and fortunately this proves to be so. We fly to Barcelona, spend a week on the coast playing, volleyball on the beach, swimming, taking a little too much sun, wine, brandy, and dancing. We get on really well and prove there really is safety in numbers. We return to Barcelona for sight-seeing, we visit Montserrat in the mountains which flank the city and see the famous Black Virgin in the Benedictine Monastery of Santa Maria which is beautiful. The Black Virgin is a statue of a black Madonna and child and is the patron saint of Barcelona. The Catholics in Spain have many Virgins such as Esperanza which means hope, Dolores for sorrow, Consuelo for consolation and many more, most people are named after a Saint and in parts of Spain their Saint's day is more important than their birthday. We are undecided regarding the Bull Fighting, the overall opinion being that we should not judge without first-hand experience, so we agree to go to a bullfight in Barcelona. We know a little about the history, that this was originally a way for poor young men to bring esteem to their families and put bread to the table, it forms part of the culture and tradition of the country. Farmers are usually pretty tough, after all they breed and care for animals then send them to slaughter for the food industry. However, after the initial spectacular music and pageantry with the exotic and elegant bullfighters, a horse is gored despite wearing protection. This followed by the long slow process of wounding, confusing, debilitating and finally killing the bull has a sobering effect on our group. These lads who are mostly big, strong and muscular became very quiet and almost pallid. We leave in silence and it takes a while to restore the high spirits of the group, fortunately this proves to be the only damper on the otherwise fabulous holiday. This is one of the few, if not the only time that I work with horses and have a balanced life. Also, the work is relatively easy, some of the horses like the bucker adding a little spice to life, but all is quite manageable, controlled and ordered.

The Head Groom has his own potions for most of the day-to-day horse ailments from thrush to mud-rash, saddle-sores or sprained tendons. He has a cupboard full of jars and bottles and makes up his own concoctions, but he refuses to share his secrets. "It has taken me a lifetime of experience to learn all this" is his reply to my curiosity. Even Percy is not impressed by his attitude. He has the old-fashioned mentality that knowledge is power and to share knowledge diminishes your power. Well, that is his choice to my way of thinking it is akin to a third world mentality, where the dictator doesn't want his people to have education so he can control them, too blind to see that enriching the people would also enrich the country. Whenever these minor ailments occur, I consult my notes and read up on all the options, then I observe our Head Groom and his potions without asking too many questions, to avoid raising the alarm that I may be after his power and knowledge!

The vet is quite the opposite and appreciates my interest. PILGRIM the mare in my charge is very moody, she always seems cross and irritable she is ticklish to handle and kicks and stamps her feet at the slightest provocation. She is obviously not happy so at the end of the season the vet gives her a thorough examination and discovers she has a cystic ovary which requires an operation.

The operation takes place at the yard. I lead the mare round to the barn which has been scrubbed out and prepared with rubber mats, the vet injects her, and she sinks gently to her knees and onto her side. The Head Groom stays in charge of her head and Percy holds her tail. I don rubber gloves, hold the instrument tray and squat down beside the vet as he carefully shaves a long rectangle on the mare's side disinfects and makes a long straight incision. Surgery is very basic and physical he delves his hand inside the mare and pulls out a round object which he examines "that one is fine, hold it," with which he places the warm ovary in my hands and delves his hand deeper inside the mare. Eventually he pulls out the other ovary, which was indeed covered with nodules, he unceremoniously cuts it off and plonks it into the kidney dish, he takes the good ovary from me and pushes it back inside the mare then begins cleaning up and stitching. The stitches are individual, and I have to cut the thread after each one. I marvel at the speed with which the wound heals and the mare recovers. Hopefully after a summer's rest at grass she will feel like a new woman next season.

One day out hunting when I arrive with the second horse the Major says they have had a quiet morning and I can hunt with them. I am on JOSIMON his new horse which Jack has successfully shown as a Heavy Weight Hunter and he had even been placed at the Horse of the Year Show. However, JOSIMON is new to the hunting field and gets rather excited, he is controllable, but it means you can't relax for a second, I have to concentrate and ride every stride. Joy is also out on her little mare and their neighbour an elderly lady on Jester, her little chestnut horse, which is full of spunk, so a good day is had by all. At one point we are waiting in a queue and the hounds which are ahead veer left. Master doesn't hesitate he leaves the queue and puts his brave old horse at a big blind hedge, so cutting off the corner. I don't hesitate and set out after him, the horse takes off beautifully but lo and behold on the other side there is a huge drop. I ruefully remember the adage "Look before you leap". I think we will never land, it seems as though we are air borne for an eternity and I have no contact with the saddle, fortunately for me he doesn't peck on landing and we don't part company. I pull up alongside the Major who is standing quietly in the corner of the field observing the hounds. He glances sideways at us and raises his eyebrows. His only comment is "Well now we know he can jump!"

I still have to warm-up, or rather calm-down my Lady's side-saddle horse before she mounts which normally consists of either hacking to the meet or cantering up and down the grass verges before my Lady mounts. "My Lady" as everyone addresses her is a true lady and a lovely person, she invites us for dinner one evening. The men are all away, so there is her daughter Meryl, My Lady, Joy, and myself. We have a delightful evening and discuss everything from women's rights to a horse's diet. It surprises me how natural, relaxed, and normal they are. After dinner we sit round an open fire, Meryl sits on the floor and finding a small hole in her tights begins by poking her finger into it until it becomes a gaping abyss, I observe with mild astonishment as she finally pulls her tights to shreds and throws the remnants onto the open fire. Her mother reprimands her lightly and Meryl confesses she hates dressing up especially wearing tights and heels. I sympathize with her for I feel much the same, whereas Joy and My Lady obviously delight in following the latest trends in fashion enthusiastically exchanging views on the latest styles. My Lady reminds me wistfully of my own mother who is an equally elegant lady who also has a tomboy for a daughter.

I spend two seasons in Leicestershire, and they are happy times. The Head Groom likes to put me to the test and loves to stick up big jumps for me, or throw me up on the bucker, but I don't mind. The second season one of the

Major's horses is behaving strangely sometimes he shakes his head and gets very agitated. I have known MURPHY since he came over from Ireland to Jack's and was subsequently bought by the Major. He is a big horse a good 17:2hh and he has proved to be a superb hunter. We have the vet out and he checks his ears and gives him blood tests. Unfortunately, one day when we are out on road exercise and Percy is riding him, he has a funny turn and then takes off at a gallop shaking his head wildly, he runs straight into a lamp post and both Percy and the horse break a leg it is awful. Poor MURPHY has to be put down, following an autopsy they discover the poor horse had a brain tumour. Even with more sophisticated equipment for detecting these things there is little that could have been done, except perhaps we would have stopped riding him. Poor Percy comes to work with his leg in plaster but can't ride so he cleans my tack in the afternoon whilst I ride the extra horses which is fine with me.

The summer between the two hunting seasons I go back to Jack for the showing season. There are two others riding for him and a full string of horses to show. I enjoy going to all the county shows, although it means very long days, sometimes, we have to start at 4 a.m. to get all the horses plaited up before loading and driving to the show, otherwise we go the day before and stay overnight if the show is too far away.

We youngsters usually sleep in the horsebox or even sometimes in a stable next to the horses, it is like camping out. One night I am sleeping in a stable when suddenly I am awoken by the trembling of the ground beneath me and a great thundering which sounds like galloping horses. I leap up thinking horses have escaped only to see a string of Shire horses being led past the stable at a walk. They are magnificent creatures, enormous and very heavy with huge feet. A horse walks in a four-time rhythm moving one foot at a time, the gallop is also four-time but with a moment of suspension, hence the confusion. Together with the rumbling and vibrating of the ground, it sounds like a herd of galloping horses and in reality, it is just four Shire Horses walking past the stable.

Jack is so good to me, when he has two horses in the Championship, he gives me one to ride. At one smaller local show in Moreton-in-Marsh the owner of the winner of the heavyweight class is there, so Jack decides to ride his horse in the championship. He knows full well that the winner of the lightweight class, which is a lovely chestnut horse, will win hands down. So, I get to ride the lovely lightweight horse who is a dream to ride and win my first Championship. I make a glorious round of honour to the cheering crowds and the local paper follows me out of the arena to ask me if they can take photographs. I am still ridiculously shy, I blush and politely decline, for which in hindsight I could have kicked myself. So often we are our own worst enemy!

The Royal show is a highlight of the summer, a glorious show usually synonymous with strawberries with cream and champagne. We are all looking forward to it and most of the owners are going to come with us so there are lots of distractions and much excitement. In the morning I am in charge of plaiting the horses and checking their leg protectors and bandages. We load the horses and pile into the cab setting off in great spirits with several cars following in convoy.

We arrive at the showground in Stoneleigh and unload the horses. We have booked stables so unpack the horsebox and settle in, only to discover, when there is less than an hour before the first class, we have forgotten all the saddles! Jack takes off in one of the cars and rushes back for them. Luckily, we have the bridles, so I and another girl have to warm up the first two horses bareback which is bordering on lethal as they are both four-year olds, new to showing and very excited making it no easy task. They are spooking at all the strange sights and smells so rather than warming them up it is a question of calming them down! Jack arrives just in time to saddle up and ride into the ring!

Despite the shaky start all the horses are placed in the top four and two win their classes so there are plenty of strawberries with cream and the champagne flows, as does the euphoria all the way home amid the array of cups and rosettes.

On the first of September I go back to Leicestershire, the men have already brought the horses up from their summer rest in the fields and have started walking exercise. I am quite happy to go back, it is a comfortable job, a good lifestyle and a better wage than I have ever earned. I stay for another season and towards the end somewhat sadly announce that I will not be back the following year. I say I have been not only enjoyed the job but also become fond of everyone, but I need to move on as I still have a lot to learn. I tell Joy's family one Sunday when we are all together, they really have taken me in as one of the family. On Sunday they always have a "gin and it" (gin and martini) before lunch which gives me Dutch courage. I have already talked to Joy about my plans, so it is not a complete surprise, all the same we shed a few tears.

We are, however, to remain in touch and I am to go back a year later to be Joy's bridesmaid when she marries local farmer Philip when he returns after a spell in Australia. Later I become godmother to their first son. Joy insists, although I tell her in no uncertain terms that I am highly unsuitable as I have neither a fixed abode nor a steady income.

I am quite sad to leave these good people but nonetheless convinced I am making the right decision, Jack, as always, is my mentor and I express a desire to do some show jumping, so on his recommendation go off to the south of England to do and intensive course.

Chapter 5

Buckinghamshire and Warwickshire

I have longed to jump ever since I saw Marion Coakes with little Stroller and Anne Moore with Psalm at the Horse of the Year show. When showing there with Jack we had a box for the evening show jumping and we were right next to the ring, sitting almost underneath one of those enormous fences. Some riders even strapped their stirrups to the girth because they were completely airborne over the fence, miraculously landing together. I had a touch of that sensation over a huge drop fence out hunting and it was so thrilling.

So, I sign up for the intensive jumping course in Buckinghamshire with Pat Thorne nee Pharazan who had been on the New Zealand Olympic team. She also still breeds thoroughbreds in New Zealand including EYESPY 111 Mark Todd's Sydney Bronze medal eventer. I take myself off to learn some new skills, there are about six of us on the course four of whom are there with their own competition horses, they are a friendly crowd, and we live and work together. The seat, or way of riding is different from the showing or the dressage seat, the muscles you use are different too, I am surprised to find muscles I didn't know I had.

First, I have to shorten my stirrups four holes and canter round the field for twenty minutes in poised position, this is with the weight off the saddle and down through the knees. Then rising for three strides and sitting for three to be totally balanced and flexible and move your weight without unbalancing the horse in fact using it to help him poising between fences and sitting for the last three strides. Another key factor is seeing the stride and measuring the distance to the fences which is not as easy as it looks. The more collected the horse, the shorter the stride and the easier it is to place him for take-off. There are standard measurements for strides between fences, but every horse has a different stride which also varies depending on speed and degree of collection.

I find having an eye for three strides most helpful and to know whether to hold or push depending on the kind of fence and what comes next, be it an upright fence, a sharp turn or a spread. There are more techniques than I had realised. For the exams, the main concept had been "forward and straight with rhythm" and to present the horse to the centre of the fence at ninety degrees which is certainly the safest and easiest way.

Now I have to learn to jump at an angle or one side of a fence to facilitate tricky turns or cut corners and change legs over the fence, so there is plenty to practice. The combinations are not always standard, sometimes they include a tricky distance. Maybe you have to decide whether to push on for one long stride or hold back for two short ones. A spread in the middle followed by an upright is tricky, it is so easy to flatten and have the last one down, so lots of transitions on and back so the horse is supple and quick to respond remaining collected and balanced. The only horse available for me to compete on is a bit lazy but as in my pony days I find my electric seat and manage to inspire him. We compete a little in Grade C and Newcomers, although at home we jump higher and train with some grade A jumpers. This means that when we go to a show the jumps look small which is a great advantage and confidence booster. At one show I am in the collecting ring taking turns to jump the practice fence when a familiar voice shouts my name from the ringside, it is a friend from the showing world who marvels at my jumping those "huge fences". Ironic really as I had done exactly the same at the major shows only a few months previously it had been me who had marvelled from the ringside.

It is the horses who do the jumping, the rider only indicates the jump and helps where possible with angle, distances, and speed. Most important of all trying not to interfere, allowing the horse to stretch his head and neck and use his back or "bascule" over the fence. It is not as difficult as I had imagined and made easier when I am taught to slide my hands forward along the crest of the horse's neck to allow him to stretch. This way it is so much easier to maintain an even contact. Previously I had been taught to keep a straight line from elbow through hand to the horse's mouth which is not so easy to judge or maintain over a fence.

To chill out once a week we go for a mad hack, we box the horses to the New Forest which is beautiful riding country. One girl is celebrating her 21st birthday and invites us all to her home in Surrey, a super home and an unforgettable party with marquee, live music and flowing champagne. Sniggy, as we all called her is an unassuming, friendly girl, one would never have guessed her background. She has her own horse, but he is quite an ordinary fellow compared with the posh imported German horses or thoroughbred crosses of some of the others. I smile to myself they must live in palaces I muse, but the great thing about horses is they are a great leveller.

All in all, an interesting, and fun few months. I finish the course and return to Jack's with an even stronger desire to jump! Jack has a few little brushes jumps on a cinder track in the form of a jumping lane. We use this to teach the young horses to "leave the ground" as Jack says, but he vows to build more jumps for me. There is also a boy from New Zealand staying with Jack who has done a bit of eventing. He is too good looking to be true and unfortunately, he knows it and has a ball that year breaking a few hearts on the way. I feel he is too hard on the horses as well as the girls and when he challenges me to a game of chess in his room I accept reluctantly. I am no expert, but I manage to beat him, thanks to hours spent playing with my father as a child. When he makes advances, I tell him he is fun as a friend, but not my type as he has a cruel streak, I don't like the way he treats his horse, a comment which logically doesn't go down too well. I had seen him lose his temper with a young horse which threw its head around. I believe the horse only protested because his hands were too hard and then he hit it over the head, totally unforgivable. To my relief he avoids me completely after that episode, which is hardly surprising, later I realise that sometimes horses, like children, can push our patience to its limits, I also realise that I too was cruel in making such comments!

Jack is a brilliant horseman but, as often is the case, a hopeless businessman. He makes me a proposition; he wants me to be his partner 50-50 and I will take over the administration. Talk about the blind leading the blind. I am completely unqualified and when I point this out, he just says "You can't be worse than me". A friend had always managed his affairs, but he had unfortunately died rather suddenly since when the bills and correspondence had simple piled up on the desk. The offer came as a surprise, but I thought it over and consulted my father who kindly offered to help me out with any queries. It is too good an offer to turn down, although to be honest I still have itchy feet. I sleep on the idea, consult my parents, and decide we should give it a year's trial for both our sakes.

The next day I spend the morning riding and go into the office after lunch. The desk is piled with papers and unopened post. First, I open everything and put it into some kind of order. As I sort through the papers, I become increasingly anxious and wonder what I have let myself in for. There are a number of red-letter bills threatening to take legal proceedings and two solicitor's letters. I am shocked and go to find Jack, who is not in the least concerned. He grins at me "No problem, we have some fantastic horses to sell and if they get nasty Stella Cardiff will help me out, it won't be the first time!" he uncorks a bottle of good French wine and seems more concerned with the bouquet of the red wine than the red-letter bills. Stella Cardiff is a wealthy client who funded Jack's tour of the United States with a string of show horses. She also owns the house and stables where Jack operates which she rents to him for a pittance. She so values his talent with horses she overlooks his financial shortcomings.

Luckily enough we have a string of clients that week and sure enough the next day sell a four-year-old for 1,000 guineas, 1,100 pounds. Odd how horses and rams are sold in guineas and horse racing too uses the currency. It has been hard day we have been showing horse after horse, in hand then ridden. Beforehand they have to be prepared as if they were going to a show, still it has all been worthwhile.

We retire to the house to crack open a bottle of champagne and settle-up. Jack ceremoniously hands me the check introducing me as his new partner and secretary. I thank them both and leave them to finish celebrating whilst I head for the office to decide which debts to pay off first. When I emerge, I go back to the yard to supervise the evening feed and on my return to the house Jack is nowhere to be found. I find his wife Sheelagh in the kitchen she says vaguely she thinks he had gone off in the Horsebox. I run out of the back of the house and sure enough the Horsebox is not there.

Jack rings about an hour later to say he will be late home. He delivered the horse we sold to the new owner and went on to see some spectacular young horses on the way home! Sure, enough when I go back to the office the check book is missing and my heart sinks, but there is nothing I can do, only wait and see. The next morning the Horsebox is back and a lovely young horse in the stable which had been vacated. There is no sign of Jack so the three of us are feeding and mucking out when one of the girls comes round from the barn with some clean shavings. She says she is sure she heard a noise coming from the Horsebox. A little later I go round and sure enough there is a loud clonk from the Horsebox. I open the little side door and to my surprise there is a horse inside. We don't have a spare stable, so Jack just loosed him in the Horsebox and shoved in some food and water! He had sold one horse and bought two more!!!!

Jack has friends in all areas of the horse world and is famous for buying valuable racehorses which don't have the speed but have a wonderful pedigree. He retrains them for showing or competing and sells them on accordingly. So, we regularly go up to Newmarket to Fred Winter's yard to buy young racehorses and sometimes he sends us on to other yards in the area. I love those visits, the stables and the horses are so beautifully kept, obviously there is no shortage of money in the racing world! The training of a racehorse is completely different they are trained to gallop and lean on the bit. To teach them to slow down when they feel pressure on the reins and get them used to leg and seat aids takes a bit of doing. Jack is such a brilliant rider he is capable of taking a horse off the racecourse and into the show ring. He is so relaxed, he sings, riding on almost no contact and of course the gallop is spectacular then he will calmly circle to stop. That is all very well but the judges and the clients need to be able to ride them too! He has a gift with young horses for the same reason, he is so relaxed he gives them confidence.

Many problems with horses arise as a result of fear or confusion. They are big animals but extremely sensitive. If a rider is afraid, the horse senses it, he doesn't realise the rider is afraid of him, rather he feels if the rider is afraid there must be something really terrifying somewhere. The more the horse tenses and the more the nervous the rider becomes means they go from bad to worse.

We, the riders, also have limited patience and if a horse doesn't respond immediately to our commands, we repeat them stronger or get cross with him. The repeating of aids leads to the term "nagsman" for a rider, and "nag" for a horse. However, nagging has the same effect on horses as it does on people. The best way to survive a nagger is to switch off and ignore them, so a horse that is subjected to kick, kick, kick becomes dead to the leg. All riders think they are giving the same aids, or commands, but like handshakes no two people have the same feel. We are different weights, have different leg lengths so an aid behind the girth from one rider is totally different pressure and position from another. Horses are incredible if they can work it out and understand us, I never cease to be amazed by their intelligence and patience. Moreover horses, like people, are creatures of habit so it is essential to create good habits from the beginning as, also like us, it is very hard to change a bad habit. This means it is not easy to retrain a horse or to overcome a bad habit.

Clients also send Jack problem horses to retrain. One such horse is a beautiful big bay horse who is perfectly sweet in the stable, however, as soon as you mount him, he stands straight up on his hind legs and refuses to move forward. Jack is always quiet usually singing or whistling softly. He instructs me to tack up the horse and put on the German-reins, these run from the girth between the font legs and through the bit to the hands so drawing the head down acting as a pulley. I lead the horse into the yard and up to the mounting block. Jack gently drew the reins up so the horses head is lowered. He instructs me to mount the horse and maintain the reins in the same position whatever happens and just keep going forward. As I alight in the saddle the horse lunges, he can't rear on his hind legs with his head down. Next, he ran backwards as fast as he can bumps into the wall and lunges forward again, Jack encourages him with a well-timed whack up the backside and he takes off at a gallop. As best I can I steer down the drive and onto the road. We gallop all the way to the next village then reduce to a spanking trot all the way round the block. I don't loosen the reins until we were back in the yard where I hug, pat and praise him. After three days the moment I land it the saddle the horse flies forward, he is a quick learner. The owners come to see me ride him unassisted and with no problem. They take him home very happy with the results.

Unfortunately, a month later they are back to square one, as frequently happens, once a horse has had a bad habit you always have to be careful, one slip and you lose control again. However, Jack's method had worked for us.

No truer saying than that of "Pride goeth before a fall". One Saturday I have a family "do" so ask Jack if I can leave about 11 am to make it home in time for lunch. Jack says it is fine if I ride four horses before leaving. One of them is a four-year-old, just broken and the last time I rode him in the schooling field as we passed the gate, he stopped dead and reared up on his hind legs. Pride: I think "I can deal with this", I put on the German reins as we had with the problem horse thinking to myself that this will solve the problem. So off we go, he is going nicely forward so I have the German reins quite slack. Suddenly he digs in his toes and up he goes on his hind legs. I am a split second too late taking up the German reins and the result is a disastrous fall. The poor horse rears, loses his balance and falls over backwards on top of me. Fortunately, there had been a lot of rain and the ground was soft, so he buried my right leg in the mud mercifully pulling the stirrup off the saddle. The horse is lying on top of me, he struggles to his feet and takes off at a gallop through the gate and down the middle of the road back towards the stables. I struggle to my feet, but there is a shooting pain in my groin. As I make my way slowly back towards the stables someone from the village recognises me in passing and gives me a lift. Jack is furious, he is beside himself as the valuable young horse gallops into the yard with his back, the saddle and even his neck and head plastered in mud, no rider and a stirrup missing. What is more there could have been a terrible accident on the road. I hobble painfully into the yard and go straight to the horse's stable to check him over and clean him up. Jack follows me asking me angrily what the hell I think I am doing putting the German reins on a four-year-old. In a strained voice I reply that he had been rearing and as we had cured the other horse of rearing that way, I thought I would try it with this one. Jack raises his eyes to heaven and tells me that is a typical case of a little knowledge being dangerous. He tells me never to do anything like that again without consulting him. Message received and understood. Luckily, the horse seems fine and not even upset I settle him down and hobble into the yard. "What's up with you?" Jack asks a little impatiently, this is too much the tears began to roll down my cheeks and I actually swear, "It bloody hurts," I retort, although my pride is as badly hurt as my groin, "I'm going for an x-ray," is my parting shot. On the way to the car, I call into the office, of course my National Insurance stamps haven't been paid so I grab the book and will have to go and queue in the post office to update it on my way to the hospital. Jack meets me by the car, "Can you drive?" he asks a little more concerned, but then barks at me again, "This is a tough business my girl and if you aren't tough enough it is better if you get out now!"

At the hospital they eye up my riding gear, it is obvious the doctor considers any pain I may be in to be totally self-inflicted. However, he sends me for an x-ray fortunately and amazingly, considering half a ton of horse has landed on top of me, nothing is broken. However, my pelvis has been displaced on one side, there is a gap, so all the muscles and tendons have been pulled, hence the pain. He tells me to keep my leg up and as still as possible for two weeks and it will probably go back into place.

My parents are due to go abroad on holiday the next day, so on the way home I buy a box of oranges on the side of the road and ring Jack when I get home. I assure my parents that I will be fine and binge on oranges with my leg up for four days but can't wait to get back on a horse. My groin is still painful but now bearable. I find Jack and apologize; he too says he is sorry he was so hard on me and welcomes me back. It is acceptable to make mistakes if we make sure we learn from them.

However, before long I put my foot in it once more. I am breaking a lovely thoroughbred four-year-old gelding by PRINCE ABYSS. I teach him to wear the tack, lunge, and long-rein. Jack supervises us the first time I mount him in the stable then I long rein him through the village to an indoor school where I mount him and ride him home. He behaves like and angel. Jack says for the next step he will bring a horse down to the school and we will ride away from home and to the next village together with the horse as a "Nanny". The first day Jack promises to follow me down to the school he has an unexpected visit from a client and doesn't appear. The second day there is a delivery of horse feed and he can't make it in time and the third day he forgets. On the fourth day I wait for ages as he has promised to come. The horse is getting bored, fidgety, and impatient so I decide to go it alone. He goes away from home when I ask him, and I praise him effusively. However, when we arrive at the crossroads a motor bike comes very noisily towards us. The startled horse leaps in the air and whips round at the same time depositing me in the middle of the road, I am unhurt but mortified. Needless to say, Jack is not pleased.

The next day he accompanies me, and all goes well, we trot and even have a few strides of canter. The following day he wakes me at 5am. He tells me to clip the young horse as hounds are meeting down the road and I am to take him. His wife is to accompany me on one of the children's ponies as a "Nanny". We trot steadily to the next village and all goes well. The meet is almost over, and they are moving off. Sheila says, "Let's carry on a bit." We stay at the back and trot down the road then follow the others down a bridle path. At the end, and the only way out, is over a post and rails fence. Sheila jumps it. The young horse stops dead, and then he becomes very agitated as he finds he is alone, and all the other horses are on the other side of the fence. I turn him around and try again. He stops dead and then gives an enormous cat jump. I lose my stirrups and as we land, he gives an enormous buck and yet again I hit the dust or rather mud. Someone catches him for me, I climb back on board and we continue. When we finally reach a road, we made our way quietly back home, by which time having been ridden for three hours poor boy is really tired and as quiet as a lamb.

I have yet another nasty experience when I am long reining a young horse in the lunging ring. There is a low wall on the one side beyond which there is an open field. I am lunging him with two reins, the outside rein running from the bit round his quarters to my hand, both reins are long, and one is trailing on the ground behind me. I bring him down to a walk and asked him to change the rein which we have done successfully in the stable. I am a fraction slow in collecting the rein that had been trailing and I have already freed the other one. At which precise moment the horse spooks at a cat, he takes off and I am just behind him. He is strong and pulls me off my feet. I fall flat on my face and the reins tangled behind my back. He is dragging me across the arena. He picks up speed and jumps the wall. Miraculously the reins free from behind my back and I am left face down with my head inches from the stone wall. That really shakes me, what is more I am not wearing a hat. The horse is careering round the field with the two long reins trailing. I feel the blood drain from my head and my heart races, I am terrified he will become entangled in the reins and break a leg. Fortunately, he stops beside the far hedge to talk to the horses on the other side and I manage to retrieve him unharmed. I confess to Jack but make light of the incident!

I am not the only one to suffer mishaps it is part and parcel of this life. We are schooling one day in the big flat forty-acre field. I am riding the middleweight and Jack is riding the heavyweight. Our objective is to develop the gallop, especially for the Heavyweight. The lighter horses usually have a good gallop, but the heavier ones are rather cumbersome. Accordingly, a heavyweight with a really, good, gallop is sure to be a winner. We have a few gallops side by side to encourage the horses to race. The big horse is really beginning to enjoy himself and flatten out. Jack tells me to walk round and cool off while he has one last gallop on his own. He is on the far side of the field and really going fast when I realise something was not quite right. I see Jack is leaning forward grabbing the horse's bridle on one side trying to pull him round in a huge circle. Then he swings himself off the horse still hanging onto his head and tries to use his own legs as brakes. It is a miracle he doesn't break both legs as they seemed tangled with the horse's legs, eventually they stop. The bit has broken, a perfectly good, fairly new, loose ring German snaffle, it could have caused a fatal accident.

Fortunately, we also have some moments of glory and fun too, although at one show Jack has another mishap. The judges pull him into second place with his friend and rival Douglas Bunn in first place. Nearly all the exhibitors know each other, they are old cronies. I go into the ring to help Jack prepare the horse for the in-hand section of the judging. I run a damp cloth down the horse's black legs which cleans off any dust and leaves them shiny. There is a lot of banter going on, Jack says to his colleague who is standing first, "Well if you are going to beat me today at least do it in style." With which he takes the damp cloth from me and stoops to wipe the hind leg of the horse standing first. The horse obviously hasn't seen him and is startled. He jumps, landing squarely on Jack's foot. Jack jokes, "Well you can beat me, but you don't have to kill me off at the same time." He is obviously in pain but soldiers on. There is a horseshoe mark on his boot that has almost cut through the thick leather. He refuses to let us take his boot off and rides in three more classes.

When we get home, we can't get his boot off, so I drive him to the hospital and they cut it off. His boot is full of blood and he has two broken toes. They clean him up and put a plaster on his foot and lower leg. The next day he is back on a horse, although he needs quite a lot of help to mount and dismount.

We have a small hunter to sell, he has been a champion in hand, but now the owner can't stop him and has sent him to Jack to sell. Sheila usually deals with the small hunters, but she rides him once in double bridle with a gag and a martingale, in other words the strongest brakes she can find. She vows she will never ride him again and sends him to Jack's yard. I ride him in the same gear, working constantly and using circles manage not to lose control but he is hard work.

The Master of the Heythrop Hunt wants a horse for his wife, with a snaffle mouth, in other words easy to control. Jack wants me to take this horse hunting to show her, he is a very attractive horse. Sheila says Jack is mad! He tells me he will use a roller snaffle which is a lot stronger, but still a snaffle and off we go. To cap it all I forget my gloves. At the meet he behaves beautifully. When we set off, I fix one hand on his neck and use the other to prevent him breaking out of a trot. We get to the first covert riding alongside the lady. We canter across the first field and I manage to keep him in check.

Then we are queueing to go through a gate and a few people decide to jump the hedge. The lady client indicates for me to jump the hedge. I point him at the hedge which he jumps perfectly, but on landing he tears the reins out of my already bleeding hands and takes off at a flat-out gallop. As luck would have it, we are up on the point-to-point racecourse so with all my might I steer him away from the hunt and round the racecourse, I have never been so fast in my life. The second time round he blows up and I manage to get him back under control. I make my way back to join the hunt not sure how much the client has witnessed of our exhibition. When we reach the road, I realise that he has lost a shoe, the perfect excuse to go home. I find the lady client and inform her that the horse has lost a shoe, so I am taking him home, to which she replies stiffly that she has seen enough. Unfortunately, the next day the little horse has a tendon like a sausage and has to be fired.

Firing is an old-fashioned method of shortening overstretched tendons literally by burning them. They can be pin fired, or bar fired depending on the severity of the damage to the tendon. The leg then swells up and must be terribly painful but usually the horse is sound after a long slow recovery. Unfortunately, it leaves scars showing the horse has had a tendon problem, this means he is practically unsaleable or at least causes a huge drop in value. Luckily, Sheila backs me up saying it was entirely Jack's fault, but I feel dreadful for the poor little horse.

There is an influx of new people, Sally comes from Scotland to work with us and learn the art of showing. This is fantastic for me as we are more the same age. We start going out in the evenings. One night we go out dancing and when we get back Jack is already up, making the morning tea. He raises his eyebrows and says, "You two have ten minutes to get changed!" Sally is from a sheep farm in the Scottish borders. Later I am invited up there to her wedding which is held at her home. An unusual family, Sally is one of nine children and they have all been educated at home by Sally's mother. Apparently in the winter when it snows, they are completely cut off from the nearest village, sometimes for a month at a time. They are all delightful and have gone on to do well in life, there is a teacher, a nurse, a solicitor. One brother, who is extremely handsome, stays to work the sheep farm with his father and Sally is horse mad like me. She marries a handsome farmer and goes to live in a house in Yorkshire which had belonged to her grandfather. Sally tells me fascinating tales of her youth. They ride sturdy ponies to cover the thousands of acres. They hunt the foxes which attack their sheep and sometimes the children have to be live earth stoppers. In other words, they have to stand in front of the fox's lair and stop the hunted fox from going to ground. Sally says she was terrified. Also, they have to help with lambing from an early age, sheering too, it was a quite tough life. I have the opportunity of helping Sally sheer her pet ewe by hand, jolly hard work as we used hand sheers. I love having Sally at Jack's, it is so good to have someone of my age to talk to and share ideas with.

There are two clients staying, so Sally and I temporarily move into the attic. There is a girl who comes with her new show horse to learn the ropes of the show ring. Jack insists she should be part of the team but whereas Sally and I are downstairs in the morning in ten minutes, it takes her nearly an hour as she makes her face up and paints her nails, before emerging from her room like a model. There is also the boy from New Zealand, he has an eventer and is good looking, but Sally and I don't like the way he treats his horse, so he doesn't stand a chance. Another client, who doesn't live in, but comes every day is Lady Betsy Profumo. She comes to ride her horse and always wears pink gloves, which fascinates me.

How it came about is uncertain, but Jack is asked to organize two week's hunting in Leicestershire for a Spanish Duke who is said to be a pretender to the throne. We have two months to find and prepare six well behaved quality hunters. Jack has a lorry load of horses shipped over from Ireland. They are all six or seven years old so ready to get fit and work and I have the job of jumping them all and even doing a few working hunter classes.

We rent a yard in Leicestershire near Market Harborough which also means I can catch up with old friends. We hunt every day with the Fernie and the Quorn. Chris Cullen the vet comes with us with his horse. He shocks us all by washing his horse from head to foot after hunting, he hoses him with cold water! Of course, he is clipped out, but washing except for tail and feet is definitely frowned upon. It is certainly quicker, and the horse must feel great afterwards. The steamy, sweating, muddy horse has a cold shower and is then wrapped in warm rugs. We always remove all the dry mud using a rubber curry comb and brushing, jolly hard work and uncomfortable for the horse too.

Jack and I stay at a small hotel near the horses. Halfway through the week, we are getting ready to go hunting and Jack can't find his stock pin. He finds a huge nappy pin, but we are hunting with the "big wigs" as he called them, he asks me if I will swop and lend him my stock pin. I have in fact a very good gold pin with sentimental value, my parents gave it to me when I passed my exams. Unfortunately, Jack loses that one too so we both end the week wearing nappy pins on our stocks! The Duke is quite young, tall dark and handsome but rather shy and his English is a little broken. Not surprisingly he is tired in the evenings and often prefers to have dinner quietly with us and retire early rather than socialize although he isn't short of invitations. He is an average horseman but only has problems with one of the horses, a chestnut gelding, he says he pulls. That is lucky for me as I get to hunt him for the rest of the week, and he is a terrific jumper. There is a jovial atmosphere in the yard, Jack has taken a barrel of Guinness, as always! The Duke is initiated into the habit of Guinness in the tack room and he seems more relaxed and happier there than anywhere.

When we get home, Jack promises he will buy me a stock pin to replace mine. He never goes near shops and has precious little time, so I am sure that although his intentions are good it is highly unlikely to materialize. The household is charming, if a little chaotic. Their daughter Selina, who is six years old, wakes up one morning shouting her bed is all wet. On investigation her little Jack Russel terrier has had six puppies in her bed! To my horror Jack cuts off their tails with the kitchen scissors, I nearly pass out and the puppies' cries haunt me, also the sight of the sad looking mother licking her babies' wounds. When I challenge him about it, he explains they are working dogs and go down fox holes. He says it has always been done that way and if it is done in the first few hours after birth it heals straight away. Their tails are cut short so that the men can pull them out of the holes without being bitten and this often saved their lives, the dogs that is. I am not convinced, there are so many aspects of "country life" I have a hard time accepting.

One of the puppies is smaller than the others and terribly nervous. The puppies are well bred and already people are waiting to buy them. My heart goes out to the smallest puppy so whenever I can I help her to feed and cuddle her. I go to Jack and ask if I can have the puppy instead of a stock-pin. As I choose the runt of the litter Jack readily agrees. So, I acquire Fleur, she is a small Jack Russel terrier with rather long legs, she is white except for two large black patches over her eyes and she becomes my shadow. She is a perfect little dog, she will run with the horses for hours, or be happy with ten minutes exercise here and there if we are travelling When I am in the car, she protects me, my uncle calls her "Fang" as she curls her lip and shows her teeth at him, she doesn't like men. Hardly surprising when her first encounter with a man was when she had her tail chopped off. When the attendants at the petrol stations approach the car and especially if one rests his hand on the sill, she launches herself from the back shelf snarling ferociously, so the burliest of men jump away. I know I should stop her, but she makes me feel so safe that tiny dog!

Every year Jack goes to Dublin to ride at Ballsbridge that wonderful International Horse Show. He rides for Nat Galway-Greer, a dealer, breeder, and producer of thoroughbreds. As Sheelagh is Irish, they take advantage of the Dublin show to have their summer family holiday and see Sheelagh's family. The first summer they leave me in charge in England and all goes well, with the exception of the unfortunate death of the children's hamster, about which I feel dreadful, but apparently, he was quite old.

As the following year approaches the family is busy preparing for their annual trip to Ireland. We are all having lunch around the big square table in the kitchen when Jack has a phone call from Nat who says that his nagsman (rider) had left and he has no-one to prepare the horses for the show, so he is going to turn them all out and forget it. Jack said "No way! I'm putting my best girl on the next plane." Nat argues "The horses are green and have not been out of their stables for a week and there is no way a girl can handle them." To which Jack replies "We don't ride fresh horses we lunge them first, she will sort them out." He hangs up and turns to me, "Pack your bags you're on the next plane to Ireland."

Chapter 6
Ireland

A new adventure in Ireland, everything happens so fast, following Jack's instructions I rush upstairs and pack my case while he rings round for a seat on the next available flight to Dublin. He secures a flight and I ring my parents, then hasty goodbyes and we bundle everything into the car and set off for the airport.

I realise that although I know the name of man I am going to ride for, I have no address or phone number. Jack is driving at the time so he tells me he will give me the details at the airport. We are held up in traffic and arrive barely in time to catch the flight. Jack is rushing me through and giving me instructions about the horses. I protest that I still have no contact details to which he replies, "Hurry up or you will miss the plane, don't worry you can't miss him he is tall with blue eyes!" with which he turns abruptly and leaves.

I am the last passenger to board the plane, I hurriedly take my seat smiling apologetically at my fellow passengers who look as though they have been seated and waiting for some time. Once settled I think about the bizarre situation, I am in. I am going to Ireland; I know neither where I am going nor for how long. All I know is that I will be met by a tall man with blue eyes called Nat. I don't even have much money on me, maybe just enough to ring England if I find myself stranded. We land on time; I collect my luggage and emerge somewhat dubiously. There, right by the exit, is a tall, elderly, gentleman with piercing blue eyes. He spots me immediately and almost takes my case from me before introducing himself with his lovely soft Irish brogue. What a relief, so far so good!

We leave the airport in a large rather old Bentley. Leaving Dublin behind we make our way to county Meath and the small village of Dunboyne. On the edge of the village, we turn down a long drive lined with trees and draw up outside the house. We are greeted by Mrs Galway Greer, who has a no-nonsense air about her, and their daughter Betty who is a little older than me, probably in her thirties. Betty is tall and slim with brown curly hair and a warm friendly smile I take to her immediately.

I am shown to a room adjacent to the kitchen which was obviously the maid's room in the past. The bed has a feather mattress and the whole house feels like stepping back in time. They explain that they had a full team of staff, but they all now live in the village with their families.

I leave my belongings in my room and am ushered into the sitting room for afternoon tea poured from a silver tea pot into fine china cups and served with cakes and tiny sandwiches. After tea Betty and Nat take me down to the stables. We emerge through the back door into a beautiful walled garden halfway along the wall on the left there is a large wooden door which leads directly into the tack room. In the tack room three men are finishing their tea, they are the head groom and two assistant grooms. They seem a little tongue tied when Nat introduces me. As we passed through the tack room into the yard Betty explains that they have never had a girl in the yard before, so logically they are a little sceptical and uncomfortable.

We emerge into a long stable yard. A small wiry man with a mass of white hair is emerging from one of the stables, skip in hand, his mouth literally drops open when he sees me. One of the men behind us lets out a roar of laughter and banters "Bad luck Snowy she only likes red heads," the others chuckle, at least it breaks the ice. However, I feel sorry for Snowy, I greet him, but he doesn't speak, neither does he take his eyes off me, he remains riveted to the spot as we make our way down the yard. There are ten stables and in these are the horses I have to prepare for the show. Nat says obviously I can't ride all ten every day, so he has hired a young jockey to ride with me under my instructions.

We emerged into another yard where the brood mares and young stock are stabled. Nat also breeds racehorses and sells many to England. The next morning, I am told to be in the yard at 7:30am sharp to meet Tommy the jockey and work the first two horses before breakfast. I am not allowed to muck out or groom, only ride. As I enter the yard, I come face to face with Snowy, to my horror and surprise he has dyed his hair red! Tommy explains that Snowy lives next door and is a simple soul.

I am not even allowed to tack-up, the horses are prepared and led into the yard for me to mount. As Jack instructed, I insist on lunging them first, although it is clear the staff including Tommy think I am mad. I am glad I insist, the first

70

two set off bucking and squealing like broncos. Jack always says they need to get that out of their system and why fight them from on top, they can't concentrate on their work with all that accumulated, electric, energy to deal with.

Tommy and I mount the first two horses and ride towards the schooling field. I have asked Tommy to lengthen his stirrups and use his legs to teach the horses the correct aids. He pulls a face and says, "Sure can't we just have a bit of tippety tip first?" tippety-tip being a flat-out gallop. I give a wry smile I am partial to a bit of tippety-tip myself, soon the tippety-tip replaces the lunging before we settle down to work. The horses are beautiful looking but very green and we have barely a month to get them ready. Just to get them to canter on the correct leg is quite a challenge for Tommy as well as the horses. They all develop a great gallop of course. Luckily, they are all shown in double bridles, this helps considerably with collection, and through riding together two or three of them developed spectacular extended trots.

My favourite, although I know one shouldn't have favourites, is the lightweight, his name is "SPLENDID" and he really is true to his name. The horses and riders rest on Sunday and "SPLENDID" comes out bucking on Monday mornings. More so if we begin with a "tippety tip", he just can't contain himself, much to Nat's amusement. When he is telling the tale to the family over lunch Mrs Greer shakes her head and referring to me comments "I knew she was a bold lass". I am quite pleased with myself, understanding she is implying that I am brave. However, a few days later, the little dog comes into the sitting room and does a puddle on the carpet, Mrs Greer leaps to her feet angrily shouting, "You, bold lassie you!" I realise that in that part of the world "bold" means naughty and not brave as I had supposed.

When the blacksmith comes, we spend a long time with each horse. A good blacksmith can change a horse's way of moving. One of the horses is a little pigeon toed, he turned his toes in, so shaping the hoof to bring more weight bearing on the inside straightens the horse's leg also probably avoiding tendon problems in the future. The same goes for cow hocks and sickle hocks, or a horse that dishes or swings his legs to the side when he trots. Nat is there with his chalk, I trot the horse in question in hand up and down, they discuss his action and mark the hoof with chalk. The blacksmith trims accordingly and the process is repeated. Also varying the weight and shape of the shoe, higher or lower heels, rolled toes, three quarter shoes etc. They say no foot no horse I really begin to appreciate the saying.

I am amused by the tea-time ritual, the men have their tea in the tack room as usual, the blacksmith has his tea in the kitchen with the cook and I have to pull off my boots and go through to the living room with the family.

The food is delicious, there are home-made cakes twice a day with morning coffee and afternoon tea. Normally I never ate cakes but when I try to refuse politely Madam scoffs and tells me not to be silly or "bold". There are two eggs as part of a full-scale breakfast every morning. At lunch time I have a problem, I have the habit of eating what I least like first and saving the best for last. In Ireland potatoes are part of the staple diet so the helpings are generous at every meal. I am not keen on potatoes so wolf them first, but as soon as I place the last mouthful of potato into my mouth the maid hastily steps forward and serves me more before I can protest. I put on a stone and a half in a month despite all the riding.

Betty, the daughter, although older than me, is a good companion. We play tennis and croquet on the lawn and Betty studies the bloodlines and selects the appropriate stallions for the brood mares. They take me racing as they have several home-bred horses in training. I am impressed as Betty knows the breeding, history and form of most of the horses running. She knows which horses run better on soft ground and those that prefer hard ground. She knows which horses have beaten which, the ones at the peak of their form and those building up for a particular race, she is a fount of knowledge.

Jack comes over a week before the show, Tommy goes back to his racing and Jack and I ride together. He seems quite pleased with the horses and the work we have done. The week of the show we all move into Dublin. Ballsbridge is a beautiful, old, established showground with excellent stabling. Nat has promised me that if "SPLENDID" gets into the Championship I can ride him, sadly he comes second. All the horses are placed and two win their classes, so there is plenty to celebrate and the spirits are high. Jack wants to take me home, but Nat won't hear of it. He even persuades Jack that he needs to keep me for another month after the show to help him prepare the two-year-olds for the Doncaster Sales and then to hold the fort whilst he is away, and I am more than willing to comply. They reach an agreement; Nat will find better young horses for Jack and I can stay for another month.

Most of the horses we take to the show are sold there and then. We take a few home and people come to try them, but my role changes from intensive riding to a little riding and preparing the youngsters for Doncaster they have to give a good show in hand trotting steadily in a straight line, standing square and being quiet to handle whilst having their legs and teeth etc. examined and I love working with young horses.

Nat takes me with him all over Ireland trying horses with a view to buying. Ireland is rightly called the "Emerald Isle", what a beautiful country. I learn so much from Nat and as with everything the more you learn, the more you realise how little you know. We mostly visit farmers who have home bred young horses for sale. What wonderful horse country everyone has horses?

On one occasion we drive down to County Wexford to see a four-year-old, a lovely big horse with a floating trot and a natural cadence. The farmer's son rides the horse, he gives us a good show and then it is my turn. I shorten the stirrups and take up the reins and we move forward. He is so green I feel he has no brakes and no steering, yet the boy had ridden him so well. Somehow, I manage to trot and canter on both reins, but it is really hard work, I feel he is stopping and starting and wiggling like a snake I can't hold him together. I take him back and dismount thanking his owner, when asked my opinion my only comment is that he is a little green. However, I add he is spectacular to look at and a lovely mover, so no doubt has a lot of potential. Nat as always is reserved, he is always a man of few words, we have tea and take our leave. In the car he is silent for a while then asks me what I thought of the horse. He listens to me in silence as I repeat the comments I made to the owner, then gently asks "Didn't you notice his knees?" He tells me never to buy a horse with flat knees, back at the knee or with small knees as he is sure to have tendon trouble sooner or later, better a horse over at the knee than back at the knee! I learn to examine knees, hocks, pasterns, fetlocks and feet with new eyes and value the importance of these over good looks and flashy movers. Also, the importance of checking the teeth for the age as Nat said the Irish are full of Blarney, charming, but full of Blarney.

Finally, the two-year olds are ready to leave for Doncaster and I am to stay on to work with the yearlings, also to school a lovely cob for Betty to hunt. In this part of Ireland, the fields are divided by huge banks so that is a new challenge, teaching a horse to negotiate the banks. One day, before he leaves, Nat invites me into his study and makes me a proposition. He wants me to stay on to hunt with Betty, who is a nervous rider, and he is sure I would give her confidence. That way I can bring on young horses and continue supervising the handling of the young livestock. He tells me to think about it and give him an answer when he gets back. While Nat is away Jack rings three times desperate for me to get back as soon as possible. I am in a quandary, on the one hand it is very tempting, I have a very comfortable life in Dunboyne, I think hunting in Ireland would be fun, I could still learn a lot from Nat and financially I would be better off. However, Jack has been my mentor helping me over a good many years, apart from which I am supposed to be his partner even though financially speaking he is a disaster. My conscience prevails and I opt to go back to Jack. When Nat comes home, I thank him saying that I was very tempted but felt I couldn't let Jack down. After all I came to Ireland on his behalf and the original idea was for a month and I have already been there for three months.

With genuine sadness I bid them goodbye and thank everyone. I am even sad to leave old Snowy who now stammers a few words to me every day. It is surprising how fond one can become of people in such a short time, I feel badly about leaving Betty too as she has been so kind to me, but whatever decision I take I will feel guilty. From the quiet order of the Irish Stud Farm to the organized chaos of Jack's dealing and showing yard.

It is good to be back; Sally has been holding the fort in my absence and it is good to see her again. We are busy as always in fact have to rent two other yards in the village to accommodate all the horses. A client comes looking for an event horse, Jack true to his word has made another arena and put up a few jumps, I show them a couple of horses and Jack is chatting to the client. As I finished showing them the second horse Jack calls after me "Bring out that lovely four-year-old". There are at least six four-year olds I asked which one. "The bay one," he replies, at least four of them are bay! I make an educated guess and appear on a bay four-year-old I have never ridden. He goes reasonably well but I am quite sure he has never jumped in his life and Jack says, "Just pop the gate my dear", I pretend I haven't heard him the first time and circle so I can jump it going towards the stables. Talk about throwing your heart over first, I wrap my legs round the horse and encouraged him with everything I can muster. He hesitates and then stands right back taking the most enormous leap. The client is delighted and buys him, what a brave, honest, young horse.

There is a gentleman in the village who has a huge black horse called Othello. He sends him to me to teach him to jump. Nigel lives with his mother in a big old Cotswold stone house in the village and invites me to dinner one evening. The dinner is very formal, and his mother is a true matriarch. I learn a lot about the village history and apparently their house is haunted. It had originally been a farmhouse in the 15th century, since when it has been renovated and extended.

Nigel says that every spring they are awoken at about four am by the strong smell of bacon wafting up from the kitchen. When they go downstairs to investigate, there is no one there, but the aroma persists and when they return upstairs there is a figure at the end of the corridor which goes into the spare room and slams the door. This always coincides with the lambing season and as soon as the first lambs appear in the area so does the ghost. They say they are not at all frightened of their ghost and have become quite used to him. Nigel takes me to Stratford theatre followed dinner a couple of times and invites me to the Polo in Cirencester. We go in his Bentley with his mother of course and a picnic hamper fit for a royalty. I really enjoy these excursions, but Jack and Sally began to tease me. I think they are silly, Nigel must be getting on for forty besides which he never made any attempt even hold my hand, so I dismiss the idea.

However, one day, unbeknown to me, he presents himself at my parent's house with some flowers for my mother and asks for my hand in marriage. My parents are thoroughly taken by surprise and tell him that is a question for me to answer. I am mortified, I explain as gently as I can that I am not ready to settle down, but he takes it quite badly. I can't believe how easily one can unwittingly hurt someone.

Jack has another fall and goes to the hospital as he is in a lot of pain. They x-ray his spine, and the doctor tells him he is riddled with arthritis so will have to give up riding. He is more angry than anything else and merely says "Stupid man how can I give up riding I don't know how to do anything else and I don't want to do anything else!" He avoids the doctors from then on and looks for any alternative that is going. He has copper bracelets, swallows' vitamins and minerals and drinks cider vinegar with honey every morning. Of course, he still rides, mounting is difficult, I give him a leg up and he puts his foot in the stirrup then very slowly lifts his other leg over the horse and even more slowly sits up. Sometimes it is difficult to keep the horse still whilst he goes through this process, especially the young ones, which he still insists on riding. However, once in the saddle he can still ride anything, he has a way with horses all of them go beautifully for him.

Brain and Cullen, the vets, have an excellent reputation in the horse world and are very good to Jack. They teach me to give injections, administer wormers, use a stethoscope to check hearts, to file teeth, remove stitches and much more, so usually they deliver the medication and let me administer it. We have one horrible accident with a lovely black gelding, a thoroughbred with a scopey jump, we are preparing for eventing. Jack decides to clip him, the clipping box is in a garage so is spacious, the clippers and grooming machine hang from the roof beams on meat hooks. Most horses if they have not had a bad experience like an electric shock or been burnt or nicked don't mind being clipped except maybe round the head and ears because of the noise. There are some however that panic which is what happened in this case. Jack merely switches on the machine and the horse goes crazy, he rears hits his head on the ceiling, breaks his head-collar and comes down on the meat hook which goes straight through his eye it is a horrific scene and Jack is trapped in the corner but his screams for help could have been heard in the next village. I call the vet and the fire brigade although it seems like forever, they were both there within 20 minutes. The vet tranquilizes the horse and the firemen cut through the meat hook. They operate there and there and then. The vet extracts the meat hook cleans the wound and stitches as best he can, but the poor horse loses his eye although the wound heals well.

The horse adapts quite well to using only one eye, we ride him, and he is wonderful but of course dashed are his prospects of being a top eventer. Fortunately, we find a perfect home for him, but it is still a tragic waste. The vet who operates has been known to accept a horse in exchange for a huge bill. Jack owes him a considerable sum and he loves the handsome, well bred, horse even though he has only one eye, so waives our large bill and takes him home. I still can't get my head round the precarious financial situation. Fortunately, Jack has lots of charm and is much loved in the horse world, but I find some of his methods more Irish, no offence intended, than English. I adore the Irish and to be fair Nat Galway-Greer runs a very tight ship and although large sums of money are still agreed on a handshake, a handshake is respected and considered legally binding.

Jack wins the Hunter Championships at the Royal Show and the Horse of the Year Show not to mention many more up and down the country. As a result, we also sell a horse for the British Event team and have an influx of new clients buying show horses. To celebrate Jack decides to have a Black Velvet party. Guinness and champagne flow and the house is brimming with people they come from far and wide and chat, dance, eat and drink into the small hours. I have never seen Jack in this light before, he is the life and soul of the party and Sheelagh the belle of the dance floor. My parents also come plus some old cronies from the Warwickshire Yeomanry as well as people from all walks of the horse world, racing, show jumping, eventing, showing, and breeding. The inter connections make realise that the horse world is really small. The house is old and rambling with lovely inglenook fireplaces and exposed beams, but it is in a terrible state of disrepair. Luckily for the party it looks fabulous by candlelight with the log fires burning.

Jack rents the house for very little from Mrs Cardiff, the owner of the largest estate in the area, she sponsored his circuit in the States years ago and he rents her stables and school when he has an overflow. She offers to sell the house to him for a song, just the land it stood on is worth more than the figure she mentioned. Jack is not interested he would rather buy more horses. It is hard to understand him sometimes especially as he has a family.

Six new horses arrive from Ireland, we have to provisionally find extra stables in the village. We concentrate on them for the next two weeks and Jack gets me to jump them all. He selects the four with the best bascule and says we are going to take them up to Yorkshire for Harvey Smith and Trevor Banks to try. This is shortly after Harvey Smith's two finger incident when he lost the £2,000 prize money at Hickstead for making the rude "V" sign although he said he was using the victory "V" sign! Not for the first time, Sheelagh and I think Jack is mad. These are green horses from Ireland which have probably never even been to a show. I am quite sure none of them have ever seen a coloured pole in their lives, and we are presenting them as prospective grade A show jumpers.

Jack is jovially confident, as always, so we load up the four horses and set off for Yorkshire. We arrive and unload the horses, put them into stables and I set about preparing the first horse. First, I trot him up in hand, then I mount and they tell me to warm him up in a small indoor school. The men come in shortly afterwards and begin putting up jumps, first a cross pole then a vertical which they higher every time I clear it. When the jump is over three feet the first horse just knocks it down every time. Disheartened I take him back to his stable and bring out the next one. This is a mare, and she is very flighty; in fact, I only dare to canter in a circle because I am sure we will never be able to stop if we canter in a straight line. When it comes to jumping, I walk her round the corner because once I line her up to the jump, she takes off, but she clears every jump by a foot and they love her. The next horse is very spooky and shies at everything so when I ride him towards the jump he hesitates and then cat jumps, he does have springs in his heels but when the jump gets higher, he stops dead. Harvey gives him a whack up the backside and tells me if he stops again, I will be the one to get a whack on the backside, fortunately he doesn't stop again but sends the poles flying, not very successful. I go back for the last horse, he is big over 17hh so to me the jumps now look small and he jumps well despite being so big in such a small school, he is the only one that feels like a real show jumper and they like him too.

I settle the horses and we go to the house where we all sit round the huge kitchen table. Here I see another side to the famous show jumper, he has a reputation for being tough and a bit rough, but here I see a quiet hard-working family man drinking milk because he is suffering from a stomach ulcer. Following this episode, I see him in a different light and am delighted later when his son follows in his footsteps. We leave two horses there and go home happy with the other two, a good day's work, Jack was right after all. We are riding on the crest of a wave and so Jack broaches me about formalizing our partnership. I love working with him and we have had a brilliantly successful year, but apart from the financial situation which has hardly improved despite the success, I don't feel ready to settle down, I still have a yen to travel. When I tell him how I feel he is as understanding and as supportive as ever saying he quite understands and would have felt the same at my age, which makes me feel really guilty.

However, I begin researching and it doesn't take as long as I anticipated to find something that interests me. It is in the form of an advertisement in Horse and Hound which reads as follows: "English speaking man, who forms part of the Swiss Show Jumping Team, seeks girl to take full charge of five show jumpers and travel the European Circuit. She must be capable of schooling flatwork and driving a car with trailer. Veterinary experience is essential." Perfect, horses and travelling and being paid for it. I apply immediately sending my qualifications, experience, credentials and references with a covering letter.

I don't expect to hear anything for some time so am surprised a few days later one lunch time when there is a phone call. Jack answers the phone, then peers over his glasses at me "Peter Reid from Switzerland for you." I take the phone, Peter Reid has a bright cultured voice, he asks me a few questions then if my passport is valid and how soon can I start. I am a little taken aback and reply that it depends on my current boss. I tell him Jack is aware that I have applied for the job, but I can't leave him in the lurch, so he asked to speak directly to Jack. They speak for some time then Jack hangs up. "I asked him to wait a couple of weeks until I find a replacement. But really I want to check him out as

I don't like the wording in the advert "English speaking man seeks girl" sounds fishy to me." Good old Jack looking out for me as always. First, he rings Ted Edgar who is in Warwickshire not far away and asks him if he has come across this Peter Reid at the International Shows. Ted confirms that he knows who he is, a wiry little fellow with more enthusiasm than style, and not to worry as he had an amazon of a wife. Apparently, she is six feet tall, a blond Italian from a wealthy family. He assures Jack that I won't stand a chance.

So, I begin to prepare for my move, I am sad to leave, but feel this is an opportunity not to be missed. Jack, noble as ever, wishes me good luck and says I will be welcome back anytime. As fate has it, I never go back to work for him but in the future am to have horse dealings with him and seek his advice frequently. I also coincide with him and Nat the following year at the Dublin Show when I am there with the Swiss Team.

The end of Jack's story is both tragic and beautiful. Several years later, about eight years after he was told by the doctor he would never ride again, he is at his favourite Dublin Show having won the Hunter Championship yet again on one of Nat's horses. They are celebrating in the Members Bar when he is approached by a member of the committee and invited to take the role of Judge the following year. This fulfils a lifelong dream for Jack and there is certainly no-one better qualified to judge hunters. He is so thrilled he invites everyone for a drink to celebrate. He is thoroughly elated and then says he is going to ride the four-year-old Champion as someone is interested in buying him. He is happily cantering round his favourite showground when he slips from the saddle and dies before he hits the ground, from a heart attack. How sad he will never judge at his favourite show, but how wonderful he dies in one of his favourite places doing what he most loves, riding a horse.

Chapter 7

Switzerland

I prepare for my trip to Switzerland. My mother says I should take thermal underwear and a fur coat. I hate fur coats, but they all insist I should take my Grandmother's old fur jacket. I take gloves, hats, and thick socks anyone would think I was going to the North Pole. My parents are supportive as always, my father simply instructs me to always have enough cash handy so that if I am not happy, I can go to the airport and catch a flight home.

It is hard to know what to take as I am probably going for at least a year. I want a few books and the riding gear is bulky and heavy what with boots, jackets, and hat. When I get to the airport my luggage is well overweight and the cost of excess baggage is excessive. I refuse point blank to pay such a sum, so opening my case, I load my father with the books and shoes etc. until I am within the weight allowance. Fond farewells, thanks to everyone for their support and wondering what lies ahead, I take my leave.

Once more I am on a flight into the unknown. I am met by Peter Reid, a wiry, jovial young man with a shock of dark wavy hair who shakes hands effusively and welcomes me to Switzerland. He ushers me into an old green Jaguar and asks me if I am happy to drive the Jaguar with a trailer. He warns me to remember to keep to the right-hand side of the road and be careful to go the other way round the Islands!

We drive out of Geneva towards the Jura Mountains to a small village called La Rippe, right on the Swiss French border. First, he takes me to his house just outside the village, an imposing, square, modern, house where I meet his "amazon of a wife" Adrienne, who is in fact very sweet, she speaks very little English but calls her husband "Luv Luv". I also meet Marie the maid who lives in, she is a pretty girl a little plump and quite young. Her first comment, in French of course, is to ask me if all English people have such big teeth and wear such funny clothes. She is very outspoken, but she makes me laugh.

The house is open plan, spacious and modern with a wide staircase and balconies on the two upper floors overlooking the entrance hall. I have the use of a bathroom, but my accommodation is to be in the village.

The stables are adjacent to the house. They are new too, big airy stables with windows overlooking the house, so the horses can put their heads out. There is a wide passage so you can tie the horses up and work undercover. The horses are all different and eye me with mild curiosity. Then Peter takes me to the village to my accommodation. It is only a short walk and initially I think it may be quite nice to be in the village but when I see where I am to live my heart sinks. My new home is behind one of the big houses on the main street, across a yard and up some wooden steps above the chickens. It consists of a kitchenette with a sink, a small fridge, two gas rings, a small table and two chairs, then a small bedroom with a single bed and an armchair. The wardrobe is outside the room as there is no space, so anyone can access it. I have to do something about that. The toilet is downstairs next to the chickens, it is raised on a platform in a shed and I have to share it with an Italian family. Peter looks embarrassed and apologizes, he explains, in his defence, that the previous girl had been very dirty, untidy and noisy in the house. As a result, they decided never again would they have a groom living in and unfortunately there wasn't much choice in the little village. I am to have my breakfast and lunch in the main house where I can also use the bathroom and the washing machine.

The next day is Sunday so I will ride with Peter and get to know my charges. Peter and his wife Adrienne work in Geneva during the week so I will see him for five minutes in the morning and again briefly in the evening to report.

Before going to bed I seek out my landlord, having brushed up on my French, I insist on having my "armoire dans la chambre". The landlord is a big serious man and not pleased at having his weekend disturbed by a crazy English girl. He says there is no room in the bedroom, but I insist, I say I would rather have the armchair outside and the wardrobe inside. Reluctantly he promises to see to it the next day, even though it is Sunday. No way am I unpacking my belongings until I have the wardrobe in my room. The next morning, I don my riding gear and set off for the stables. I see a lady crossing the yard but my "Bonjour Madame" is greeted with a lowering of the gaze as the lady scuttles past me as fast as she can. There is another lady peeping through a window, I smile but she withdraws and hastily draws the curtain. I meet Peter in the kitchen, and he gives me a set of keys for the stables and the house. We go to the stables together and feed the horses. For the past week he has only removed the wet bedding and put more on top we do the same, I can clean them out properly on Monday. Then we have breakfast with Madame, served by Marie a wonderful bowl of coffee with croissants. I love the way they cover the bread or croissants with butter and jam and then dunk it all in the coffee which looks disgusting but is delicious. Breakfast is the only thing I liked about my school exchange in France. At last, to the horses, first Peter rides his favourite, CASANOVA who has a similar build to his owner, if anything even thinner. He is palomino with lovely cream mane and tail and golden body. He has some Arab blood, although he is taller than an Arab, he has a very pretty head with a slightly dished face, a typically Arab trait, and from what Peter tells me he has the stamina of an Arab as he is tireless. His stable name is KIKI which I am told has sexual connotations, quite appropriate considering his name. This horse is the reason for the requirement stipulating veterinary experience, apparently when nervous, or with the change of climate as experienced when travelling from one country to another, he is prone to asthma attacks. This implies that when travelling I have to keep a careful eye on him and when his flanks or nostrils show signs of laboured breathing, I have to inject him quickly with antibiotics and cortisone. I am to ride Madame's horse PICKWICK. He is a thoroughbred ex-racehorse, a tall, bright chestnut, gelding with a long thin neck and over at the knee, I am surprised they jump him, but apparently Madame only competes in local shows, mostly at the club, and hacks out with her husband at the weekends. None of the horses have been out for a week as the previous girl had left earlier than agreed. There is nowhere to lunge so Peter says it will be a good test to make sure I can manage the horses! The riding country is fantastic all cart tracks open fields with no fences. There is a long flat valley flanked by woods on the foothills of the Jura mountains so plenty of hill work too.

We reach a long stretch of grass and Pickwick gives three enormous bucks. I manage not to fall off but am completely taken by surprise and impressed by the height of the bucks, so obviously he can jump! Peter laughs and says they always gallop there, with which he takes off. Two more bucks and Pickwick takes off too, we pull up just before a wire fence enclosing somebody's property. There are six strands of barbed wire standing about five foot high and barely visible. Peter tells me that once KIKI jumped it, he had been fresh and Peter couldn't stop him, but clever KIKI saw it at the last minute and cleared it. Obviously riding out with Peter is going to be quite an adventure. The next two horses are O'MALLY an Irish three quarter bred grey horse, good looking with lovely dapples and iron grey mane and tail. Peter rides O'MALLY, he is the young prospect just five years old and competing in grade C. I ride JOLLY JOKER another chestnut gelding famous for his buck, but I am prepared this time and manage to avoid a bucking spectacle. JOKER is grade A, not as brilliant as KIKI but he is on standby for the team. There are just these four when I arrive but later there are two more additions, CHALLENGER, another grade A chestnut gelding, so named after the shuttle, needless to say before its disaster. Finally, CRACKERS an attractive bay four-year-old who really suits Peter they are both a bit crackers.

I am quite happy working alone and soon get the stables, horses, and tack ship shape. Peter seems happy and comments that the horses are looking really fit, well and smart with their pulled manes and tails. He is also impressed that I clean the tack every day. The horses are lovely I have occasional problems with O'MALLY he will nap in certain places. One place where it takes me twenty minutes to get him past there is a pig farm, so I think this must be the reason as some horses are terrified of pigs. He always goes past in the end, but he is not a forward going horse like the others and Peter likes horses that love to go. He also starts refusing when the fences get over 4ft, so Peter sells him to a man who just wants to jump at local shows which is perfect.

Riding and looking after four horses a day is fine. Peter only rides at weekends and at shows. Occasionally mid-week, in the evening, I take two horses into Geneva to the club for him to jump them in the indoor school. I soon learn his methods, it is simple, he uses placing poles and increases the height and or spread of a single fence little by little until they are jumping, accurately and confidently, fences bigger than they usually encounter in competition. Peter says this allows him to cut corners, take risks and get away with it, especially with KIKI who is so brave, agile, and generous. I am sure part of his success is due to the fact that the horses are not over jumped, they have fun and variety, galloping in the country, climbing mountains and jumping logs, so when they do jump, they really enjoy themselves and it is reflected in their performance. During the week I give them all some flat work to improve suppleness, agility, balance and obedience, hill work and long steady trots and canters on the flat with lots of transitions and soon they are muscled up and bursting with health. I also ask

Peter for linseed and barley to boil to give them a big mash once a week specially to try to get some weight on KIKI.

The first International Show is in Turin. Peter is going with the 2nd team. He was in the 1st team with his first International horse PLAYBOY who sadly died. So, with only KIKI as a top-class horse he is relegated to the second team, he is hoping that JOKER, CHALLENGER or CRACKERS will replace his beloved PLAYBOY so giving him another chance to be in the first team.

We go to Turin with the car and trailer and Madame comes too. A relief for me as Peter drives most of the way especially through the Simplon Pass where there is a still ice and snow. We also get held up at the border and I speak no Italian so am relieved I am not alone. The scenery is spectacular through the mountains we stop a couple of times, but it is a long journey, and we are glad when we finally arrive. The stables have been provisionally set up in a huge warehouse alongside the arena. We unload the horses, food, and equipment and the Reids are about to leave when I stop them. I remind them that I speak no Italian, have no money, and have no idea where to go or where I am to stay.

Peter hands me some lira and Adrienne goes to speak to the only other group already installed. They are the Italian military team the grooms for the fantastic D'Inzeo brothers amongst others, but not one of them speaks English. Adrienne tells me to go over to them as soon as I have finished with the horses and they will look after me. Apparently, all grooms have to go to the secretary for the details of accommodation.

Before I have finished the four men come over and signal to me to go with them. We go to the secretary and I am given the reservation for a hotel, I am about to look for a taxi when one of the men says "Mangare" and beckons for me to go with them. There is no sign of a taxi, so I follow them. Five of us squeezed into a little Fiat off we go into the centre of Turin and we stop outside a restaurant. I gather that one of the grooms is from Turin and knows the owners. We have a meal and I pay my share; the wine flows and the atmosphere is jovial. I am getting nervous as I have no idea where I am nor where I will spend the night. When I try to get my message across, they all grin at me saying there is no problem. From there we squeeze back into the car and after a short drive draw up outside a tall block of flats we pile into the lift and go up to the 11th floor, obviously one of them lives there.

An attractive, dark eyed girl with a baby on her hip opens the door. Inside there are another five children, we all sit round the kitchen table and more food and drink are brought out. I can't join in the conversation, so I get on the floor and play with the children, I don't understand a word they are saying either. By this time, it is after midnight, I muse that I have until 7 a.m. to find my way back to the horses. At around 1:30am everyone is kissing everyone, the children too, and we take our leave.

After a half hour drive, we pull up outside a small hotel and one of the men gets out and signals to me to do the same. It seems he is staying at the same place. There is a sleepy porter watching T.V.in the lobby, he hands us our keys, my colleague points to his watch and the foyer. I understand he will meet me there at 6:30. I eventually settle into my room which is simple but clean and fall sound asleep, what a crazy day. True to his word at 6:30 the fellow is waiting for me. We walk for about twenty minutes and arrive at the stadium. To my relief the horses seem fine I check Kiki's breathing which appears to be normal, and he seems calm. The horses tuck into their breakfast while I see to their beds. I have checked them over and am rolling bandages when my friend from the hotel turns up and with a friendly grin says "Mangare?" I am surprised but this time I accompany him happily, the Italians are perfect gentlemen.

The Italian team have wonderful equipment they have a mobile kitchen complete with a barrel of wine, more spaghetti than I had ever seen in my life, more tins of tomatoes than you would find in the supermarket and coffee. Someone has bought fresh bread and milk and we tuck into a hearty breakfast. I am introduced to bread and olive oil and by the end of the week I am hooked. I find it delicious much to my surprise as I remembered as a child my grandmother bought a small bottle of olive oil from the chemist, she made me drink a tea spoonful which I found utterly disgusting. I have breakfast and lunch with the Italians for the whole week and every evening we go to the little restaurant.

Peter comes to ride for the first three days to acclimatize the horses and the warehouse slowly fills with horses. I find some people who speak English and I even bump into Ted Edgar washing his boots under the tap, he doesn't recognize me of course but I thank him anyway for his recommendation. Peter and his team give a creditable performance in Turin without covering themselves in glory but come home with a few rosettes and quite content. We continue to tour Europe with the second team going to the smaller International shows and travelling mainly by rail and road.

We go to Lisbon by train from Geneva. We take the horses to the station in Geneva and literally have an empty wagon. There are some old hands there who show me how to divide the wagon into partitions with ropes and bed down the horses. I travel with them in the wagon with the door slightly open for ventilation.

The horses walk onto the wagon with no problem, and I tie them up with a nice fat hay net, so they munched away happily. I have to take horse feed, plus all the tack and equipment not to mention my own things and food for the journey plus the paperwork. It is not the most comfortable journey; I wedge myself between hay bales and sacks of oats but in a way, it is nice to travel with the horses. Transport has been laid on at the other end, I will have three days to ride the horses and acclimatize them then Peter will fly in just for the competition. The horses are stabled in a warehouse with provisional stables similar to those in Turin and I stay in a small hotel nearby.

Travelling alone and especially eating alone in hotels and restaurants I have acquired the habit of reading avidly to overcome my shyness. It comes to the point that I cannot sit down to eat without a book propped up in front of me. Lisbon is a lovely old city, and it is so nice to have time to explore. I visited briefly with Jean on a school trip with OXFAM we went on a cruise to Algeria and stopped in Lisbon on the way home, the port is just as I remembered it. I meet my Italian friends again and they insist I join them for lunch. One evening we all go to a discotheque and they are just like the big brothers I never had. We all dance together and later when a Portuguese boy asks me to dance, they take it in turns to go behind him and check thumbs up or down to see if I am okay. When the boy gets a bit fresh and I pull a face one of them rapidly comes between us gesticulating dramatically proclaiming "Hey Amor mio!" so sweeping me away, we still can't hold a conversation, but we laugh a lot.

We do however have a complication with the transport, the railway tracks in Spain being wider than those in France we have to change trains at Irun a small town in the Basque country of Spain right on the border. All goes smoothly on the way there, however, on the return journey there is a rail strike in France, so we are pushed up a siding and left there. There are about six wagons of horses and we are left there for three days. We run out of money and food for the horses and ourselves, so we take it in turns to look after the horses whilst the others go in search of sustenance and water. Being in a siding we have no platform so can't take the horses off the train, it is desperately uncomfortable for man and beast. There are a lot of curious barefoot gypsy children who live nearby, at one point I am eating oranges and they come begging for the peel apparently, they dry it and use it as fuel. We are in a poor suburb of the small town and soon we have bought all the carrots and apples in the area. When finally, an engine shunts up to move us, we let out a heartfelt cheer, it is nervous relief!

Another memorable train trip is to Lac Lugano in the Italian part of Switzerland a beautiful setting and we are stabled at a farm up the mountain with beautiful views. There is a Scottish girl looking after a horse belonging to a friend of Peter's also staying there and we girls share a room in the farmhouse, it is a humble affair, the farmer's wife has a string of children and works from dawn to dusk. One evening we are about to head down the mountain to find some supper and the farmer offers us a lift. We exchange glances, we are not keen, but it seems churlish to refuse. We climb in and soon realise he is taking us away from our destination, when we protest, he gesticulates and jabbers in Italian, we understand it will only be for a few minutes. We draw up outside a modern building, he beckons to us to follow him, inside there was a large room with an extravagant fireplace and a bar where several other men are drinking. We both refuse a drink and wonder what on earth we have let ourselves in for. Then he ushers us through a door at the end of the room. To our horror we find ourselves in a chicken factory. It seems as though there are millions of chickens packed together the noise and the stench are stifling. A pulley runs round the ceiling where the poor chickens are strung up by their feet, electrocuted then plucked. The farmer proudly thumps his chest implying that all this belongs to him, we both felt sick.

Fortunately seeing we are neither impressed nor interested in the company, the drink, or his factory he pulls a face, after much gesticulating and insistence from two desperate girls he reluctantly takes us down to the town. Although neither of us speak the language we glean enough information to realise that all this has been created through contraband tobacco passed over the border up in the mountains. We feel sorry for his poor wife who obviously knows nothing about it and certainly doesn't reap the benefits. Apart from this incident it is quite a pleasant stay we ride the horses down to the showground and back again. There are other horses at the farm, but their grooms are not staying there. As usual Peter arrives just in time to ride in the competition and leaves after his last class telling me transport has been arranged with the same man who took us up to the farm when we arrived.

On the morning of departure, we are all packed and ready. Transport arrives for the other horses and my friend and I are left until last. The same man who brought me up arrives but says he has come for my friend. I make frantic signals for him to return for me and the horses, he just shrugs. I wait anxiously for half an hour and no one comes. I am desperate the train is due to leave in half an hour.

I open the trunk grab a saddle and bridle throw it onto one of the horses and we fly down the mountain in a highly uncontrolled manner. We gallop into the station yard and the man who is supposed to do the transport is leaning against an outdoor bar drinking. I leap off the horse hurling abuse at him and gesticulating frantically.

Fortunately for me the other grooms rally round, one speaks a little Italian and talks to the man then asks me if I have any money. I have a little, for food for the two-day trip and to buy straw which Peter said would be at the station but there is none left I part with half of the money. The man is persuaded to go and fetch the other two horses, trunk etc. and my Italian speaking colleague accompanies him telling me to calm down.

I find my wagon, there is no straw anywhere and I can't travel three horses for two days without straw. One of the other grooms offers to hold my horse and I run to a row of cars, there is a man sitting at the wheel of his old pick-up. I wave the bit of money I have left at him shouting "Paja paja" he signals to me to get in I don't think twice there is no time. He drives me to a chicken farm; this really is a chicken plagued trip. There is some straw in a loft, it is very short, dusty and poor quality but beggars can't be choosers, the obliging driver helps me put four bales into the back of his pickup and takes me back to the station. We arrive at the same time as the horses. I have just got the horses, straw and belongings into the wagon when the train whistle gives a shrill blast. One of the other grooms asks me if I have any food, my reply is negative and they all chip in and give me apples nuts and crisps to keep me going.

Later they told me that my Scottish boss is not known for his generosity and haggled refusing to pay the full price for the transport hence the man had no intention of doing the job. Thanks to the intervention of my colleague, we were not left up the mountain. Ironically, Peter had left a note pinned in our wagon wishing us a good journey!

Despite everything I am happy working for Peter, true the accommodation leaves a lot to be desired, but it is paid for, plus most of my food, I have the use of a car and 400 Swiss francs a month, which for me is a fortune. The hundred-franc notes are huge, and Peter always pays me in cash. Peter may be a bit cheeky, but he is good fun and accepts all my suggestions regarding the horses. However, I do have words with him about the near disastrous transport incident in Lugano, he is contrite and assures me it will never happen again.

I have spruced up my humble little abode and made it quite bright and homely. One day Peter drops off some papers for me and is quite impressed with the transformation. I also meet an English girl, Diana who is looking after horses in the next village we meet out riding, she rides a rather overweight chestnut called LUCIFER whose owner has jumped a bit but no longer competes. My day off is Tuesday, as frequently we are travelling back from shows on Monday, so sometimes I meet up with Diana. A strange girl obviously from a well to do family but her parents divorced when she was tiny, she was sent to boarding school from the age of seven and later to Finishing School in Switzerland. She ran away from finishing school, got herself a job with horses and fell in love with a Swiss farmer called Rudi. We have a delivery of hay brought by Jean, who owns the farm adjacent to Rudi's, soon we were all going out together and going to all of village Fetes.

Jean is Swiss German, and the family farm must have been very splendid in its day it would have been a majestic mansion, sadly it is rather run down, his brother and family live in one wing and Jean and his parents in the other. There is third wing which Jean's bother has converted into flats which they rent out. Jean looks after the farm with his father. They have a good herd of Dairy cows, so he is tied because of the milking, I help him sometimes on my day off and he is very, good to me. He always asks me where I would like to go on my next day off and one day, I say I would love to see Mont Blanc, the highest mountain in the Alps, so he takes me there. We go to Chamonix the site of the first Winter Olympics. I am not disappointed, it is majestic and imposing yet retains a certain air of mystery, below the snow-capped peak the harsh lines of rock are softened by gentle swirls of cloud and has inspired writers and poets like Byron and Coleridge.

When I mention that I would like to learn to ski Jean buys me skis and takes me skiing, he is too good to be true, I scarcely dare show interest in anything for he rushes off to fulfil my slightest whim.

We go skiing with our Swiss friends to try out my new skis. They have all been skiing since they were three years old, I tell them I have never skied in my life, but they laugh, saying I am fit and ride horses so it will be easy. I don my skis, shunt across the car park which is fine, and I make it to the first ski lift, so far so good. The ski lift is a tow bar, I have no idea you stand up and be pulled and I sit down instead of letting it pull me, my skis fly in the air and I unceremoniously fall flat on my back about ten yards up the slope. How embarrassing, I climb down and queue again, next time I am nearly halfway up and I cross my skis and once more bite the snow. At my third attempt I manage to get to the top, the others have skied down the first run and are on their way up again! When I finally get to the top of the lift, I peer down the first run and it looks ominously steep. The others are on their way to pick up the next tow bar which is down a gentle slope, so I follow getting a gentle feel of gliding along on the snow which is lovely. I repeat the operation up a third lift and almost reach the summit of the mountain. The views are breath-taking, the air crisp and fresh and the snow sparkling in the sunshine and I am pleased with myself as I have finally mastered the tow bar.

By this time most of my friends are on their third descent. The descent looks very steep. I begin snow ploughing, gingerly and at an angle, they ask me what on earth I am doing as it will take me forever to get down that way. They tell me to put my skis together and turn with my heels. I aim diagonally across the run and put my skis together. Wow what speed I pick up almost straight away, I try to push with my heels to no avail I crash into a snowbank. I dig myself out and position myself pointing at a safe snowbank between the trees on the other side of the run and repeat the operation. Miraculously I get down the mountain in one piece.

The next day I am so stiff I can hardly walk, and I am covered with bruises. I tell Peter I think I might do better on snowshoes than skis, he finds the whole thing amusing. The horses have special snowshoes which consist of a plastic plate between the hoof and the shoe, this prevents the snow from balling in their hooves, even so galloping behind Peter is like being pelted with snowballs.

I am surprised to see a military weapon in Jean's house and question him about it. Military Service is compulsory for all the Swiss men and once completed they each have a piece of military equipment to maintain, Jean has the weapon, one friend has a Land Rover and another a horse!

Jean's parents are sweet but speak no French and of course no English. His mother is not well and is taken to hospital, so I go and do some cooking and housework for them on my day off. The kitchen is immense with a long refractory table which seats at least twelve people. In the larder there is a row of large wooden barrels, peering inside I discovered that they contained flour, sugar, salt, and one full of honey, I quite enjoy cooking on the old range and here I learn to use garlic and olive oil. There is definitely a French influence in the culinary department plus of course the wonderful Swiss cheeses and fondues.

They take the cows up to the mountains for the summer, this is an age-old tradition, and I am lucky enough to be around the day they are due to go. They put bells round their necks with garlands of flowers and drive them on foot up the mountain which takes all day. It is a long slow climb but eventually we emerge into a beautiful green valley high in the mountains. All traces of snow have disappeared giving way to lush green grass so inviting for the cows, although they must have been tired, they frolicked with joy jangling their bells. Jean, his brother, and his father take turns throughout the summer, every weekend the other two go up with supplies and change over. Whoever stays lives in a small stone house which must have been there for centuries. The water supply consists of a hose pipe coming in through the window from a small stream outside and into an old stone sink the drain goes out through a hole in the wall, very primitive. Whoever is on duty milks the cows and makes cheese as there is no way the milk can be collected, hence the wonderful selection of Swiss cheeses, in this case Gruyere from the Canton de Vaud. Next to the dairy there are vats and a huge stone hand churn where they make the cheese by hand and shape it on a stone slab, then it is carefully wrapped in muslin, so whoever is there works hard. At the weekend they take fresh bread and made a huge cheese fondue which really is delicious, simply melted cheese with a little home-made kirsch or schnapps, this is pure alcohol made in this case from home grown apples or cherries. It is so beautiful up there, wildflowers of all colours of the rainbow and sparkling streams of cool, clear water, one breathes peace and tranquillity. The silence is only broken by the gurgling of the stream and the occasional jingle of a cow bell, truly Heidi country.

There are plenty of shows in Germany, France and Switzerland as well as Italy and Portugal. There are shows all year round plus team training clinics so life is busy which means I can't go home for Christmas. It will be the first time I have been away for the duration of Christmas. I am riding towards the mountains on Christmas Eve when snowflakes begin to fall, and I suddenly feel very nostalgic. I make an effort, I decorate my little home and Jean and I have put up a huge natural Christmas tree in his house with real candles, it is quite fun lighting them all in the evening and then blowing them out, the aroma of the hot wax on the pine needles is wonderful, miraculously there isn't a fire.

On Wednesday evening before Christmas, I take two horses into Geneva to the club for Peter to jump and on the way back it begins to snow heavily. Luckily, the Jaguar has had its winter tyres fitted, but even so it is not the best vehicle for ungritted snowy roads at night with a trailer and two horses in tow. I drive slowly, visibility is down to a few yards and the windscreen wipers can hardly cope with the volume of snow. Once out of the city I am glad of the poles to indicate the sides of the road as there is just a white blanket of snow as no vehicles have been down the road. I make it through the village but there is a dip in the road between the village and the stables I accelerate a little hoping to make it up the hill the other side. Halfway up we grind to a halt, the wheels start to spin, I brake but we slither backwards, and the trailer jack knifes. We are blocking the entire road. I put on the hazard lights and lock the car. The wind is howling, and it is still snowing hard, blizzard conditions. I unload the two horses and lead them home, they are so excited they almost carried me up the hill, my feet barely touch the ground. At least being between the horses I am protected from the driving snow and it is such a relief when we finally arrive home. Once safely inside the stables we shake off the snow we are drenched. I settle the horses and go to the house to ring the Gendarme and warn them about the blocked road. The only person likely to come down that road tonight is Peter who is due to come home with Adrianne, but he has rung Marie to say that they will stay the night in Geneva.

There are two famous winter shows in Switzerland, one at St Moritz and the other at Davos. The arenas being on the frozen lake, the snow on top of the ice is harrowed and makes perfect going.

St Moritz is my first show on ice, and I travel with the horses by train. Adrianne kindly lends me a full-length sheepskin coat and the horses have nice woollen hoods to keep their ears warm. We travel in the train with the door ajar, at thirty degrees below zero. I go on ahead with the horses to acclimatize them as usual. Apart from the cold there is the altitude over 1,800 meters. The Winter Olympics and the World Championships were held there so the installations are excellent. I ride the horses in the morning and take myself off to the ski school in the afternoon, the nursery slopes are a piece of cake and at a gentle speed I learn to turn, stop, and have some sort of control. I am not very elegant on skis but definitely safer.

The horses wear huge studs, long ones on the outside which have to be put in out on the snow as it was hard for the horses to walk on the firm ground, it is like wearing uneven heels. I stuff the stud holes with cotton wool to protect the thread and become very adept at screwing and unscrewing these huge studs. The horses go well, and we also compete in skijoring which means "ski driving" in Norwegian. I ride O'Mally and pull Peter behind on the skis. We compete in the slalom races and we do quite well considering it is our first time, thanks to Peter's skill on the skis combined with my gymkhana instinct! On the last evening everyone is invited to dinner at the summit, grooms, riders, trainers, and families. Peter tells me that we will come down by sledge in the moonlight. I have seen a lot of horses and sledges which act as taxis and assume that is what he means. We go up by cable car, have a lovely dinner by candlelight with log fires. We then emerge into the crisp freezing air and everyone is given a small toboggan and sets off down the road which is steep with hairpin bends. Silly me, I have forgotten my gloves and am not ideally dressed for the occasion, but we laugh, race, and crash our way down the mountain which proves to be a perfect finale to a fabulous show.

When we get back, I go skiing again with my friends. We go to San Cerque which is near La Rippe but just over the French border. I have the use of the little Fiat, the system is good in Switzerland we have one set of number plates which I put on the Jaguar when I am towing the horses and put them on the Fiat when I am pottering around on my day off.

Jean is busy, so I take two friends and we pile into the Fiat. As we are crossing the border a Gendarme pulls me over and says we can drive no farther, the tyres are bald!

Peter is furious with me for trying to cross the border and more so when he receives a whacking fine as well as having to change the tyres!

We are near the border with France and frequently cross it on our rides out. There is a stone on the edge of the field denoting the border, but it is open country with no fence. We sometimes cross the border together to go to Divonne where there is a racetrack for trotters and if they are not holding races Peter and I have our own races. We have splendid long gallops side by side. One day I venture over there on my own to give Joker a gallop, on the way home a Gendarme jumps out of the hedge and demands my passport and the horse's papers. I apologize and say I have left my handbag at home; he is not amused and threatens to detain me next time. Peter just laughs and says we should just gallop across the border and the gendarme will never catch us!

I have been in Switzerland for a full year, and I haven't been home for a visit. Finally, I take time to go home and strangely when my parents meet me at the airport, I understand them perfectly but find it quite uncomfortable and awkward to reply in English. In the beginning Peter spoke to me in English but Adrianne and Marie only speak French so as my French improved, we all now speak

French. The same happened with my friends and even if I happen to be alone with Diana, we seem to speak French. Is it possible to forget your mother tongue?

Chapter 8

Europe

I feel very strange being back in England. I visit friends and Jack of course. My father is Investments Secretary for a large Insurance Company. A colleague of his, one of the Directors, with whom he has worked for many years, is retiring and has bought a lovely property in the Cotswolds. He asks my father to take me over to see them and give them some advice regarding the stables.

They live in small village with a Post office, a Church and a village hall but no shop and no pub. Their house is down a No Through Road which leads to a bridle path. There are straddle stones outside the house and the house itself is old and rambling with two wings forming two sides of a cobbled yard with a fountain in the centre. The stables form the other two sides facing the house and both are built of beautiful mellow Cotswold stone. The stables have solid oak doors with brass fittings and are roofed with beautiful old tiles beneath which there is a sizeable loft. There are four large loose boxes a feed room and a tack room. To the right of the entrance there is a huge Cotswold stone barn, and it is all in very, good condition.

Behind the stables there are two paddocks a small one acre and a four-acre with old turf grazing, ridge and furrow and good fencing. In the garden there is a well and a small Cotswold stone building inside which there is a long wooden seat with three holes, one of them smaller, this is the original bathroom! The Egerton's know nothing about horses, but they all agree it is a pity not to have horses looking over the stable doors of such beautiful stables. I say I am sure they will have no trouble renting the installations. However, I warn them to be careful, as some horsey people can be a bit loud and untidy, and the stables are in close proximity to the house. I think to myself, rather wistfully, this is a dream yard for some lucky person.

My holiday comes to an end and I go back to Switzerland. Before my holiday Peter had fenced off a paddock behind the stables so whilst I was away the horses had taken it in turns to be loosed so they had a little holiday too. I set to work getting them fit again. We go to several team training sessions mostly in the German part of Switzerland. One such course in Germany is quite testing, but Peter is a very determined rider and meets all of the challenges. They are selecting the team for the Olympics in Mexico. Peter isn't selected as he still has only one top class horse although two of the others are competing well in grade A competitions, they haven't quite won enough to prove themselves worthy of a place at the Olympics.

However, Peter is promoted to the first team. This good news comes as we are preparing to go to Palermo with the second team, so we go to Munich instead. Peter's friend goes off to Palermo in his place but sadly there is a terrible tragedy. The horses are loaded onto the ferry to go across to the island. The vehicles are loaded into the hold with the horses on board and the doors closed. When they arrive and open the hold most of the horses have died through lack of oxygen. Those lovely horses, it is shocking. Peter's friend only has one horse which he adores, and he is devastated.

Peter says if I had been there, it wouldn't have happened. That is a terrific vote of confidence, but I am so glad I wasn't there. I probably would have insisted on travelling with the horses especially for KIKI and I would have died with them as once at sea it would have been impossible to open the hold even if I had raised the alarm. The European circuit for the first team is different from the circuit for the second team which we have already done. This means all the shows will be new for me, except Dublin and The Horse of the Year Show in London which I already know. For the trip to Munich I drive to Paul Weir's place, he is German/Austrian, but his wife Monica Bachman is Swiss and on the team. We have already had training clinics at their home. Paul is an experienced and brilliant rider who later becomes a course builder. From there we transfer into a huge modern German transporter with other members of the team. This modern transporter has a padded semi-circular, protectors in front of each horse's head which also prevents the horses from biting each other.

I load KIKI and when the man clicks the protector into position KIKI panics. He must be claustrophobic. I instinctively cover his eyes with both hands. I remember reading in Black Beauty when there was a fire, the horses have to be blindfold in order to lead them to safety. KIKI stops thrashing about and stands snorting loudly. I ask the man if he can remove it, but he can't as it is hinged to the vehicle, and he says it is dangerous to leave it loose. I ask him to hold his hands over the horse's eyes whilst I take off my jumper and use it to blindfold KIKI. Also, I ask permission to travel with him because if the blindfold slips, he will panic and probably cause an accident. Poor KIKI, I hold him and talk to him all the way. The journey seems never ending and we are so relieved to arrive in one piece.

Munich is a spectacular show, the horses go well, and I make new friends, we enjoy our free time and I even get to drive a bright green Lamborghini when we go out one night. I tell Peter about the problem KIKI has with the transporter and on the way home I blindfold him before they fasten the head protector, but still travel with him.

We are selected for Dublin and I look forward to seeing Jack and Nat again. We fly the horses to Dublin; I drive them to the airport and out onto the tarmac.

Peter comes with me to take the trailer home. The plane is rather old and is obviously a freight plane. The nose cone is open, and a huge wide ramp has been fitted. In the body of the plane there are partitions for the horses in rows of four. KIKI loads well and is in the front row. There are a few seats on the sides, and I notice rather dubiously there is tape holding one of the inner windows in place. The plane is closed, and we take our seats, we are warned that if a horse kicks through its partition it will be shot to avoid the risk of their kicking through the side of the plane in which case, we would all go down. We taxi towards the runway and as the plane turns to line up for take-off KIKI goes into panic mode. I am with him in a flash, but he is stuck half on his side thrashing against the partition with his hooves. Fortunately, two strong men rush towards us and my heart thumps I could never face Peter if anything untoward happened to KIKI. To my relief I realise they have come to my aid. One gets hold of his tail and the other his head and they literally lift him up back onto his feet. They tell me to keep his head up as high as possible so he can't get down. The cockpit is above us just in front of KIKI. There is a trapdoor and some steps leading up to a space between the pilots. The pilots hear the rumpus and one of them shouts down to me that I can't stay where I am for take-off. His colleague explains the situation and they tell me to go up into the cockpit and lie down between the pilots on my stomach holding KIKI's head through the trap door. All of this takes place as we are picking up speed for take-off.

Fortunately, KIKI is happier about the take-off than the U turn on the runway and we arrive in one piece. It is fabulous to be at Ballsbridge again, such a lovely old showground. I settle the horses in and go in search of Jack and Nat. I find Sheelagh at a ringside watching Jack ride she immediately invites me to have supper with them. Sheelagh is Irish, hence their holidays in Ireland and she met Jack when he went with Nat to try a horse belonging to her father. The horse was playing her up, Jack says she was too nice. Jack is never rough with horses but has a way of saying "Hey that's enough" and the horses all seem to respond to him, as did the horse belonging to Sheelagh's father. Jack went home with his horse and his daughter! She is bright, she is pretty and has gentle Irish charm. I spend the evening with them catching up. They always rent a house for the show and say I can stay there with them. However, apart from the fact that they are already overcrowded, I have been provided with accommodation.

There is a Dutch girl, Mina, staying at the same hotel. She has her horses next to mine, so we team up. Dutch people have a gift for languages, she speaks Dutch, German, French, English and some Italian. I meet my Italian friends again and Mina is soon chatting away to them. There is a boy there I haven't seen before. He is tall and blond, a mounted policeman from Palermo and I gather he usually rides a motor bike. He seems very protective towards me and is kind and helpful. One night, quite late, he accompanies me to the stables, I like to give KIKI an extra feed last thing at night as I am desperately trying to keep weight on him and with all the travelling and his nerves it isn't easy. As we approach the stables some of the Italians are there in a small group and Mina emerges from one of the stables with another of them. I go towards her, but Mina waves for me to go away and slips into the stable with another man. My chaperone hurries me away shaking his head. I am worried about her and wait up, when she appears later at the hotel I asked if everything is okay and she just shrugs saying, "These Italians you sleep with one and you sleep with them all!" but she seems more amused than perturbed. I can't relate such behaviour with the kind, polite boys I know. I realise that I am naïve, and I suppose in some strange way that has protected me. All the same I consider I have been very, lucky, either that or I have a guardian angel! My mother always says that if I fell off the top of Marks and Spencer's, (at that time the highest building in Birmingham), I would land on a feather bed!

The main feature of the Show Jumping in Dublin is the incorporation of the Irish Bank which is new for Show Jumping and causes problems even for some of the most experienced horses and competitors. If they aren't Irish and haven't been hunting in Ireland, they will probably never have encountered such an obstacle. It is not easy to find a bank of those characteristics to school over; it features in the Nations Cup which is a big testing course. KIKI and Peter are the only members of the Swiss Team to go clear with Peter's determination and Kiki's agility they make nothing of it and don't hesitate at the bank. Peter says it is because he is used to scrambling up and down the Mountains at home. I also jump the horses up and downhill over fallen trees and dykes. Peter is quite impressed when I show him some of the places we jump. They are small compared with what he jumps in the ring, but they are solid, if you hit a show jump it falls down but if you hit a solid fence like a tree you can go base over apex. I still prefer cross country!

We also win the prize for the best turned out horse, which we also won in Munich and Aachen where KIKI was third and I won a case of German beer. The clipping, trimming, and plaiting I learned with Jack and the show horses, plus the checks and sharks' teeth marks on their quarters make them look stunning compared with many of the jumpers. Jack wins the Hunter Championship so there is plenty to celebrate, however, all good things come to an end. We are due to be picked up to go to the airport at 5 a.m. and I decide to sleep at the stables, my faithful friend and protector, the lovely guy from Palermo, comes and sleeps in the next stable and helps me to load the horses. It is strange we can't even hold a conversation. Our relationship is purely platonic with no demands, but he has helped me so much during this trip which I truly appreciate. We decide to sedate KIKI for the return journey to avoid the risk of losing him if he panics again and breaks through his partition. We were very lucky on the outbound journey, if it had not been for the two strong men on the plane, I dread to think what would have happened, the timing is essential, and the vet leaves me the me an injection together with strict instructions. All goes well and we load KIKI with no problem. I hold him until we are lined up on the runway for take-off then take my seat on the side of the plane. Absolutely no problems until we land when poor Kiki is still a little drunk and he staggers when I go to lead him forward, so I don't dare to take him down the huge ramp. We have to stay on board for another 20 minutes until he can walk in a straight line before disembarking.

Once more I am destined to spend Christmas in Switzerland. Peter's mother, who is Scottish and lives in Lausanne, invites me to join them for a Christmas meal in one of the best Restaurants in Geneva, overlooking Lac Leman. She is a nice lady and means well. The restaurant is very elegant, and I am enjoying the treat. Suddenly Peter's mother whispers in my ear, "My dear I don't know about etiquette in England but here it is frightfully bad manners to have your hands on your lap". I am devastated, I work with horses, so my nails are cut short, scrubbed clean and not varnished apart from which I wear no jewellery. I observe the other female guests at the table with their elegantly draped hands, long painted nails, and exquisite jewellery. I always feel that in England we are sticklers for etiquette, but this takes the biscuit! To complete the evening, they all order Steak Tartare, being ignorant of the dish and struggling with the sophisticated French Menu I decide to order the same. When I see the raw meat mixed lovingly by the Maître with raw eggs, my heart sinks. Fortunately, it is delicious although at this point, I begin to feel some empathy with vegetarians.

I decorate my little home on Christmas Eve and am waiting for Jean. When he arrives, he is obviously very, upset, it transpires that his mother has just died. I visited her in hospital with Jean, but as a family they speak Swiss German, and I hadn't grasped the seriousness of the situation. I go to their house and cook for Jean and his Father on Christmas day; the dim light of the candle lit Christmas tree seems melancholic this year and casts a shadow over these lovely warm people. At first the Swiss people seemed a little unfriendly and cold but once they know and accept you, they are the most supportive and generous people imaginable. Even the old ladies dressed in black in the village, who initially peeped through their windows at me without so much as a "Bonjour", now give me food and gifts and fuss over me. Jean's mother is laid out at home, this I find disconcerting. In my brief encounters with death, I have never had contact with the person after they died. In England they are taken to the funeral parlour and I have only seen the closed coffin at the funeral. On the day of the funeral, I stay at the house to prepare the wake, a cold buffet for everyone who attends the funeral. Some gentlemen in black bring the coffin and with some difficulty they lay her as gently as they can inside. Jean, his brother and two of the men carry the coffin on their shoulders and the mourners make their way on foot, in procession, behind the coffin all the way to the village church, and then to the cemetery.

This winter we are going skiing every Tuesday which is my day off and I never excel but enjoy it immensely especially when it is sunny. I love the fresh air, the crisp snow, the gentle swishing sound of the skis cutting through the snow and the mountains which are so beautiful. My Swiss friends know these mountains like the back of their hands and take me on beautiful virgin runs, happy days indeed.

My mother writes to say she would like to come and visit me as she doesn't know Switzerland. When I tell Peter and Adrianne, they immediately say she must stay in their house, however, my mother insists she wants to stay with me. I put my mother in my bed and borrow a camp bed which I put up for myself at night and push under the bed in the day. I have got used to my little home and am really quite fond of it. One problem which concerns me regarding having my mother to stay is the lack of a bathroom. I share a toilet downstairs with an Italian family and in the winter, there is an electric heater in front of the toilet to prevent it from freezing. One night when I go down there is a rat sitting comfortably in front of the heater washing his face, I let out a piercing scream! Funny I loved animals, but I still scream. The Italian neighbour emerges and bursts out laughing when I tell him, the rat having run away by then terrified by my scream. He tells me to bang on the door first and they will disappear. So, I tell my mother if she wants to go to the loo I will go down first and check that no one is there! The weather is below freezing, the calor gas heater warms us quickly but I have to switch it off at night and in the morning the condensation that runs down the walls has frozen into icicles. My mother is duly horrified. Peter and Adrianne bend over backwards to entertain her. They put on a dinner party with English speaking friends, show her films of the highlights of our travels together and invite her to a good restaurant, but mother remains cool!

She accompanies me in the Jaguar when I take the horses into Geneva for training at the club, but as she doesn't like horses and is unimpressed by the posh horsey set, she does not enthuse. The happiest times are when we go out with Jean and his father, we even take her skiing, but she doesn't get farther than the end of the car park before falling flat on her back, whereby she gets the giggles. When we finally get her back on her feet, she decides enough is enough, it is not her sport and she prefers to call it a day. However, she does enjoy the wine, the kirsch, and the fondue in the lovely mountain setting. Watching the ski slopes through the window in front of a log fire she agrees is lovely. Even though they can't communicate there is a feeling of empathy between my mother and Jean's father. Not only are their languages different but their backgrounds could not be more diverse. When my mother takes her leave, Peter tells me to take her to the airport in the Jaguar. Peter and Adrianne bid her good-bye and tell her she will be welcome any time and next time they beg her stay with them as she will be more comfortable. Mother's reply is terse, "Thank you, but I shall never return to Switzerland, I have seen enough!"

Diana marries Rudi, gives up her job and moves into the farm, they live in a small attic but seem to be happy. In no time Diana is expecting a baby, I know nothing about babies or having them but try to help my friend as much as I can. Diana seeks my company more and more, since her mother died and she ran away from Finishing School she has had little or no contact with her father, who has re-married. She sits cross legged on my bed and lights a cigarette inhaling deeply and allowing the smoke to trickle slowly from her lungs escaping through her nose and the corners of her mouth. The worry lines on her brow soften as if the smoke has taken away some of her anxiety. Smoking may be socially acceptable, but I am sure it isn't good for the baby, and I try in vain to encourage her to smoke less. Diana says the doctor hasn't told her not to smoke and it is important she stays calm; it is evident she is anything but calm and she insists that smoking helps her!

One night it is dark and snowing when Diana arrives unexpectedly at my little home. She is driving the Land Rover saying she is having pains and the baby is due any time. I ask her if Rudi knows where she is. Apparently not, she says that he is busy calving. I get her back into the Land Rover and drive her home trying to sound calm and telling her to relax and breathe. I screech to a halt in the yard and run into the barn dragging Rudi out. We make it to the hospital just in time and she gives birth to a beautiful little girl.

Jean rents one of his barns to a man called Maurice who breeds horses rather indiscriminately, they are all small and narrow, sad looking creatures. I can't imagine who is going to give the poor things a home let alone buy them. Maurice takes a shine to me, convinced we have something in common. I keep finding gifts hanging forlornly on my door when I get home. He even comes to the stables. I carry on working trying not to be rude but reminding him that I am going out with Jean. This is a fact he knows only too well, but he is still persistent. One evening when I am walking home, he springs out of the hedge and nearly frightens me to death. I let out one of my piercing screams which startles him. I tell him in no uncertain terms to stop following me or I will call the Gendarme.

One day I leave my watch at Jean's. I am riding with Peter the next day and he suggests we ride over to Jean's to pick it up. As we ride up the drive through the avenue of trees he is really surprised and asks if they rent it. When I tell him that it has been in the family for generations, he says it is a lovely property and must have been magnificent in its day which is certainly true.

We have a really good season; the horses are in fantastic form and Peter is speculating over the coming season when I receive a letter from my father's friend. He makes me an offer, he says he will lend me some money to set up a horse business on his property, we will be partners, he will do the books and I can pay back the loan over a period of two years. I am bowled over and walk around in a daze for the next few days. This is the opportunity of a lifetime to run my own yard. I have had two great years in Switzerland and travelled pretty well all over Europe, so really it would be a question of repetition from now on, plus the fact I want to compete myself. I know it is now or never and I will always regret it if I don't seize the opportunity, offers like this only come once in a lifetime.

I make my decision and go to talk to Peter before replying. He understands but is very disappointed. He says he was planning to apply for Swiss Nationality for me so I can compete, and I can compete on Pickwick as they want to start a family. In Switzerland you can't compete if you were not a Swiss national. I am touched, I tell him I have been very happy and loved the experience, but this for me is the opportunity of a lifetime and I may never have the chance again to run my own business. Reluctantly Peter agrees, he asks if I will stay until he finds someone else and if I will show them how I work, as his horses have never been so well and successful. I thank him for his comprehension and say of course I will help him especially for the sake of the horses as I have become so fond of them, we have shared so many adventures together. However, I am not prepared for the reaction of my friends and even my grumpy landlord who almost sheds a tear. It has taken a long time to get to know and gain the confidence of these people but once they accepted me, they really took me into their hearts and homes. Now they cannot conceive that I am not going to be part of their lives forever. They simply do not understand my reasoning. I am mortified the last thing I want is to hurt or offend these good people, but it seems inevitable.

Jean especially is heartbroken; he looks at me mournfully and asks me if I remember when his mother was in hospital dying and she had said how content and at peace she felt knowing that I am going to look after him. This is the first I have heard of it as Jean and his mother always spoke Swiss German and I hadn't understood a word. It is sad, a year later Jean and some friends visit me in

England, they have been to a European Agricultural meeting in London and come to see me for the day. We have a meal together and I show them around. As they are leaving Jean takes me to one side and tells me there is a nice lady with a little girl who wants to marry him. He first wants to know if there was any chance, I will go back and marry him, if not, he will go home and marry her. I am speechless and even more so when he shows me scars on his wrists and tells me he wanted to end everything when I left. I go cold all over and think I am going to pass out. He has been so good to me, but I had no idea I had caused so much pain. There are no words to say how sorry I am that he has been hurt. I only say I hope with all my heart he will find happiness because he deserves the very best, he is a truly lovely person.

Diana too says she will have no one from the same background to confide in and talk to. I tell her another girl is coming from England to replace me. My friend retorts it won't be the same as we have shared so much together, which is true enough. The new girl arrives, I feel guilty about leaving the horses too. I write down all the idiosyncrasies of each horse, emphasizing the special care that KIKI requires especially regarding travelling, how to manage him in the German transporters, the planes and control his breathing. She seems to be a nice girl and quite competent but even, so I leave with a heavy heart. Peter thanks me for the best two years he and his horses have ever had and says he will probably come over and see me for a day's hunting. It never materializes as shortly after I leave, they start a family, and he has other priorities.

On my last morning I go to say goodbye to the horses, and it is my turn to have a broken heart. They are so different, but I love each one of them. JOKER with his naughty bucks, he is cheeky but there is nothing nasty about him, he almost apologizes when he is a bit too bumptious, a loveable naughty boy. PICKWICK is the dear old gentleman, wise and kind even if he did nearly buck me off on my first day. CHALLENGER really tries hard he is such an honest horse; he always does his best and gives his all. CRACKERS is the baby and it has been lovely to see him grow and develop from a green baby into a confident adolescent. One should never have favourites, but it is almost impossible to avoid, I have shared so much with KIKI and his beautiful deer like eyes looked knowingly into mine. I wrap my arms round his neck and the tears rolled down my cheeks. I implore the new girl to take special care of him. I think how true the saying is "Parting is such sweet sorrow," indeed a bitter-sweet pill although the decision is mine and mine alone. It is also true that you cannot have your cake and eat it, and nothing is perfect, sadly we have to make choices in life.

Regarding KIKI it is as though we both know something when I bid him farewell. Several years later when I am visiting Geneva, I ring Peter and we have a long chat. Peter and Adrianne have a lovely daughter and now have ponies. When I ask after KIKI there is silence for a moment then he tells me he hoped I wouldn't ask. A year after I left, they were on their way to a show in Germany and Kiki panicked in the German transporter, he kicked right through the side of the vehicle and broke his leg, he had to be put down there and then, I gasp. He asks me please not to say anything he knows full well I warned them about his fear, but they weren't able to control his panic and it resulted in tragedy.

Chapter 9

The Cotswolds

I go home, sad to leave horses and friends behind, but in a state of anticipation at the prospect of setting up my own little business. My father picks me up from the airport and I spend a night at home. I set off for the Cotswolds the next day full of anticipation. Mrs Egerton shows me to a large bedroom on the second floor in the wing opposite the main row of boxes. Mr Egerton's office is on the floor below. I move in and we have our first meeting, he opens an account in the name of their joint business "The Egerton-Hutt Stables" and transfers the loan. I waste no time, I clean everything thoroughly and buy feed bins, water buckets, hay-nets, saddle racks, basic tack, saddle, bridle, head-collars, ropes, lunging gear, rugs, rollers blankets, clippers, grooming kit, wheelbarrow, broom, fork and shovel. These are only the essentials I could go on ad infinitum.

I have the use of the Land Rover and need a trailer, I can't splash out on a top of the range model but settle for an Ivor Williams for two horses and have a second floor put in for security. At the vets I once saw the effects of terrible accident when a horse put his foot through the floor of a trailer, and it haunted me.

Mr. Egerton is a Chartered Accountant, he is brilliant, meticulous, and as wise as an owl. He refuses to be rushed, an excellent example for me as I tend to be impulsive. I always try to fit a quart into a pint pot, in other words I take on too much. It has taken me years of concentrated effort to try to slow down, plan carefully and say, "NO" in order not to bite off more than I can chew. Finding the balance still evades me at times often I fly into his office asking for the papers to transport horses, for entries for competitions or bills for clients who waiting or with horses loaded up ready to leave with the time calculated to the last second. When I am obviously flapping Mr Egerton purposely goes slower and says, "Good Morning" peering at me disapprovingly over his spectacles, only when I respond appropriately he will say, "Take a seat". Clearly, he isn't going to give me the paperwork until I consent. Then he peers at me once more, over his spectacles, and enquires mildly, "Where is the fire?" This makes me smile and relax realizing that my behaviour is bordering on hysterical!

Mrs. Egerton is a practicing catholic although her husband is very involved with the Church of England, but they respect each other and it works perfectly for them. They sing in the choir together sharing their passion for music. She is a sweetie, she loves high society and mixing with the horsey set, also she is a wonderful cook. She makes her own bread and wonderful ginger biscuits which she stuffs into my pockets to "keep me going".

Robert, their younger son, lives at home, he is a member of the Sealed Knot and works with firearms. He collects relics from the war, and these are aspects I find hard to come to terms with. Despite which he is a kind and gentle person and he is so persistent I ended up going out with him. It is a very difficult situation; I am stressed with the amount of work and sometimes impatient and bad tempered as I feel trapped. In truth I treat him rather badly which he really doesn't deserve.

Joseph the older son goes to Oxford and later works for MacMillan publishers, he is undoubtedly brilliant but a strong character and he and I clash especially when he interferes with the stables. For example, he has a load of logs delivered and stacked in front of the stables, I can't even open the doors properly to get the horses out. He says there are doors at the back, which there are, but they are not stable doors and awkward to open. Furthermore, they open onto the manure heap not the ideal way for clients to access their horses! I move the logs to the barn which does not go down well. He has some ingenious ideas which at the time sound mad but with time prove to be innovative and ecological. He talks about using horse manure for energy and heating. I am selling the manure to the mushroom growers apart from loss of income I don't fancy humping it all to the other side of the property on some wild madcap scheme which might not even work! He often comes home at weekends, sometimes with friends to go Beagling, normally we manage to get along and his father is a brilliant mediator when we come to loggerheads.

Jack is delighted for me; he immediately recommends a good feed supplier and introduces me to a gentleman farmer who lives nearby and sells me hay and straw at a good price. Mr Warlock, the epitome of a gentleman farmer is an unusual character, he is tall and dark, his wife is also exceptionally tall. They invite Jack and me to tea, shaking hands over the deal for hay and straw which is to include delivery. Mr Warlock hunts avidly and has recently bought an appropriately tall horse from Jack, who, as always is happy to be my mentor also saying he will be sending me horses.

Now all I need is horses!

I begin by introducing myself to the neighbours in the village. For such a small community there are a lot of horsey people. Mrs Bulkley or Biddie, as everyone calls her, is the next-door neighbour. She is a bit of a recluse and a little eccentric but from a top-drawer background. She follows the racing avidly, has a couple of home bred racehorses, keeps a few cattle and lives with and for her dogs especially her devoted lurcher. Her house is somewhat chaotic and run down, but she is very friendly, knowledgeable and extremely interesting to talk to about anything concerning horses. In the afternoons she is always watching the racing on the television, sprawled on the sofa with all her dogs and she likes to summon me to go in to talk "horse" with her. Her son is a Brigadier and occasionally visits her, but she will never go out. Apparently, she lived in High Society and sadly she and her husband divorced in the days when divorce was simply unacceptable in those circles, since when she has hidden herself away in that tiny village, such a waste!

Sir John and Lady Aird live opposite Mrs Bulkley, they have a sizeable farm and keep their own hunters in a rather basic fashion. They are looked after by Dickie who looks and rides like a racing jockey, but he proves to be invaluable helping to me when I am breaking young horses. As he rides past the yard every day, he is happy to accompany me when I take a young horse out for the first time. Lady Aird is a delight, she is young and outgoing, she flies round the village on a bicycle, even when heavily pregnant, and she talks to everyone. Our first encounter being when she sweeps into the yard on her "sit up and beg" bicycle shouting at the top of her voice she is desperate for garlic, any chance she can borrow some! They soon have small children and can be seen up and down the lane as a family with ponies, dogs and bicycles. In fact, she is the first to offer me assistance saying she will tell their friend George who rents a cottage in the lane and hunts on Saturdays.

Sure, enough George turns out to be our very first client. George has red hair and he rides a bright chestnut mare called MARY STUART, they are both charming if a little eccentric. MARY STUART is lovely she is forward and active and when she gets nervous, she paces, in other words she walks in two-time like a camel, she makes me laugh. Sometimes she paces when she sees sheep in a field in the distance. I think perhaps she needed spectacles as she is not afraid of sheep up close. I start getting her fit, clean and trimmed. George comes down to ride her one weekend. He seems very impressed when I lead her out of the stable with her mane pulled and damped down and her hooves oiled, he says she had been transformed in a couple of weeks. They make a dashing pair. George hunts in pink with his top hat and he asks me if I mind if he leaves his boots in the tack room, of course I don't mind and end up making his boots shine as much as his lovely mare.

George is charming and much admired by the elite young ladies of the Heythrop. He arrives in his Jenson sports car to spend the weekend in the cottage and hunts on Saturdays together with his friend David. Out hunting he sometimes asks me if there is another way to go in order to escape the madding crowd and his admirers. As I am not an eligible suiter, I imagine he feels entirely safe with me and I thoroughly enjoy his company. I usually hunt Jan's four year old on Saturdays and we have some great days. Occasionally in the evening, George invites me over to the cottage for supper and he and David cook. Their culinary skills are impressive, simple fare, but delicious especially George's delicious banana flambe, and we chat away into the small hours. On Sunday George usually goes to church in the village where Mr Egerton is Church Warden and Choirmaster. On Sunday I usually walk the horses that have hunted on Saturday round the village to check they are sound and stretch their legs. I just jump on their rugs and ride them round the village and past the church so often coinciding with the church goers.

Sometimes George hunts on Wednesday when the meets are around Woodstock nearer to London. I take MARY STUART in the Land Rover and trailer, leave them near the meet and drive George's Jenson home. At the end of the day George drives MARY home. We leave the Land Rover on the side of the road and do not even to lock it, there is never a problem. On the occasional Saturday when George can't come, he asks me to hunt her, and it is pure pleasure to hunt MARY STUART.

Mrs Dammers who lives at the end of the lane is a dear, elderly lady who has bred and shown horses all her life. She has downsized so now breeds Dartmoor ponies, among which are some little champions, and the foals are just adorable. She has a four-year-old pony she wants broken to sell for showing and asks me if I will take him, I am a little concerned I am too heavy for him but she assures me her "Darties" as she calls them can carry a farmer all day long. Mrs Dammers crossed her last winning, thoroughbred, champion show mare with a Connemara pony stallion hoping the result would be a small, manageable, horse for her to ride in her old age. Unfortunately, dear VIGO has inherited the looks and knee action of his father and the hot temperament of his mother, so Mrs. Dammers says she would also like me to have him to hunt for a season so horse number three. She also has a friend in Wales who breeds show ponies, which are like miniature thoroughbreds, and she is sure she will send some for breaking and schooling. Jan Woolley has a livery yard in the village asks me to ride her young horses. I start with a four-year-old, a nice-looking bay horse called MONSOON. I usually hunt him one day per week and show jump him another, so without leaving the village I have the yard full of horses and plenty of work lined up. The idea is to have some hunter liveries, horses to get fit and produce for their owners to hunt and these clients pay by standing order which creates a regular income or the "milk money". We are in the heart of the Heythrop country, apart from Leicestershire it is one of the most popular hunts being nearer to London. I will also take horses to break, school or prepare for competition and we decide to invest in a young horse for me to bring on compete and sell, so there really is plenty of work.

Mrs. Dammer's VIGO has been turned out. She lent him to a girl to hunter trial, but he ran away with her. I lead him home have him shod, wormed, vaccinated and checked by the vet. Then I start by tacking him up and lunging him in the paddock, he is very fizzy. When he calms down a little, I take him back to the stables and mount. I have to work hard to keep him in walk, I walk him to the next village and back, about an hour by the time we get back by which time he is in a lather and will walk all of four strides before I have to check him again to prevent him running off. For a whole week I lunge him in trot and canter and only ride him at a walk until he settles, then I begin with long slow sitting trots, riding every stride to keep the rhythm and prevent him from racing off. Mrs Dammers has a small Indoor School where I begin cantering him in circles with masses of transitions using lots of half halts until I can keep him under control. Mrs Dammers says I must gallop him before I take him hunting. She has a large field which is flat at the bottom leading up a long steep hill. I canter circles at the bottom and then slide into a gallop uphill. The hill helps with the braking process although he is still as powerful when we reach the top.

The Heythrop hunt four days a week, Wednesday and Saturday are the most popular days, so I am to hunt Vigo on Monday and Friday which are the quieter days. The first day I take him I am given a lift and accompanied by Mr Warlock. VIGO is by this time is going well on his own, but the added excitement of being with fifty other horses and going cross country is another story. We park and hack the last two miles to the meet, he behaves quite well at the meet but once we move off, I have to work very hard to keep him under control. I keep him in trot when the others were cantering, and when I canter it was like riding a racehorse down to the start. We jump a few fences which he does beautifully, and we hunt until 4 p.m. when it is getting dark. Even after that long day he shows no sign of slowing down, Mr Warlock walks his horse the last mile back to the trailer but Vigo jiggles and jogs sideways all the way. Mr Warlock raised his lucifer eyebrows and asks if VIGO ever gets tired, the answer to that is "No never" I sleep well that night!

I persevere and take him hunting two days a week. By always keeping him steady and never letting him race off, eventually he settles. After a couple of months Mrs Dammers says she wants to come out and see how he is behaving. Fortunately, he is angelic, he behaves like a perfect gentleman at the meet and we are able to stand and chat whilst having a stirrup cup. We move off to the first covert and must queue along the side of a ploughed field. The horses are crammed together, it is cold, and we have to wait for a good twenty minutes. Mrs. Dammers is in the lane on the other side of the hedge and cannot believe that VIGO is so patient. The truth being it is hard for him to fidget when he is up to his hocks in mud.

Finally hounds break away and all the horses squeeze through the gate into a huge grass field, lovely old turf and a long straight gallop slightly downhill. As I have always held him in a steady canter VIGO does not attempt to rush off, we just slide into a glorious balanced gallop. Towards the left-hand side of the field there is a strip of bare earth, a horse on my left goes to cross over to the other side. They have a crashing fall. A pipeline has recently been laid and filled in with loose earth, so the horse suddenly sinks up to his knees and with the speed he is going turns a somersault. Fortunately, neither horse nor rider is seriously injured but both are badly shaken. Everyone says the danger was obvious and how foolish she was to ride across it at that speed. I secretly think I have had a lucky escape, I stayed with the crowd so Mrs Dammers could see her horse behave amongst the other horses. Normally, in order to keep Vigo calm, I try to avoid riding in the middle of a crowd of horses in which case it could easily have happened to us.

Mrs. Dammers is thrilled with her little horse but wants me to continue hunting him twice a week for the rest of the season. I am very fond of dear VIGO by this time as he is really settling to the job in hand, enjoying himself and jumping well. I also have her four-year-old Dartmoor pony to break in which is going nicely, I have to borrow a tiny saddle and bridle from Mrs Dammers as none of my tack fits him. He is a good little pony and soon I am riding him down the lane and round the fields. Mrs. Dammers decides to try him, she is tiny and looks much better on him than me. She is happy on the pony and says she really doesn't think she will ever ride her dear VIGO, but neither will she sell him, but she is quite happy for me to ride him. She also says I can use her indoor school whenever I want, and she spoils me! There is a bridle path next to Mrs Dammer's gate and when she sees me ride past, she always runs out to ask me if I will be going past again with another horse. If I said "yes", she leaves a glass of port on the gatepost for me!

Mrs. Dammer's friend Joy Hillman from Wales, who breeds show ponies, also sends me a pony to break. RUMOUR is 14:2hh and beautiful, a miniature thoroughbred, a glossy dark bay, and he moves like a dream, he floats with a natural cadence pointing his pretty little toes in such a proud fashion. He comes with a wardrobe of clothes an assortment of rugs, bandages and boots for all occasions. I have strict instructions not to work him without brushing boots in front and behind, overreach boots and knee pads. It takes nearly as long to get him ready as to work him!

It takes me approximately six weeks to break a horse in order to be able to stop, start, steer and ride quietly in walk, trot and canter. Of course, they are all different. RUMOUR has been handled and shown in hand since he was a baby and he has won a considerable number of prizes. This means he has also learned a few naughty tricks and got a few bad habits, but fortunately he is an honest little fellow. When he tries to be naughty, he doesn't try again when he realises he can't get away with it. So, I just have to be quiet but very firm. I ride him in Mrs Dammers School and then all over her farm. I teach him to open gates and jump logs and straw bales and generally have fun. Mrs Dammers rides out with me one day on the Dartmoor pony, but is horrified when I say I have jumped him. Joy comes to see me ride him and seems satisfied, but she says she wants me to keep him and school him for the show ring as he will have to be shown by a child. So, I keep him for another couple of months and when Joy comes back, we gave her a super show in the big field. He has a spectacular extended trot; we canter on both legs and finally the gallop which is also impressive as he resembles the mini racehorse he is and to my astonishment Joy sells him for 10,000 pounds! To me this is an absolute fortune and I now understand all the protection and Mrs Dammers' concern when I told her I had been jumping logs and bales! I am relieved I did not know his value when I was working with him as we would not have had half the fun.

The Rector rides into the yard on his old mare a few days before RUMOUR is due to go home. He has three churches to look after and he visits his parishioners, many of whom are farmers, by horse. He is a short wiry, middle aged, friendly fellow and has become a close friend of Mr Egerton who apart from being Church Warden is Choirmaster for two parishes and manages the accounts for all three. Now he also manages the accounts for our little horse business, and he is still the treasurer for the Birmingham Bach Society so he has a busy retirement. The Rector says he will have to stop riding his old mare as she is very stiff with arthritis and stumbling. He is somewhat downhearted as he adores her and has been riding her round his parishes for the last 15 years. However, he has bred from her and as a result has a lovely four-year-old mare, who is unbroken, hence he would like me to break her in. He says it is strictly business and he wants to pay the going rate. I say I would be delighted and arrange to pick up the mare who is turned out behind the Rectory in the next village. Mr Egerton tells me on no account am I to charge the Rector, he will cover costs from his own pocket if necessary. The home bred mare is a quality, bay, mare, she has not been handled much but is quiet, trusting and a quick learner. After five weeks I ride her alone to the next village and up to the Rectory, the next day the Rector comes over, I help him mount and accompany him on VIGO, we ride round his parishes and she behaves impeccably. The next day I ride her over to the Rectory again to leave her there to begin her new role in life. The Rector and his wife invite me in for tea and he pushes an envelope into my hand, I refuse it saying Mr Egerton had forbidden me to accept anything and it has been a pleasure. He becomes rather agitated so eventually I take it but say I will hand it to Mr Egerton who will only return it to him. I reiterate that it has been a pleasure, the mare is a delight and if ever I can do anything for him not to hesitate to ask me.

He raises his eyebrows peers at me over his rimless spectacles, "You could sing in the church choir, we desperately need people". I am a little taken aback and retort that I cannot sing, to which he informs me that I have an excellent teacher living under the same roof. How can I refuse? So somewhat reluctantly I accompany Mr Egerton to choir practice the following Tuesday evening. It turns out to be an enjoyable experience, we rehearse in the Broadwell Church on Tuesday evenings and then adjourn to the local pub, "The Fox", right next door. It also entails singing at the morning service in Evenlode and Evensong in Broadwell. This implies an extra early start on Sundays to see to the horses before church. George's face is a picture when he sees me in the choir stalls on Sunday morning, he is thoroughly amused, and I get a lot of leg pull. I learn a lot from the Egertons, they begin to educate me musically and on winter evenings we sit round the fire listening to music and following the score. Mrs Egerton is contralto so I must try to follow the soprano line. My father loved classical music but of the powerful kind his favourites being Bach's Brandenburg Concerto and Wagner's Ride of the Valkyries. I remember he liked to play The Ride of the Valkyries, the dance of the witches, at full volume despite my mother's protests.

Wendy, my friend from the Academy where we took our B.H.S. exams, rings me. She is working for John who also took his exams with us and is racing and eventing. He has been point-to-pointing a horse called QUENTIN HOUSE but wants to sell him. Wendy says John is a not a good jockey and always falls off but the horse jumps really well so would be perfect if I wanted to have a go at racing. She says they just want a good home, so he is very cheap for the quality of horse. I consult Mr Egerton regarding the financial situation and Wendy brings him over. He does move a bit strangely behind, but the vet passes him as sound and we buy him for 400 pounds. When we buy QUENTIN, he is already clipped and quite fit, so I get my point-to-point pass and decide to take him hunting on Wednesdays to qualify him, I am now hunting four days a week.

Hunting days, I begin work at 5:30am, I have the horses fed and the beds done by 7am. Then I exercise the horses not hunting and plait the horse or horses going hunting, I always sew the plates and never use rubber bands. The horses are turned out like show horses, fit to go to Wembley. After hunting all day, I clean and settle the hunters then I work with the young horses again. I like to work them twice a day, little and often and each time making a little more progress in their training.

QUENTIN is easy to handle, box, shoe and clip, he is a lovely hack and will go anywhere never shying at anything. The first time I take him hunting it is a poor day and we spend most of the time hanging around or struggling across ploughed fields. The next time hounds run well, and we gallop across lovely turf, he flies. There is a big hedge at the far end of a grass field, a few people jump it, but most go for the gate. I think this is a great opportunity to try him out as he has already point to pointed and this will be exactly his kind of fence, I line him up and he takes off perfectly then in mid-air it feels as though there is an ejector seat under the saddle, I am sent flying sky high and can do nothing about it. I land on the other side of the hedge and QUENTIN gallops on and jumps two more big hedges without me. Embarrassing to say the least, fortunately someone catches him for me. I thank them and re-mount, saying "As you see he can jump, and he is for sale". I take him to a local trainer's schooling fences, first fence fine, at the second he uses the ejector seat again. I try all ways and find it impossible to stay on board when he humps his back in mid-air, he has developed it to a fine art. I remember Wendy saying that John is a bad jockey and just falls off, now I know why. Ironically, John is short listed for the British Eventing team so he can't be such a bad rider. This explains why such a quality horse was sold so cheaply, but to go on falling off him will do my reputation no good and obviously we are never going to win a race. I change my tactic, he is sound and easy to handle and ride, except for the jumping. I find a perfect home for him, a retired gentleman farmer who just wants to ride round his estate to check the fences and stock but likes a quality horse as he had point to pointed in his youth. I sell QUENTIN at a small profit which just covers the cost of keeping him for those few months. I don't blame Wendy; the horse is loveable and a delight to look after and Wendy obviously never jumped him!

Jan who has the livery yard on the village green asks me to ride another four-year-old, I go over to her yard and ride him in Jan's orchard. Another bay gelding, he is huge for his age and a lovely ride. I hunt him with Jan on her old Russian horse Bez. Initially I accompany Jan who goes quietly and never jumps. He proves to have a good jump and loves jumping so Jan tells me to go ahead, from then on, I hunt with George and other friends. One day I find myself with David Tatlow and company, I follow them as they are taking their own line and they jump some big fences following which Jan also wants me to show jump him.

There is a large indoor school in Stow on the Wold where they hold indoor jumping on Sundays throughout the winter, so Sunday becomes an extremely busy day. I have to get up extra early to have the horses mucked out fed and walked out before singing in church, sometimes my parents come over for lunch and I go show jumping in the afternoon, then church again followed by feeding and settling the horses for the night.

Sadly, I have one of the worst experiences imaginable with one of Jan's liveries, a 14:2hh show jumping pony. He is then 14 years old and semi-retired from competition. The girl who owns him wants to go hunting. As Jan doesn't jump, she asks me to chaperone the girl, I am riding her young horse MONSOON that day. Considering MONSOON is still green and only four years old I assume that the girl will jump far bigger fences than us. We ride together happily and jump a few fences. Suddenly we see a small group of horses gallop down a field and jump what looks like quite a small hedge at the end. We set off after them and I line MONSOON up to the hedge, when we are in mid-air, I see there is a huge blind ditch on the other side, I scream back to the girl "Kick on it's wide!" MONSOON being a baby has the tendency to jump everything very big and has no problem clearing the ditch. However, the pony show jumps the hedge, so her forelegs don't quite reach far enough and plunge into the ditch, her chest hitting the edge with a sickening thud. She slips back into the abyss of a ditch which proves to be very deep. It was completely blind, being choked with weeds, so from the other side it looked like a grass track not a ditch. Fortunately, the girl is fine although shaken. I get her off the pony who after several attempts is unable to get out of the ditch. I put the girl on MONSOON and tell her to ride up to the road and ask for help, then find Jan and go home with her. Seeing her safely trotting up the field, I go back to the pony, I manage to take off her saddle to see if she can move more easily but she cannot. Then her breathing became laboured, I feel hot tears of despair run down my cheeks and weep uncontrollably into her mane begging her forgiveness, I can't bear to face what I know in my heart of hearts is inevitable. I spend nearly an hour in the ditch gently stroking the pony until a vet arrives with a farmer and a tractor. The vet examines her and says she has internal injuries and must have punctured a lung; her breathing is getting worse and worse. He says the kindest thing was to put her to sleep there and then or she will certainly endure terrible suffering and still probably not make it. I can't speak I am choked with tears, but I stay until the pony goes peacefully to sleep. The vet kindly takes me back to Jan's where the girl and her parents are waiting. It is a dreadful moment I want the earth to open and swallow me up, I have never felt so miserable and guilty, I say it was unforgiveable of me not to have been more careful. I will never forgive myself and offer to find another pony for them. Although I know nothing can replace the little mare, I would do anything to help them. They are very understanding and insist it was an accident. Furthermore, they say it was the best way for the pony to go, she had a wonderful life and now won't suffer old age with colic and arthritis. Their kindness just made me feel even more wretched.

Jack rings me up to say he had a well-bred four-year-old, by Game Rights who is a very popular sire. He says Sheelagh tried to break him, but he went berserk and broke all the tack, according to Jack he just needs my patience. I agree to go and see him. He is a real beauty and moves like a dream. If I can get him going, he will be worth four times what Jack is asking for him. Mr Egerton encourages me, and we decide to go ahead, I give Jack a cheque and bring him home. He is lovely in the stable, but I go very slowly with him putting an elastic bandage round his girth and tightening it little by little. I lunge him and long-rein him with no problem. When it comes to the saddle, I am very gentle and tighten the girth little by little, turning him and moving him so he feels it, he is fine. Suddenly one day when I am lunging him a rabbit pops out of the hedge, he shies and explodes bucking like a bronco. He leaps high in the air with his legs straight and his head between his knees just like the horses in the American Rodeos. Luckily, I have put a breast plate on him, so he doesn't displace the saddle. I eventually slow him down and he finally stops and stands shaking and sweating poor thing. Having calmed and reassured him I gently move him forward; he is nervous but fortunately keeps his four feet on the ground.

Working him twice a day these incidents occur less and less. I mount him in the stable with no problem, I long-rein him down the lane climb aboard, he carried me home without incident, I really felt we are overcoming the problem. Then I mount in the yard and Earnie the gardener comes round the corner with a wheelbarrow and startles him, he launches into a series of bronco bucks. Although they are high, and his head is between his knees it is not too difficult to stay on board. We bucked round the yard for a full ten minutes then Dickie appears on one of the Aird's hunters and offers to come to my rescue, so I ride him round the next village with Dickie and he is fine.

The next day I ride him in Mrs Dammer's indoor school I am convinced we have overcome the problem. I decided to ride him straight out alone, he goes like a dream we trot and canter, he even goes through the ford in the next village without a lead. I am so pleased with him, then walking back through the village a noisy rattling lorry comes past and startles him and once more he launches into his bronco bucks. Mrs Bulkley invites me to go round to her house, she never goes out but knows what everybody is doing within a radius of ten miles. She tells me she has heard I am having trouble with a young horse that bucks. Some horses are cold backed like the horse I rode in Leicestershire, but this is not his case. Mrs Bulkley says she thinks it could be the girth. I have tried different girths but Mrs Bulkley has an elastic girth which for me is quite a novelty, an invention. She explains that as it stretches it will not feel tight with sudden movement which is probably what triggers his bucking fits. This makes sense and seems like a wonderful invention, no-one I know has one and it amazes me how, being the recluse, she is, she not only knows about them but possesses one which she kindly offers to lend me. Although I ride him and he really is a beautiful boy, I feel I cannot sell him without telling the prospective owners his history and about the girth. Consequently, when I have an offer from a lady, who wants a challenge and a quality horse at a reasonable price, I accept, once more I have not lost money but neither have I made a great profit. I just could not sell him without telling them the whole story. I realise that buying and selling horses is not my forte!

The artist Penelope Fleming lives in the village. She has been to the Egerton's to paint their portraits and the one of their son Rob is particularly good. He is wearing his Sealed Knot uniform and a jaunty wide brimmed hat complete with feather. She depicts men far better than women for some reason. Albeit certain things and people upset her. There is a cottage in our lane built with local Cotswold stone although it is not a historic building. However, the owners have added stone buttresses just because they like the look of them. Penelope is horrified, she says it ruins the beautiful lines of the lane! She also becomes distraught when her neighbour levels the ridge and furrow on the land behind their house, she insists that apart from being beautiful, especially with the evening shadows, it has ruined her view and is destroying the heritage of the village! She goes to great lengths to explain the wonders of undulating the field in this manner to provide natural drainage and increase the area of grazing. Furthermore, it dates back to the middle ages when it was ingeniously created by their system of ploughing. However, she has a gypsy caravan in her garden which blocks this particular neighbour's view, but that according to Penelope is fine as it is a beautiful hand painted work of art to enhance their view! Supposedly this is a question of artistic license. Penelope is charming towards me; she invites me to supper in her cottage. She also invites me to go Scottish country dancing with her once a week, which I do whenever I can. Penelope's mother is a successful authoress, but she writes crime stories of which Penelope does not approve and her Father is a Harley Street Eye Specialist. The family home is in Broadway and she invites me to a summer concert there, it is in a beautiful setting. Penelope's brother is there, I have seen him before in the village. He too is a little eccentric, he tends never to wear shoes, which might be normal in South Africa but in England in the winter is highly unusual to say the least. During the interval he brings me a glass of champagne and whisks me away to the bottom of the lawn to have rose petal races down the stream, he is bizarre but harmless.

Suddenly a whole year has flown by, despite the fact I have not made a great success of buying and selling, with the steady income from the liveries and schooling we have made a profit. Sufficient for me to pay Mr Egerton back his loan in full which is very satisfactory. I have worked seven days a week and very long hours, but it has also paid for my hunting and competing, so I have enjoyed the experience. In addition, I have had enquiries for more hunter liveries next season which means eight months increased guaranteed income.

Chapter 10
Evenlode

The summer passes by in a flash, through Jan in the village I have also been asked to Instruct at Pony Club Camp. They have excellent facilities with full a show jumping and cross-country course. Apart from being fun, if exhausting, I meet a lot more people from another sector of the local horse community. Later someone from the pony club rings me to enquire whether I can transport two ponies for Riding for the Disabled. I duly collect the ponies and take them over to the venue. The lady in charge asks me if I can stay and help. I am asked to lead a pony ridden by a boy called Andrew. Andrew was one of the thalidomide babies, that awful drug to stop morning sickness in the first months of pregnancy which left so many babies disfigured. Andrew is about 14 years old; he is open, friendly and extremely intelligent. He has no arms just three fingers at shoulder level. The equipment is ingenious, he has ladder reins so he can manage to shorten and lengthen his reins himself using his little fingers at shoulder level. He also has an incredible sense of balance bearing in mind he can never hold on to the saddle if he feels insecure.

I am terrified of physical disability. As a child I belonged to the brownies and in the guide group which followed our meeting there was a girl with one arm amputated just below the elbow. She always had her sleeve rolled up and the little red stump exposed. I had nightmares that I had to dance round the campfire next to this girl and hold her stump. I refused to join the guides but never told anyone why.

I am fine with Andrew while I keep looking into his eyes. He is a lovely boy; we chat away and I begin to feel quite at ease with him. When it is time for him to dismount, we all line up and are instructed to help our rider dismount. I ask Andrew how he dismounts. He says he will lean forward; I must hold his hands then he will swing his leg over the pony's rump and so dismount. I feel the blood

120

drain from my head as panic seizes me. Andrew knows I am terrified and reassures me, telling me to take my time it will be fine. My knees feel weak, but I keep looking into his kind blue eyes, he leans forward and as soon as I felt his warm soft fingers in mine all my fears evaporate. I feel a rush of gratitude and love towards Andrew, what a compassionate and brave, boy. I continue helping the group, sometimes Instructing too, it is extremely rewarding. I find I am now fine with the physically handicapped, but we have some children from Mencap which I find disconcerting as there is little or no eye contact especially when they make erratic movements or unintelligible sounds.

I have a busy summer, whilst out hunting the previous season I met Colonel Tilke's daughter Celia from the Academy. She married a farmer and they live in the Monday country. She rings me and tells me that she has bred two foals from her fabulous dressage mare AZARETTE, one is a three-year -old and the other four. Her sister Judith has tried to break in the four-year-old but got into difficulties and fell off, so she asks me to have the two of them to break. When she brings them over her father comes with her, his only comment being "I don't know whether you deserve this, but it is a very nice yard".

After my experience with the horse Sheelagh had problems with, I wonder if this will be a similar challenge but luckily it proves to be plain sailing. I work both young mares twice a day and fortunately the older one has not been traumatized by her earlier mishap. Six weeks later I can mount them in the yard and ride them out alone. The beauty of the long reining is that they learn to go everywhere alone in front. They understand the voice commands with patience and without trauma, so it is easy to repeat the procedure sitting quietly on board. This for me is a proven method and I prefer working alone with the young horses as we are totally focused on each other. It is so thrilling once they understand I never cease to be amazed at how noble and generous they are. I always feel it is a great honour when a young horse accepts you and allows you to ride him or her. After six weeks I ring Celia, who comes over and chooses to ride the three-year-old as she still doesn't trust the four-year-old after the incident with her sister. Her father comes to watch. I have trimmed their manes and tails and oiled their hooves, so they look smart. I lead the three-year-old out into the yard and help Celia to mount, to my surprise she is quite nervous, what a reversal of roles. I mount the four-year-old and we ride side by side down the lane, they behave impeccably we meet dogs, a tractor and a bicycle and they don't hesitate, I am so proud of them. We ride down to Mrs Dammers', I previously asked her permission, and she loves to be involved. I know Celia will be more at home riding in a school and there we trot and canter on both reins. Even her father grudgingly admits I have done a good job, to which my dear friend Mrs Dammers sings my praises, bless her. Celia is happy and she asks me to hunt the four-year-old for her. It will be so much easier now I know the country, and I know I can go quietly with Jan until the babies get their confidence and settle then little by little start jumping them. I hunt the little mare once a week and after a couple of months hounds are meeting near where Celia lives, and she and her husband come out in the car to follow. By this time the mare is jumping nicely in that part of the country there are lovely stone walls to jump and practically no ditches. After a couple of hours, I ride up to the car followers on the road to find Celia thinking that is probably enough. As we are chatting on the road hounds run away across the bottom of an adjacent field. Celia wants us to continue and the mare is still fresh enough. Her husband goes to open the gate but finds it is chained and locked, I tell him not to worry and we jump the wall, it is a fair size, but I am confident that with all the other horses on the other side the little mare will jump it happily which she does. Celia was duly elated although she had bred her with dressage in mind. As I well remember AZARETTE was not a great jumper, but her daughter seems to love it.

Nicola and Simon are new clients and send their horses to me as hunter liveries. Simon rides a lovely black gelding who is as good as gold and Nicola rides a naughty little grey mare side saddle. She has been very successful showing side saddle and is a plucky rider because the mare has a nasty stop. Nicola and Simon have recently married and bought the vicarage in a nearby village, they are a lovely couple. They also have dogs and keep otters in their garden. Nicola's mother is also from the showing world, so they really appreciate the way I turn the horse out. I clip them out every two weeks, so they never have a whisker out of place. To go hunting they are all plaited and I sew in the plaits, it takes longer but the results are so much better, and I still frown on rubber bands, although I know they are widely used by the show jumping fraternity, many of whom do not plait at all.

In order to try to improve Nicola's mare's lack of enthusiasm for jumping we decide to go to a sponsored cross country for charity. There are three options, a big jump, a small jump or a gateway for non-jumpers. This means everyone can take part and it is all in a good cause. As it is on a Sunday my parents decide to come as I have asked them to sponsor me. I ride VIGO and jump the big fences and Nicola is going to ride alongside us and jump the smaller fences to see if the little mare will begin to enjoy her jumping. We set off and over the first five fences all goes well, by which time we are out of sight from the spectators gathered near the starting point and the finishing line. One reason I love cross country is that there is you and your horse, and the jump judges, not masses of people watching your every move. VIGO flies the next fence and whether Nicola relaxes as the mare is going so well, who knows, but she stops dead at the last minute and Nicola flies over her head and hits the fence, a solid post and rails. I rush back through the gate and jump off. The jump judge has caught the mare and Nicola does not move. As I reach her, she comes round, the jump judge meanwhile has called for the ambulance. The ambulance men want to take Nicola back in the ambulance as they say she may have concussion. Nicola is furious, she stands up and dusts the grass and mud off her clothes retorting; "No way, give me that bloody mare!" with which she snatches the reins from the jump judge and climbs back on board telling me to give her a lead over the fated fence. She is plucky and so determined we manage to complete the course with no further mishaps. However, as we triumphantly cross the finishing line we are met by my irate parents. My poor mother is as white as a sheet. No sooner had we disappeared from sight the ambulance was sent out, roaring after us. She says in no uncertain terms that if I want to kill myself, fine, but she is never ever going to attend another horse event, and she means it she keeps to her word!

Colonel MacDonald Buchanan breeds his own Polo Ponies. His stud groom has always broken in the youngsters, but he is getting quite old so needs to delegate. They have heard of me, so he rings and arranges to come for a meeting. He is a gentleman of the old school and utterly charming. He tells me they sent a three-year-old mare to be broken and the results were rather disastrous. They now have her full brother, already four years old, big and strong and totally unhandled. We discuss terms and he agrees to bring the horse over, saying he would like to visit and observe progress every two weeks. A few days later a very smart horsebox pulls into the yard. The stud groom asks which stable the horse will be going in as they have herded him into the horsebox because they had not been able to put a head-collar on him. We must put the ramp right up to the box door with the tail gates on the sides of the ramp so the only way he has to go is into the stable. It takes a while to coax him to leave the horsebox but eventually he gives a huge leap down the ramp and into the stable. We must be quick to get the gates and the ramp up and close the stable door. He is bright red chestnut with four white stockings and a wide white blaze down his face. He has a wall eye, showing the white of his eye, this adds to the impression of his being completely wild. He is snorting and his nostrils flaring red, whilst rearing on his hind legs. I shut the top door quickly as I am afraid, he will attempt to jump out over the bottom door.

The stud groom raises his eyebrows, wishes me luck saying he will return in two weeks. The smart horsebox crunches its way out of the yard and I peep through the door at our new addition. He has hay and water, so I decide to leave him quietly on his own to settle down and get used to his new environment. An hour later I feed the other horses and go into his box with his feed. He eyes me suspiciously and backs away, I put a little feed in his manger and try offering him some from my hand, but he just blows it away snorting loudly. I go in every half hour and put a handful of feed and some carrots in his manager, eventually he starts to eat. He quickly learns that I go into his stable to put food in his manger and by the next morning he follows me across the stable until he will eat with me there. I stay with him placing my hand on his shoulder and little by little stroking his neck, then his head and his body.

The next day I put a strap round his neck and have a head collar on him by the afternoon, having gained his confidence, he proves to be very trusting, although it takes a little longer to handle his legs and pick his feet up. Then I put an elastic bandage round his girth securing it round his chest and tightening it little by little, soon I have him lunging and long reining in the stable. By the time they come to see him after two weeks he is wearing a saddle and bridle and I lunge and long rein him in the open field, from there I take him out round the village and down the lane. I work him in the school and when I feel he trusts me enough loose him in the paddock to run, roll and eat grass. To my surprise he follows me round like a dog, so I have no problem catching him. I mount and dismount in the stable and finally long rein him down the lane climb aboard and ride him home.

A few days later I ride him out with Dickie, and we have some long trots and go round the Broadwell. He hesitates about going through the ford, so Dickie comes back to give us a lead. I tuck in behind him and in a flash the colt jumps on top of Dickie's mare. It is so unexpected we are both taken by surprise. Luckily, they disentangle and no harm is done, he could so easily have broken Dickie's leg. Luckily Dickie is unperturbed, but I am careful to keep my distance just in case. Then I take him up the lane and across the fields where we canter, and all goes well.

They are coming to collect him in the afternoon, so I turn him out in the paddock in the morning for a last treat. True to form I have become very fond of him. He is so trusting considering he was completely wild when he came. I ride out on another horse and there is a sudden downpour. Luckily, it isn't cold, but he is soaking wet. When they arrive, his back is still wet. I remember Jack put a piece of sacking under the numnah when the horse's back was wet which was crude but effective, still it would be a strange new experience for the young horse. He is as good as gold; I lead him out of the stable. It is blowing a gale, which always makes horses nervous, and still raining. I mount him and ride him down the lane the owner and stud groom following in the car. I give them a nice show in the indoor school, but it is small, and he isn't balanced enough to canter round the corners, I assure them he has cantered in the field and they seem more than satisfied. The next time I see the stud groom at a horse event, he is on crutches. He fell off a young horse he tells me, I go cold, "Not my boy?" I query nervously. He laughs and says that "my boy" never puts a foot wrong, it was his sister. He also tells me that the five-year-old from the same mare has turned out to be too small so they want to sell her. He says she will make a fantastic Small Hunter. She was broken at three and turned away to see if she would grow, but she has not. They ask me if they could send her to me to prepare for sale. The little mare is a small edition of her big brother but a little skinny and very scraggy as she has come straight out of the field. I set to work, I pull her mane and tail and with work and good food in a month she looks like a different horse. She proves to be a lovely ride and is ready to do novice dressage tests at Riding Club level. Mr Egerton for some reason falls in love with her and says we should buy her which we do for a very reasonable price and we call her FANNY FLETCHER as the house is called "Fletchers". I enjoy her and take her to one or two "parties" at which she behaves impeccably, and people begin to show an interest in her. Some people come to try her for a rather ambitious boy. I have seen him at shows and do not like the way he rides. After being eliminated in the show jumping once he came out of the ring and beat the horse, there is no way I will let them have the little mare. I say the mare is not suitable for what he wants as she can be moody due to her hormones and I ask a ridiculous price. Later a lovely family come to see her, mother and daughter who want to share her and she would have a very loving home as they would look after her themselves. I sell her for far less than I should because I am sure it will be the perfect home for her. We cover costs, make a small profit and I have enjoyed the little mare, but I realise, yet again, selling is not my forte.

Lady Mary Fanshawe is another new client whose husband, Colonel Fanshawe, is a gentleman from a long line of aristocrats with distinguished military careers. He has given up hunting due to ill health but has bought his wife a Connemara mare thinking she will be safe and easy to manage. ZARA is dun with a yellow body and black mane, tail and legs, quite a smart cob but a bundle of nerves. She dishes and has knee action so is not very comfortable, she shies at everything, is as stubborn as a mule and will not go in front. In the stable she is a nightmare too. When my bedroom light goes on in the morning, she starts banging the door impatiently with her hooves and doesn't stop until she gets her breakfast. In a word she is a pain. She has been in nearly all the yards in the area and been asked to leave. David Tatlow hoots with laughter when he hears she is with me and wishes me luck. Lady Mary constantly criticizes me and everyone else in the yard, on top of which she comes every single day. It comes to the point that when I see her car my stomach churns, I suppose she is just an unhappy lady.

Sadly, the Colonel dies, he was a gentle soul and meant well, but there is no way I can convince her to sell the mare. As she insists on riding out with me every day, I can't try to re-educate the mare either. One day in desperation I decide to ride ZARA in the afternoon to see if I can school her a bit, unfortunately Lady Mary comes back because she has forgotten her gloves and she is beside herself with anger. When she calms down and accepts the fact that I am only trying to help she comes full circle and asks me to take her hunting. The mare fidgets and pulls faces at all the other horses, Lady Mary always goes at the back and never jumps now I knew why. I close my legs firmly round her and hold her straight riding towards the front. At one point we are alongside the Master who affirms that the mare is highly unsuitable for an elderly lady, I could not agree more. I manage to jump her over small tiger trap at the second attempt and we came to a small ditch, the mare digs her toes in and refuses, she is really stubborn it takes me 20 minutes to get her over and a child could have jumped it. I begin to feel sorry for Lady Mary. It is no pleasure riding ZARA and that is unusual for me as I tend to fall in love with anything on four legs.

Poor Lady Mary is always losing and forgetting things and has me hunting high and low for her belongings. She had been asking me for days if I had seen her dentures and one morning when I go to clean the mare's feet there is a set of dentures neatly embedded in the mare's hoof.

Most seasons some members of the royal family come hunting with us for a day. On this day Princess Anne is out with us. The whole field is waiting in narrow enclosed cart track. I am about a third of the way down and Lady Mary at the back as usual, she is with the gate-shutters who have dutifully closed the gate behind her. Hounds suddenly run in the opposite direction, so there is a mad scramble to make an about turn, as the saying goes the last shall be first and the first shall be last. The field is confronted with Lady Mary who is now in the front nervously fumbling with the gate, and at the same time blocking the post and rails beside it which everyone wants to jump, someone shouts at the top of their voice "Bloody well get her out of the way!" Not very polite but the blood is up with the heat of the chase. Now everyone refers to poor Lady Mary as Bloody Mary, I do feel rather sorry for her. I promise myself I will try to be more patient with her in the future, although it does not last for long. It must be chemistry, odd how some people just wind you up without really doing or saying anything!

Hilary is a farmer's wife and delivers the milk in the village, she is about my age, a vibrant, hyperactive girl with long, blond hair she wears in two jaunty plaits. She is very outspoken. She calls a spade a spade in no uncertain terms and she falls out with one or two people including Penelope, they become sworn enemies. She rides the milkman's horse which still pulls the milk float during the week and Hilary takes her show jumping on Sundays, quite successfully too. She rides other people's horses and has a couple at home on the farm. She works extremely hard, she milks the cows with her husband, does the milk round and then rides the horses. The truth of the matter is that she is quite shy and awkward with people, she has a rather brash manner in order to help her overcome her insecurity. Really, she has a big heart and as often happens, people who own the least are sometimes the most generous, which is certainly true in her case. I love riding and performing but I am not very competitive. I need someone to put a bomb behind me and Hilary does just that. She competes in every equine event going in the area on horses of all shapes and sizes. As she delivers the milk, she shouts across the yard to ask me if I have a ride for the show, hunter trial, team chase or whatever is coming up. If I do not have a horse for that competition Hilary will say that she has a horse for me to ride and she will see me there, just like that, no arguments! Often, I compete on horses I have never seen before, but Hilary just tells me to get on with it and I do.

The milk man is delighted and loves what Hilary has done with his milk float mare so he buys a young horse from a local farmer. He is a lovely grey horse and in no time, they have outgrown the riding club competitions, so she begins Eventing him very successfully. She upgrades him from Novice to Intermediate in one season.

The milkman is on the crest of the wave and buys another locally bred four-year-old for her to ride, this time a lovely bay mare. Hilary persuades me to go to hunter trials with her, I am on the mare and Hilary on her eventer getting him fit for the Spring events. We have a good ride but unfortunately the mare is still very green and she stands off too far from a post and rails and bangs her knee, I feel dreadful, they are very nice about it which just makes me feel worse. I also go team chasing with Hilary, their team is called "The Rat Catchers" and they wear tweed jackets which are also known as ratcatchers. I ride a show jumping mare with loppy ears. Hilary warns me if I try to ride the fences at a gallop the mare will stop, but if I check her and show jump them for the last three strides, she will jump a house! Team chases are fun, but the courses are fairly big and solid. The four of us set off, I duly check the mare and jump the first fence beautifully but of course am left behind, I gallop like the wind overtaking the others and check before the next fence, the others laugh every time I whizz past them calling out rude comments, but we get round in pretty good time.

Hilary continues Eventing the local farm bred horse and takes him up to Advanced level, she qualifies for Burghley Horse Trials one of the biggest Events in England on a par with Badminton. Qualifying for an International Event is a great achievement for an amateur working on a shoestring. She has real guts, together with terrific determination and I love being involved with the preparation. In order to prepare for the steeple chasing we school together over point-to-point fences, I ride one of Jan's horses, jumping those fences at speed is a great feeling akin to flying!

Eventually she gets the horse so fit he is bursting at the seams with energy. She says she cannot walk on a grass verge, when his feet touch grass he takes off! That is a real test for Eventers as they must be very fit but controlled enough to do a dressage test. They go to Burghley which is pushing them both to their limits and she is worried about his legs as with so much work and feed they tend to swell. Fortunately, he passes the vet and they complete the imposing course …chapeau! Hilary all this time continues milking cows and delivering milk, I go round to her house sometimes and she also runs a home and cooks, one very competent lady.

When I compete or hunt, I start work at 5 a.m. and finish around midnight. Hilary will often appear in the yard at about ten o'clock in the evening to help me finish up, a friend indeed. As I am so busy Mr Egerton suggests his brother might come and give me a hand. Graham is retired and recently divorced so could do with a new interest. Graham knows nothing about horses but is willing to do anything and proves worth his weight in gold. He is calm and steady with a wonderful ponderous sense of humour. I like doing the beds myself, but Graham takes charge of scrubbing and filling water buckets, filling hay nets and sweeping the yard. It is amazing how helpful that is. It is such a joy to always have the yard tidy and clean and just to have an extra pair of hands to hold a horse's head still when I am clipping the ears or tricky bits. Graham is fascinated, he watches me meticulously sewing a horse's plaits and putting Vaseline round his eyes and nostrils and as I come out of the stable, he frowns at me and comments with a completely straight face "You haven't cleaned his teeth!" Imagine his surprise when a few days later I ask him to hold a horse while I file his teeth.

By the end of the second year, we had made a nice little profit despite my bungling at selling. I hated the whole scenario of buying and selling my four-legged friends. Due to increasing demand, I asked Mr Egerton if we could build two more stables in the barn. I also put new five bar gates on the paddocks, which made life a lot easier, and had the ditches cleared and hedges trimmed. With hindsight I think was foolish to invest my hard-earned money in someone else's property, however, I am very happy and have a great life even though I am as poor as a church mouse.

Mr. Goudie wants to send me a horse for the coming season. He is well into his seventies and a gentle soul, he keeps his horses at home, but has recently bought a new horse they cannot handle. The horse is a big chestnut and very good looking, initially he behaves like a gentleman, I even take him cubbing where Richard Sumner, a well-known professional approaches me. He tells me to be careful, he had a terrible problem with the horse rearing, when he couldn't stop him and put a stronger bit on him, he just stood on his hind legs the whole time. He told Mr Goudie he was totally unsuitable for him, but he refused to sell him, took him away and sent him to me. He never puts a foot wrong for the first three weeks including out cubbing, but one day I am riding back along a bridle path that runs across a huge ploughed field on the top of the hill near Chatterton when without warning or provocation he yanks the reins out of my hands and takes off at 90 miles an hour! A runaway is truly frightening, horses are creatures of flight it is one of their main defence mechanisms which usually comes into play when they panic, in which case it is impossible to communicate with them. We are heading towards the end of the path at a terrifying speed towards trees, a stone wall then the road. With all my strength I haul his head round the right, so we are heading round the ploughed field. Even so he shows no sign of slowing up, we race around the deep ploughed field until he eventually stops because he blows up and can hardly breathe. He is in a lather of sweat and shaking, I keep his head turned almost to my knee and we progress in small circles until he calms down.

I decide to tell Mr Goudie because I do not want him to ride him. He wants to take him away immediately, but I ask him to give us another opportunity. I talk to wise old Biddie who says the behaviour sounds like a brain tumour or fit, the vet is inclined to agree but says they would have to have him in the clinic and run tests with no guarantee they can do anything to help. Mr Goudie is dubious.

This disheartens me somewhat, but Jack also tells me that nothing terrifies a horse more than the feeling the rider is out of control. I wonder if I can avoid that situation, he may overcome the need to run away. Using turns and circles maybe I can convince the horse he is under control, it sort of works for a while but one day we are coming home down a cart track with hedges on both sides and no room to turn or circle. Aware of this I keep him in walk but although I am concentrating and trying to keep him calm, he suddenly lunges and gets away from me, we are going at a flat-out gallop and I can do nothing. I know there is a lane at the end of the track and on the other side of the lane a hedge. Fortunately, there isn't a car coming and I prepare myself for him to jump the hedge thinking we will then be in a field where I can turn him. It is as if he doesn't even see the hedge, he falls spread eagled into the ditch and I go flying, fortunately I keep hold of the reins.

There is a farm worker farther down the lane with his land rover, he cannot believe his eyes and is dubious when I ask him to help me get back on. When he sees he cannot dissuade me he consents to help. The man kindly holds him, I quietly turned his head to one side before mounting and we head off down the lane in minute circles until he calms down and somehow, we get back home in one piece. When Mr Goudie hears of the escapade, he says I am not to ride him again, he will turn him out on the farm with the cattle and he will never be ridden again.

He is a lucky horse, but I wish we could have found out the reasons for his behaviour. It reminds me of a horse we had at Jack's once, a lovely horse gentle and noble but when we went to ride him into the schooling field he stood on his hind legs and ran backwards which was quite out of character. Eventually when Jack consulted his friend the vet, they discovered the poor horse had angina, so when he worked, he was in pain, hence his aversion to the schooling field. Sometimes we are too quick to judge and blame a horse for bad behaviour when he is simply trying to tell us something. Mr Goudie is a lovely person, he asks me if I will consider going to work for him. He says I work far too hard. I could have my own cottage, keep a horse for myself and compete all I want just for looking after the family's three hunters. It is tempting but seems too easy, I still need more of a challenge.

Dr Silver brings me his hunter WELLINGTON, on Mr Goudie's recommendation. Dr Silver is an American eye surgeon who operates on Fifth Avenue in New York, he has bought a Manor House in a nearby village and wants to hunt. His horse WELLINGTON is a big chestnut horse and gives no problems except for clipping. Even when I am clipping another horse in the yard he goes to the back of his stable and stands shaking and sweating. When a horse is nervous about clipping, I usually find running the clippers regularly in and around their stable without doing a full clip, they become used to the noise and lose their fear, but Wellington's reaction is extreme. Some horses understandably do not like the clippers if they have been nicked or burned, clippers do tend to overheat, or if they have had an electric shock. Other horses just do not like the noise, especially around their heads and ears.

Dr Silver is aware of the problem and says the horse is booked into the vets to have a general anaesthetic, he asks me to go there to clip him. That is really weird clipping a sleeping horse, when I finish one side, they turn him over with the pulleys for me to do the other side. He is only clipped twice a season for this reason, which I am not very happy about, but Dr Silver doesn't hunt very much. He says he works seven days a week for eight months and has four months off which he plans to spend in his Manor House in England. He is a close friend of the Goudie family and I suspect he had a soft spot for Mr Goudie's daughter, who also acts as hunt secretary and is as delightful as her father.

Robin is the Estate Manager for a large neighbouring estate. He is married to Liz, they live in an idyllic cottage, have two beautiful children, two smart pointer dogs and a little thoroughbred horse which Robin hunts. They seem to me an idyllic family, they sometimes invite me round to supper when we sit round a log fire sipping wine and chatting late into the night. Robin's horse is called MANIFESTO and he looks after him himself. Robin says he can't stop him out hunting so asks me to hunt him. MANIFESTO is lovely to ride he is very fast, but I do not find him hard to stop, I just have to sit and check him, and he is very responsive. I realise Robin is totally a passenger hoping the horse will automatically slow up and stop in the right places. Manifesto is very honest and sensible, he always stops when he reaches the end of a field or a crowd, but sometimes rather abruptly slamming on the brakes at the last minute if left to his own devices. I just suggest that Robin tries using his seat to just check him back now and again.

Robin asks me if I will Point-to-Point MANIFESTO at the end of the season and ride him in the Members race, as he is already qualified. I readily accept, but only have six weeks to get him ready. I work hard and feed him up working him on the hills to get him fit without damaging his tendons. I also give him some fast work and after a month he looks like a different horse. I take him up to school over a local trainer's fences and Robin comes to watch, I am excited about riding in my first race. Robin is so impressed he decides he wants to ride him himself in the race. My heart sinks, it seems I am doomed not to ride in a Point-to-Point. Nevertheless, I continue preparing him.

On the day of the race, I take a gleaming MANIFESTO to the races. Robin and his family meet me there. It is a disaster really, but we have a wonderful day, MANIFESTO looks spectacular as he strides round the paddock and with his looks and his name people actually back him to be placed. I leg Robin up and tell him not to let him go, to keep him steady down to the start and for the first circuit. It is a pity Robin is a lot heavier than I am and he doesn't hold him back to save his energy. They make an impressive first circuit in the leading bunch jumping really well, but the poor horse blows up halfway round the second time. Fortunately, MANIFESTO is fine once he gets his breath back and Robin is euphoric. I cool, check, and settle Manifesto and we have a splendid picnic prepared by Liz with champagne and caviar, nothing but the best, while we watch the following races.

Out hunting one day I am approached by Bunny Scaramanga. Bunny is married to a gentleman farmer; she competes in Dressage and spent some time in Canada in her youth where she still has friends. I have met her previously through the pony club and seen her at a few shows. She asks me if I know someone who would like to go to Canada for the summer to look after and compete showing, dressage and jumping for an elderly lady. I think for a moment, I have been working 7days a week, 12-14 hours a day, for over two years. I have a yard full of hunter liveries which will go out to grass on May 1st for their summer rest. Instead of taking on young horses and horses to compete for the summer, I could quite easily close the yard until it is time to bring the hunters in again. On impulse I say, "Will I do?" Bunny looks taken aback but says a Canadian friend's daughter who lives in London will handling the interviews and is coming to stay next weekend. I say I will have to consult Mr. Egerton first and will confirm by phone.

Mr. Egerton is amenable and does not oppose the idea, I feel it will be good for the family too I have invaded their privacy for long enough they will probably be glad of a break from me. I know I am sometimes impatient and crotchety when I have no right to be. My fault entirely as I always take on too much, simply because I find it so hard to say "NO". The entire Egerton family have been very patient and kind. I consult my faithful livery clients and confirm their horses are to be turned out on the first of May and came back in at the end of August to give me two months to get them fit for the opening meet in November. This means it will just fit in beautifully as due to the climate in Canada all competitions are held during the summer months as they are steeped in snow for the rest of the year.

So, I ring Bunny and go to her home the following Sunday for the interview with Desi. Desi's mother looks after Lorna Casgrain's horses in the winter in Montreal. In the summer she takes them to her family's summer home in the Eastern Townships, it is there she needs someone to look after the horses and compete.

Lorna still competes in showing and dressage, sadly she has had three spinal fusions so can't jump but loves to see her horses jump. The job also involves being her companion she is a very special lady according to Desi. It is a true summer job I will have my fares paid, pocket money, full keep and perks apart from competing with the horses, sailing, canoeing, tennis and hiking. To me it sounds like a dream holiday. Although I have loved every minute of what I have been doing up to date, having worked seven days a week and 14 hours or more a day I am exhausted and need a break. Desi says she thinks I will be ideal; she offers me the job there and then and I accept.

I finish breaking the young horse I am working with, rough off the hunters and see them all safely in their summer residence. Then I thoroughly clean the stables and leave everything tidy and packed away. Graham has kindly offered to whitewash the stables during my absence so everything will be tickety boo for me to start up as soon as I get back. I give the Egertons effusive and heartfelt thanks for letting me take advantage of this opportunity and pack my bags.

Chapter 11

Canada

Canada here we come! Flights to Canada are expensive but Freddy Laker has just introduced cheap flights to New York. The Egertons have some old friends who live in New Jersey and work in Manhattan, I met them briefly when they were visiting England. I plan to visit the Marchbanks and then continue to Montreal by Greyhound, the long-distance coach service. The Marchbanks live in a beautiful Mill House in New Jersey and they are very welcoming. As Mr Marchbank works in Manhattan, he takes me in in the morning. I explore all day and go home with him in the evening. I see the usual sights, Empire State, Twin Towers, Statue of Liberty, Central Park, Wall Street, I spend a couple of hours in The United Nations and go to a matinee on Broadway. I have a busy and interesting mini holiday. I only have one mishap, on the first day I get on the over ground going in the wrong direction and end up in the Bronx. There is not a white face to be seen. An immense, black guy approaches me from behind and startles me. Then with a friendly toothy grin and a knowing nod he states, "You lost lady!" One glance at my face confirms his suspicions and he gently tells me how to cross over and go back the way I came!

I bid farewell to the Marchbanks and thank them for all their kindness. The bus drive to Montreal is beautiful, up through Vermont, New Hampshire and the White mountains, then across the border into Canada. The scenery is stunning, the magnificent Maple trees which in the Autumn, or rather Fall, are famous for their rich hues of gold, yellow, orange and red but currently equally beautiful shades of vibrant green. Then the backdrop of imposing mountains still snow-capped, farther on open rolling hills give one a feeling of freedom, space and closeness to nature. I even spot little black bears on the side of the highway; this is a great country in every sense of the word.

Mrs Casgrain meets me at the bus station, the same bizarre situation as in Ireland, being met by someone you have never seen before but instantly recognize. Desi described her quite well, she is average height and weight with short, curly, grey hair, and although known to be absent minded she has a twinkle in her eye and a sharp sense of humour. Despite being wealthy she is a simple soul; she tends to wear old jeans and lives for her animals. They have fondly nicknamed her "Foggy" as she is always in her own little world and has a tendency to forget things. Although she appears vague and humble, she has quite a history. She married a French Canadian, the love of her life, however, two weeks after the wedding her husband was posted to the war in Europe where he was killed, and she never saw him again. A tragic story, especially as she never re-married instead of which she dedicated her life to animals.

She is quite high up in the S.P.C.A, Society for the Protection of Cruelty to Animals and campaigns for animal rights. She also learned dog training in the States and took it up to Canada where she set up dog training groups. She was downhill ski champion of Canada in the days when they had to climb the mountain before the race, no ski lifts in those days. She rode and competed, having owned a horse that qualified for the Canadian team, but she refused to put her horse under such pressure. She has had three spinal fusions due to falls from skis and horses, but she still rides and skies!

She drives me into Montreal in her big brown station wagon, she asks me if I will be happy to drive it with the trailer and three horses, she is glad to hear I have plenty of experience driving with a trailer and driving on the right-hand side of the road. The only difference being that the Buic is huge and automatic but fortunately has four-wheel drive, so will be more comfortable and better for towing with than the Jaguar in Switzerland or the old Land Rover in England.

She currently has three dogs, Biddy a very elderly spaniel with warts and almost blind but much loved, Jessy a lively, cheeky, wire haired terrier and Jake a black standard poodle. She hates the way poodles have fancy clips and are dressed up with ribbons, bows, diamond collars and posh coats. She says they were wonderful water retrievers, working dogs, very intelligent and easy to train, also good at tracking, although she says Jake is not the best example as he is rather shy, poor boy.

She lives in a house in Westmount a rather elite residential area not far from the city centre. We drive into a spacious garage which leads into an extensive dog parlour including shower area and dog grooming table. The stairs lead up to the kitchen where we are met by Adrienne who has been serving the family since Mrs Casgrain was a child and still treats her as such, thus they have an odd relationship, rather akin to siblings who can't live together in harmony, yet neither can they live without each other. I am shown to my room on the next floor and then we are served a delicious meal by Adrienne who is obviously skilled and experienced in the French cuisine.

The next morning, we load the dogs into the car and take off for the stables. The horses are kept at Desi's mother's farm. Pam Dillingham is not young but has terrific energy and enthusiasm. There are horses everywhere a mixture of loose boxes and standing stalls and everything from miniature ponies to 18hh horses. There is a large outdoor arena for schooling, show jumps and a cross country course, as every year she holds competitions throughout the summer.

Mrs Casgrain only has three horses for now, TANGO a little bay mare who is rather old, BARNABY a handsome palomino gelding, a good all-rounder and easy to ride, then there is PUCK who is younger and a bit green, he is liver chestnut and has a long neck and back making it difficult for him to engage his hocks and collect. As a result, he is on his forehand and tends to lean on the bit which Mrs Casgrain finds uncomfortable, so he needs a lot of schooling. Mrs Casgrain rides BARNABY and I ride PUCK and we go out for a hack in the Arboretum an adjoining nature reserve full of beautiful trails. There we pass a compound there where they are breeding wolves.

The wildlife in Canada is extraordinary, when we walk the dogs in the woods we have to look out for porcupine, dogs being natural hunters. Jake chases one and tries to bite it, the result is a mouth full of porcupine needles which have a barb in the end making it impossible just to pull them out, the poor dog can't close his mouth and is desperately pawing and whining so he must be rushed to the vets and have them removed with pliers under anaesthetic, but dogs don't learn they still chase porcupine. Skunks are another problem when walking the dogs. If a skunk comes across a dog or another possible enemy, he will spray them. The smell is pungent, almost sickly sweet and hard to get rid of it seems to linger in your nostrils, not to mention on the dogs.

I have a couple of days to explore Montreal, named after Mount Royal, which is in the heart of the city and close to Westmount. It is an old French Colonial city and the largest in Quebec even having its own Gothic Notre Dame, in contrast there is a vast modern underground city which makes life easier for the inhabitants during the long hard winters.

The next day we pack up, load the horses in the three horses Rice Trailer and take off for North Hatley, a small town in the Eastern Townships, situated at the end of Lake Massawippi. We drive south of Montreal and soon are in open country with its rolling green hills and extensive forests. It oozes the sensation of breathing space, it gives me a profound feeling of peace and sheer joy right down to my toes, after all the frantic hard work I left behind. I am beginning to fall in love with this amazing country.

On the way Mrs Casgrain explains the situation at Robin Hill which is the family summer house. She has an older sister, Barbara who had three grown up children and numerous grandchildren hence she fills the house with her clan. Mrs Casgrain says she would like to adopt me as a niece and could I please call her "Aunt Lorna". This way she tells me she won't feel so taken over by her sister's family. Robin Hill is a large property, the house being an old, wooden structure with a veranda running the length of two sides, from which wide steps lead down to a lawn sloping downhill towards the lake. There is another lawn to the front of the house used for croquet and dog training as it is level. The stables are on the far side of the house, there are two loose boxes and two standing stalls together with feed and tack room in one building. There is a flat dressage arena and a stable full of show jumps and two paddocks running downhill parallel with the lawn, also with stables. The paddocks have old cedar wood, rail fencing and huge old trees for shade.

Racoons are very clever. I am surprised Aunt Lorna doesn't have the tack under lock and key but has a padlock on the feed bins. Racoons have little hands; they can undo bolts and turn handles and they love the horse food. There are chipmunks too, delightful little creatures with their striped backs and pouched cheeks, pretty, little rodents.

Having settled the horses, we go to the house. Aunt Lorna's sister Barbara has been there for a few days opening the house as it had been put to bed for the winter. There is a flying squirrel in the living room, and she can't get him out. The dogs are going mad and barking furiously rushing to-and-fro. Barbara has two Brittany Spaniels so the excitement and noise of five dogs chasing a flying squirrel round the house, skidding on the wooden floors and barking insanely, poor Barbara is screaming at the top of her voice "Come here damn you!" It proves quite an eventful start.

We open all the veranda doors and windows, having removed the dogs, and try to encourage the squirrel towards the open doors with brooms and mops and anything with a long handle. The squirrel runs up the curtains, so he is above the doorways then he opened his arms and legs, between his wrists and ankles there was skin forming wings and he glided across to the other end of the room, he has all three of us running up and down the room for about twenty minutes before he manages to make his exit.

Life at Robin Hill is very pleasant, I get up at seven, feed the horses and muck out then return to the house and the aroma of coffee and bacon. Aunt Lorna is very disciplined in everything, we have a full breakfast every day but small portions the perfect way to control weight, we eat everything and really enjoy the food. A small fruit juice, a fried egg and two pieces of crispy bacon, the egg she eats with a tea-spoon and the bacon with her fingers, sometimes waffles and bacon with maple syrup, all absolutely delicious, plus one piece of toast and coffee.

After breakfast we ride out together, the country is wild, dirt roads, open fields and trails that she has made over the years, she has marked the trails with coloured paint on the trees and built jumps through the woods. Next to each jump there is a wicket gate. Aunt Lorna goes through the gates and when she reaches the other side of the wood, she gives an Indian call, her call echoes round the hills, this is my cue to jump through the woods and join her, it is fun. The third horse I school on the flat or jumping and she puts up the jumps for me. Tango doesn't jump any more but sometimes I use her to give lessons to Barbara's grandchildren.

Aunt Lorna enjoys her hacks without the jumps and she still competes in a showing classes and dressage competitions. Sometimes we ride down to the village and school on the Ball Park which is a lovely large, mowed playing field. Aunt Lorna has permission for us to ride there on the understanding we pick up the droppings immediately, so she keeps a shovel down there and we clean up before we leave, it is good for us to have space to school together and practice galloping for the showing classes. All of the competitions are in the summer, so we have competitions most weekends and a wide variety. Puck and Barnaby are mostly Riding Club level, nothing too demanding but plenty of fun, dressage, jumping, showing and cross country all on the same day, the horses have a lovely life. After schooling we cool off by walking down to the lake and paddling the horses in the cool water, sometimes we take them down bareback with a head collar and rope wearing our swimsuits and swim them. I love swimming with horses, they only have their heads above water so by just holding the mane they pull you through the water, the problem is coming out of the water, when their feet touch the bottom, they sometimes plunge forward, when they are wet and slippery, and you are only wearing a swimming costume it is very easy to slither off and part company. On more than one occasion PUCK goes back to the stables without me, very embarrassing to say the least.

We ride in the mornings and the horses are turned out in their paddocks for the afternoon. So, after lunch I go to the club where Aunt Lorna has made me a member and play tennis or sail, the latter being a new activity for me. The family has little Lazers, small one-man sail boats which I learn how to manage, more or less. Sometimes I volunteer to crew in the Regattas. There is one charming, good looking boy, we have chatted on several occasions and I am quite excited when he asks me to crew for him. The day arrives and we sail down the lake in good style but coming back the wind drops, he puts up the spinnaker, to little effect, so he swings the boom out at right angles to the boat and asks me to hang on the boom to add weight. I spent two hours hanging like a monkey off the boom my back a foot off the water and when I move because my arms and legs are aching, he becomes irate and shouts at me. As a skipper he changes character completely, you can go off people!

Aunt Lorna doesn't accompany me for tennis and sailing but she loves her canoe, she has an old wooden canoe and teaches me how to paddle. We paddle down the lake to little beaches that cannot be reached by land there we picnic; it is so peaceful. There is supposed to be a black hole farther down the lake where no-one had ever reached the bottom and rumour has it that boats have disappeared there. She also loves us to go out on a moonlit night and chase the moonbeams in the water, she had a great sense of fun. Lake Massawippi is long and narrow, Robin Hill is a mile out of the village, and it is a mile across the water to the Sailing club so often I go in the canoe and sometimes even swim. I am not a strong swimmer but swimming in the lake is somehow easy.

Aunt Lorna's niece Margo comes to stay, she is dynamic. In the past she helped with the horses in the summer, and she painted all the show jumps, the wall, which is made from wood, as is almost everything in that part of Canada, Margo had painted red bricks, with Snoopy snoozing on it! She, like her aunt is full of fun and when there is a full moon, she and her friends go skinny dipping in the lake. There are about six of us, they all strip off and ran down to water. I confess I am a bit of a prude and run down in my bikini and at their insistence take it off in the water. They all laugh their socks off, take it off me and threw it up a tree, that will teach me a lesson, Canadian sense of humour!

I have terrific fun with Margo she tells her Aunt I should have a few days off and takes me hiking in the White Mountains, she belongs to the 4,000-footer club and has climbed most of the mountains over 4,000ft.in the area. Margo lends me all the equipment, we take everything in our backpacks, food, utensils, clothes, tent, sleeping bag. We go with map and compass. There are trails and the odd mountain shelter but normally we put up our tents near water planning the route accordingly. We light a fire making tea or soup from packets adding rice and we eat vast amounts of nuts, dried fruit and "gourp" a special high calorie concoction made by Margo I think it contains honey, chocolate, cereals and nuts among other things, she bakes it in the oven and breaks it into pieces when it is cold. We have to tie our hiking boots up in the trees, so the bears don't take them in the night. One night we camp above a small lake and as we are finishing supper there is a tremendous noise and thousands if not millions of tiny frogs came pouring down the mountain across our camp on their way to the lake. Many of the poor little things got stuck in our camp on the way we have frogs in our boots, rucksacks, sleeping bags, cups you name it, it takes us ages to extricate them all and what a night, the noise is like a full-blown orchestra.

Moving above the tree line there are small, scattered trees more like shrubs, we passed some fellow hikers. They say when people spend too long alone up the mountains it goes to their heads, we meet one such a guy who ceremoniously welcomes us to the Land of Lilliput. Higher up the mountain there is snow, it is paradise hiking through the cool snow with the sun on your back, we even scoop up snow into our mugs to drink. Quite high up the trail follows a narrow ridge, there is a sign warning climber to take care as there are frequent weather changes in the area, when we embark on the trail there are a few clouds but nothing ominous. About half an hour later the wind gets up, soon it is so strong we have to move on all fours clinging to the rocks there is no way we can stand up. We decide to retreat, and it is lucky we do. Near the Warning sign there is a small shelter we gratefully take refuge, just as well as the ferocious wind is followed by an almighty storm it is like something out of a horror movie. We are alone up there with no electricity or means of communication. Fortunately, the next morning we are greeted by sunshine and calm so are able to complete our climb to the summit. Mountains are strange, every time you think you are reaching the summit you find another peak in front of you, but when you do get there it is such a thrill and sense of achievement you get hooked. Whenever you see a hill or mountain on the horizon you get this massive urge to climb to the top.

Canadians are very tough, Aunt Lorna's niece Susan has a baby and two weeks after giving birth to a baby girl she comes on a small local climb to Barnstable Pinnacle carrying her baby and accompanied by her other three children, her husband Hugh, Aunt Lorna, Barbara, myself and the five dogs. We have a picnic on the top overlooking the Lake while Susan breastfeeds her new baby.

Tango is feeling her age, she is twenty-six, Aunt Lorna wants her to enjoy the summer but not put her through another winter. Consequently, we go to look at some horses with a view to buying another horse. Aunt Lorna has some friends at the other end of the lake who have horses and compete in long distance rides, we go riding with them and have lunch at their lovely lakeside property. They are very friendly, but Aunt Lorna confesses that she hates riding with them, they go everywhere at top speed, flat out butchers-boy trot or flat-out gallop for miles, uphill and downhill. The horse they have for sale only knows how to go in this way and pulls like a train if you try to steady or balance him. He is not suitable for Aunt Lorna as he is already eight years old and set in his ways, even though he is lovely looking and had a nice nature.

Later, we went to visit a neighbour who breeds Appaloosas, lovely spotted horses, and quarter horses. These stocky little horses are strong and agile it strikes me they would be great for Polo. He asks us if we are going to Sherbrooke Show which of course we have so asked me if I could show his Appaloosa stallion. They are shown Western style and I have never ridden that way. He says he will teach me it is much easier than riding English, as he calls it. It really is easier than I anticipated, the saddle is so comfortable, and it is almost impossible to fall off. I have to ride with the reins in one hand and neck rein to turn the horse. He wears a Hackamore, a bitless bridle, which I find strange. I like to have a contact with the horse's mouth, but this is quite different, the horse is so light, but nevertheless responsive. He can stop dead from a gallop and turn on a sixpence. We even do some barrel racing at which he is brilliant.

He has a half quarter horse for sale, a bay gelding called Sirocco, meaning hot wind, he will need re-schooling but has good paces and Aunt Lorna feels happy on him, so she buys him. We take Sirocco to the May Day Parade to see how he behaves in crowds; Aunt Lorna goes every year and wears fancy dress she and Barnaby have quite a reputation. Sirocco behaves very well and is quick and willing to learn, soon he is doing Novice dressage tests and jumping small courses. Puck is also coming along nicely, I never let him lean on the bit and gently asked him to flex one way and the other until he became lighter and more responsive, and the lighter he became in front and the more he engaged his hocks the better he jumps too. I know Mrs Dillingham will say he is not active enough and she is right, but even so he wins a heap of rosettes that summer and is a delight to look after. I work him in circles with the contact on the outside rein boosting the activity and his inside hind while avoiding his leaning on the bit. He tries hard, his long neck is beginning to take shape, he is muscling up with lovely quarters and Aunt Lorna even enjoys a gentle hack on him.

North Hatley is a small town but is full of amazing talent. They have a theatre called "The Piggery" as the building had actually been a piggery. There they hold plays and concerts throughout the summer and very, good they are too. These are magical evenings another of Canada's charms being the magnificent night skies. As there is so little light pollution due to the great expanses with no civilization. The night skies are studded with millions of stars, it is easy to recognize some of the most common constellations. Gazing at the stars makes me feel so minute and insignificant. When you think that each one is like our sun and surrounded by planets like earth, the universe is so vast, and we are so tiny. We frequently see shooting stars too which is supposed to be lucky.

As the summer draws to a close Aunt Lorna takes the hard decision to put Tango to sleep, she had become increasingly stiff. Even the journey back to Montreal, and certainly the long hard winter would imply a lot of suffering for her. Such a hard decision, especially as she has such a gentle nature. Her main job throughout the summer has been looking after Barbara's little grandchildren who she mainly taught to ride in the ring (which is in fact oblong and a full-sized dressage arena). Sometimes two tiny children would sit on her back and another lead her then we would take her down the garden to munch apples under the tree. They brushed her and plaited her mane and tail and loved her to bits. The sad day comes, Aunt Lorna has a hole dug in her paddock under the big tree, she says she can't bear to be present and begs me to stay with Tango and feed her carrots and apples up to the end. The vet comes and I lead her down her field, her beautiful brown eyes gaze into my very soul with a knowing, weary look. She nuzzles me gently for more apples then as she munches them the vet injects her. She falls gently to her knees and we ease her onto her side. She is sleeping peacefully, one more injection and her breathing ceases, she has gone. My eyes mist with tears I can't focus, just feel a deep sadness. Aunt Lorna has left some flowers made from material in my bedroom with a thank you note from Tango, a sad day.

David has come to scythe down the long grass around the property, he is a medical student, and his parents live a few houses down the road. Below Robin Hill Aunt Lorna has built a winter house just above the lake, it is appropriately called The Doghouse and David does a good job of clearing all the undergrowth between the house and the lake. Aunt Lorna says I can teach him to ride on Barnaby, which I do, he is very sporty, and we started working out and running in the evenings plus the odd hike with Margo and company.

His parents are wealthy neighbours, they also have a house in Barbados where they spent the winter. They lead a hectic social life and consequently drink quite heavily. David is totally against alcohol and very health conscious. His parents are always very, nice to me and invite to dinner on several occasions. We go strawberry picking and make jam in their house. David comes to shows with us too to give a hand, but it transpires his parents think I am not the right person for their son and do not encourage our friendship. They needn't worry as at the end of the summer it is time for me to return to the Cotswolds and David will go back to McGill University.

Aunt Lorna is also invited to the cocktail parties or "veranda parties" as she called them. She hates them and always insists on taking me with her for moral support, that is when she can't find an excuse not to go. Aunt Lorna and Barbara are both tee-total, except for the very occasional glass of wine, which is ironic considering the family fortune has been made from distilling alcohol, the Meagher brandy and whisky, which was later bought up by Corby, has left the two sisters very well off. Mr McTaggart, Barbara's husband on the other hand is a dour Scot who really appreciates the produce of the family business. He tends the vegetable garden where he grows wonderful sweetcorn, apart from which he is an active climber, walker, sailor and skier even though he is well into his late seventies.

Aunt Lorna is a Jazz fan, and she adores Benny Goodman. When she finds out he is playing in New York she gets tickets and we fly down for the concert, we always travel first class because of her back problems. I know nothing about jazz but enjoy the concert and Aunt Lorna's enthusiasm is infectious. Benny Goodman is well into his eighties, but he spends two hours on stage playing without a break, the clarinet is his main instrument, but he also picks up a saxophone and even a trumpet at one point, such spontaneity and energy.

The summer is drawing to a close, a few of the leaves begin to turn golden, Aunt Lorna says one year I must stay into the fall as the colours of the Maple trees in the autumn are so beautiful. Sometimes I help her training the dogs, Jess is brilliant at agility, so quick and nimble. Jake on the other hand shines at tracking. I put on a glove and then give it to Aunt Lorna, then I take off into the woods, she tells me not to worry if I get lost, Jake will find me and bring me safely home. Fifteen minutes after I have left, she lets Jake smell my glove and tells him to 'Find' he always finds me even though I have gone off the trails crossed a stream or hidden up a tree. Good old Jake!

Aunt Lorna asks me if next year I can accompany her on a trip to see her niece in California and then up the coast through the Red Woods into Canada and up to Vancouver to see a friend in Victoria. She says we can then take the sky train through the Rockies and stay at Banff before heading back to Montreal. We plan the trip for the following May, before taking the horses to North Hatley.

Meanwhile, after taking the horses back to Montreal we visit her friends in Quebec City. The O'Donnells have visited us at Robin Hill, they are friends through the dog training and have four dogs themselves. They show us round Quebec City with its delightful colonial fortified centre, narrow streets, bistros and boutiques, it feels almost European. Mrs O'Donnell makes hot muffins for breakfast every morning, they are mouth wateringly delicious. I am having lots of holiday experiences with the promise of more to come.

Back in Montreal I am fortunate to have some lessons with Mrs Dillingham, as I anticipated she makes me activate Puck a lot more, initially he is very heavy in the hand which I hate, but as his quarters came underneath him, he lightens in front and she seems pleased with the result. She kindly lets me ride other horses too and asks Aunt Lorna if I can stay with her for a few days. She herself is a very accomplished horsewoman. Her son Charles was selected for the Canadian Team with Aunt Lorna's horse ROBIN who he evented. However, Aunt Lorna didn't want them to accept as she didn't want her horse pushed to his limits. Desi Dillingham is quite high up in the Dressage world in the U.K. and Canada. Mrs Dillingham's sister is a renowned course builder, and her other daughter Shirley is also a competent rider.

I make another friend there too; Gina is an air hostess. We ride together every day when she isn't flying. She is beautiful with a mass of curly dark hair, she is spontaneous, modest, and good fun. She falls hook line and sinker for a pilot although her better judgement tells her she is treading on dangerous ground she is deliriously happy and keeps me up to date with her romance.

The following two summers with Aunt Lorna follow a similar pattern, we have our magical trip to California and British Columbia. We fly first class to Los Angeles and stay with her niece who is married to a doctor. They live in a large house on the water's edge with their boat moored at the bottom of the garden. When we arrive, we have lunch in the garden, it is a beautiful day. We are only there for half an hour and I get badly sunburnt. I go to the gym with Suzanna despite my red and white stripes which causes considerable amusement. They show us around and take us out on their boat, then we hire a car and head north up the coast through the Red Wood trees and on up into Canada and thus to Vancouver. We spend a couple of nights with my Aunt's brother and family and look round Vancouver where you can easily sail and ski in the same day.

They have beautiful parks with huge old trees it takes four of us holding hands to embrace one tree trunk. It is refreshing to see so many red squirrels too, in England they have practically disappeared, and we are overrun with the larger grey squirrels, sometimes referred to as tree rats, sadly this is as so often happens entirely due to man's intervention with nature.

We then go over to Victoria Island to stay with a friend of Aunt Lorna's, a lovely peaceful place to live it feels like going back in time. On the boat crossing we are accompanied by a school of dolphins, such playful and intelligent creatures. After a few days in this paradise, we leave the car in Vancouver and take the train through the Rocky Mountains. The train has a glass roof so you can really appreciate the scenery the beauty of which is breath-taking. The mountains are vast and the lakes the most vibrant colours, sky blue and turquoise even the photographs don't do them justice. We stay in an imposing hotel on the way, an old chateau like building with high ceilings and huge chandeliers and fireplaces overlooking Lake Louise. We share a room which is more like a suite overlooking a vast lawn leading down to a turquoise lake with a backdrop of imposing, white capped, majestic mountains interspersed with tongues of glacier. We awake in the morning to the sound of bagpipes, there is mist hovering over the lake and through the mist emerges a piper wearing his kilt and sporran, the eerie notes of the bagpipes float through the misty morning, moments to remember.

We fly back from Banff to Montreal pick up the horses and make our way to North Hatley for another glorious summer holiday! We have full house that year as a friend of Aunt Lorna's also brings her grey mare to stay with us, all too soon summer passes and yet again and it is time to go back to England. However, there is great excitement in the air as next year the Olympic Games are to be held in Montreal. Mrs Dillingham's sister has been selected to build the cross-country course for the three-day event, so there is great speculation, and everyone is making suggestions for original and outrageous fences! That is fun to do when you don't have to jump them, so I am really looking forward to the coming summer when I am also to meet dear MAYBE.

Chapter 12
Montreal

There is great excitement when I arrive in Montreal as they are preparing for the Olympic Games. Mrs Dillingham's sister has duly designed the cross-country course for the three-day event, and we have the opportunity to walk the course with her. The little Eventing, I have done has consisted of big fences built to impress the riders. When you focus on where to take off and where to land it is not such a big deal but if for example you peer down the gaping ditch that reminds you of a tomb you quake with fear. There have been protests due to accidents when horses hit these solid fences, so this seems almost to be a turning point, the challenges shift from requiring just speed and guts to requiring other skills involving negotiating tricky angles, turns, combinations and distances. To save time you need to take the shortest line which may involve jumping a wide angled corner instead of a combination. Every horse is different, just like people no-one is good at everything we all have our strong and weak points, that is what makes it so interesting.

It is fascinating walking the course with the Dillinghams discussing all the options. On the way round we see Princess Anne who is on the British Team, she is striding out the distances and discussing the line to take with her colleagues. Sadly, she takes a tumble in the cross country, really, bad luck as she had previously won silver and gold medals in the European Championships. Her mother Queen Elizabeth opens the games and other members of the Royal family are there too, to support her. The Canadians are very, proud of their link to our heritage and the Royal family, and their knowledge of our history puts me to shame. One evening, at dinner, Barbara says "Oh I would like propose a toast, today is Princess Margaret's birthday, many happy returns to her!" The Mactaggarts and the Dillinghams are English Canadians and sadly there is considerable animosity between the French and the English Canadians in Quebec, even to the point of violent demonstrations and letter bombs.

Shirley is planning to fly over all the Olympic installations and invites me to join her. The plane is tiny, like the inside of a mini, four of us including her friend the pilot squeeze in, it really is a privilege to fly low over the "The Big O" as the stadium is called, some people say it looks like a doughnut, to me it looks more like a flying saucer. Sadly, soon it is to be called "The Big Owe" due to the huge debt incurred as a result of the Games. We fly over the Olympic village and then out to Bromont where the Equestrian events are to be held. Seeing the cross-country course from the air gives us a totally different perspective from our impression when walking it the previous day. We land in the bumpy field where we left the car. Desi's friend explains it is no more expensive to buy and run a little plane than to have a car and due to the vast distances, it is quite normal for people to own small planes in Canada.

We take the horses out to North Hatley as usual and we have tickets for the Equestrian Olympics later in the summer. It is good to be back, by now it is like home from home. There is a Hardware store in the village owned by Stuart Reid. He is a big man but quiet and gentle, he keeps horses and has a home bred horse he wants to sell. More to the point he is looking for a good home for him and immediately contacts Aunt Lorna. Stuart had a big black mare to pull the sleigh in winter. She was quite a character and he sent her to an Arab stallion the result being a colt. They called him MAYBE because they weren't sure whether he would be grey like his father or 'maybe' black like his mother. Surprisingly, he is dark bay and looks more thoroughbred than Arab or Draught horse.

Aunt Lorna and I go to Stuart's house and meet his wife and children. They take us to a field behind their house where in a stable are two horses MAYBE and a little mare. He tells us Maybe is fine in the sleigh in winter but gets nervous in the summer trap, which the whole family use as a means of transport. The little mare is much quieter, and the children can ride and drive her; she is a pretty little thing with large kind eyes. MAYBE isn't very big about 15:3hh, lovely dark bay with black mane and tail, his head is fine and intelligent with a white star stripe and a snip on his nose. The narrow-crooked stripe down his nose makes him look cheeky and he has two white socks.

Aunt Lorna asks if he has been ridden, Stuart says he had sat on him but never actually ridden him he prefers to drive. MAYBE is six years old and virtually unbroken. His official name is Zabez-Hi-Hat from his Arab father's

149

line. Stuart invites us to go for a drive with him the next day. When we arrive, he has the trap all sparkling clean it is very smart. I help him to put the harness on MAYBE who fidgets a bit but is reasonably well behaved. We put him between the shafts and hitch him up. Aunt Lorna and I climb into the trap, Stuart asks me to take the reins and says he will lead MAYBE to begin with, just as well because he is keen and strong.

We make our way across the field and all goes well but as the wheels scrunch onto the gravel on the drive MAYBE gets agitated. Thank goodness Stuart is strong, Aunt Lorna is about to bail out, but Stuart begs us to keep still. He is one of these natural horsemen, he is strong, firm, and quiet he remains unruffled as MAYBE plunges, he just holds him firmly and plods determinedly in a straight line.

Once we get to the road, there is less noise on the tarmac and MAYBE settles. Stuart joins us in the trap and takes the reins, much to my relief as I have very, little experience driving. We have a long drive, MAYBE is really, active, he takes us up hill and down dale. Once we recover from the initial trauma, we all enjoy it enormously, including MAYBE. Stuart says he wants to sell him but not to anyone, he really wants Aunt Lorna to have him as he knows how well she cares for her animals. He feels MAYBE is wasted with him as he is sure he has potential. Aunt Lorna is, like me, a real softy, she agrees to have him on a month's trial so Stuart says he will bring him up to Robin Hill the very next day. So MAYBE joins us and is very excited, he was born and has lived his whole life in Stuart's field.

He has been well handled by Stuart and is used to the harness, so breaking him to the saddle does not take long. I lunge him in the tack and get him used to my commands, then I mount and dismount him in the stable. The next day I mount him in the arena and Aunt Lorna lunges us, after which I ride him off the lunge. A few days later we ride out with Aunt Lorna and Barnaby. With some horses as with some people there is an instant feeling of empathy and mutual understanding it is so with MAYBE. He is a playful character and has a few quirky habits. As he is not used to carrying weight whenever he goes from walk to trot, or trot to canter he gives a little jump. Maybe he is trying to tell me I am too heavy!

We want to start him in preliminary dressage tests, but it is so hard to get smooth transitions. We have some very funny comments from the dressage judges. Another annoying habit is putting his tongue over the bit, this can be disconcerting as it usually means you have absolutely no control. Jack taught me an effective and simple solution to this problem consisting of threating a rawhide shoelace through the middle link of the snaffle and tying it to the front of the noseband hence holding the centre of the bit up so he cannot get his tongue over the top. There are tongue bits which you can attach to the bit and lie on the tongue, but the thong was just as effective. Maybe is full of fun and due to his Arab blood, he is tireless. He takes to his new life like a duck to water everything is an adventure for him. I start him with trotting poles and small jumps, he gives enormous leaps in the beginning and loves it although he gets a bit excited.

The Olympics are approaching, on my way through New York I saw Dr Silver who asked me if he could come to the Equestrian Olympics with us, Aunt Lorna agrees and invites him to come and stay at Robin Hill. We all go for a ride; he rides Barnaby and jumps all the panels and tiger traps through the woods giving Maybe and me a nice steady lead.

Finally, the Olympics, first we go to the Dressage. I love watching the warmup arena as much as the tests, some horses are spectacular warming up and fizzle out in the arena and for others the reverse is true, they grow when they perform. The Swiss girl, Christine Stuckelberger on Granat wins the individual gold and we are lucky enough to see her warmup and perform. An impressive pair, such an inspiration, it is here I begin to appreciate, understand, and even aspire to working more on dressage. Although in my heart of hearts I still prefer jumping. The U.S and Germany also excel in the three-day eventing and Jumping, the Swiss do pretty well too, the Canadians manage a silver medal in the jumping, and we see the Eventing from start to finish, a thrilling, few days. I also go to the main stadium with David to see basketball which is his passion. After the closing ceremony, a friend of Aunt Lorna's rings her to say she is holding a clinic at her place given by Richard Meade, member of the British team. He came fourth in the Individual Event but previously won Team and Individual Golds at Munich in 1972, he has also won at Burghley and Badminton, definitely one of my idols. Aunt Lorna asks her friend if I can go to the clinic with MAYBE. I am horrified, the top Canadian riders will be attending, all Advanced Eventers. MAYBE is recently broken, unschooled and has jumped a maximum of three feet out of a trot. We have never even competed in a Novice Event. I think she is mad, we will just cause huge embarrassment, but Aunt Lorna is determined.

We move in with MAYBE, we stay in Aunt Lorna's friend's house with Richard and his then girlfriend Angela Farquhar who is delightful. It is such a treat to be able to pick his brains over breakfast and to his credit he is not at all disparaging towards MAYBE and me. Really, I am just a girl groom with a green little home bred horse, as opposed to the others on the course who are riding big well-bred horses already competing at National and even International level.

There are five of us in the clinic and we begin with individual flat work sessions. Richard is curious about my rawhide shoelace to prevent MAYBE putting his tongue over the bit. He says JACOB JONES, the horse he has just ridden in the Olympics, has the same problem so at least we were in good company. He suggests we buy a tongue piece for the bit as we won't be allowed to compete in dressage competitions with our thong! He teaches me techniques that will stand me in good stead for years to come. Working in a circle getting the horse to balance on the outside rein, freeing the inside rein a just asking for the bend, using open reining too. This way of schooling works on all kinds of horses, for the ones that rush the circle slows them down and for the lazy ones it activates the inner hind leg. The smaller the circle the harder the horse has to work. For MAYBE to steady him and maintain the rhythm we use ten-meter circles, when he settles easing him onto the straight and if he rushes again open reining onto another ten-meter circle. It works like a charm, without fighting him and keeping a nice steady contact, this Richard said gives the horse confidence. Then the use of lots of transitions and half halts until the horse is light and attentive. If a horse engages his hocks his head automatically comes perpendicular. Trying to hold or force the head into the correct position only causes resistance and tension and tightness in the wither and poll especially if the hind quarters are not engaged.

For the show jumping he uses trotting poles and a placing fence then one stride into a larger jump. Aunt Lorna is filming the whole thing which is a bit embarrassing but proves very, useful in order to see one's mistakes and try to avoid repeating them! Schooling I usually use a placing pole three meters from the fence to help the horse take off at the right place. The small placing fence is even better giving you a perfect canter stride into the fence. With this method he has us jumping a 4ft 6inch, meter wide, oxer within three days. Once MAYBE stopped dead and got very het up, he told me very quietly to get him walking forward then turn him into the combination, when we were straight and MAYBE hesitated as if to duck out, he told me to hold him straight and he gave him one sharp smack up the backside and he jumped about 6ft! Aunt Lorna shrieks and tells him off vehemently for hitting her horse, he smiles and said it won't happen again, luckily it doesn't as it is totally unnecessary after that incident MAYBE flies over everything.

Cross country is next, as luck would have it there is a complete course and it doesn't look too big especially after the show jumping, we jump ditches, drops, a coffin, a farmyard, hedges, post and rails and a tiger trap. Maybe the fact that I love cross country is transmitted to MAYBE because he goes really, well. I am so pleased with him, he really tries hard, he gives his all. On the last day we work on steeple chase, shortening our stirrups another three holes and galloping round jockey style so comfortable for horse and rider.

There are no steeplechase fences, so Richard chooses a large tiger trap. Tiger traps are easy to jump as they give you a good ground line and can be jumped both ways but this one is alongside a five-bar gate and the same height which makes it a very, big, solid fence to jump at speed. The steeple chase fences are brush so you can do just that, brush straight through them, whereas if you hit the top of the tiger trap at speed you could turn turtle. The first time MAYBE and I gallop but in a very controlled fashion, so we are reprimanded and sent to try again and go for it. Richard is right the horses respect the tiger trap. At the next attempt we go at full speed, MAYBE stands right off and cleared it by a foot, it is such a great feeling. So, we have an excellent clinic and achieve the same objectives as the Advanced horses. We are all thrilled and when Stuart sees the photos, he can't believe his eyes.

However, I do feel we asked too much too soon and stressed MAYBE, so we ease off and take part in easier competitions for the rest of the summer, with the exception of one jumping competition in the States. The arena is tiny and the fences enormous, so different from our competitions at home, it does mean there is only room to steer, MAYBE jumps round clear but is very lit up afterwards, it is judged on speed and we aren't even placed. I remember Darlene, one of the American girls who had been on the B.H.S. course, telling us about jumping at home, at her Uncle's farm she had jumped six-foot fences. She was elastic and brilliant at jumping but couldn't get her head or her body round dressage. She couldn't sit still on a horse, she had us all in tucks of laughter.

MAYBE is happy, he has varied work every day, followed by the afternoon in the paddock and parties every weekend. He doesn't like water, I take him down to the lake and after much patient persuasion he reluctantly goes into the lake and swims, however, coming out he gives huge leaps and I slip off every time.

He is a bit of a joker, he will run back up the hill towards the stables and stop to eat apples under the apple tree, where he waits for me to climb on board again. When we cool off after schooling, I often stop under the apple tree and pick him an apple as a reward. He is going well so Aunt Lorna rides him out on some hacks and takes him in some showing classes quite successfully. One day we are out hacking and get a bit carried away, so are trotting quite fast towards home as we are expecting visitors for lunch and MAYBE stops dead under the apple tree. Poor Aunt Lorna nearly goes over his ears and doesn't know what was going on until I confess, he has stopped for his apple!

This year it is my 30th birthday, which is in August, so I am usually in Canada and at least receive a couple of birthday cards from England. This year I receive no cards and on the day of my Birthday no one says a word, so I am feeling really, sorry for myself and quite depressed. We ride as usual all morning, then have our snack lunch, and as we were finishing Aunt Lorna says, "Isn't it your birthday soon?" I understand as she is foggy about things generally, so when I say "Yes, it is today" she apologizes profusely and suggests we go out for supper. I am going out with David at the time, and he hasn't mentioned going out either, so I thank her gratefully. Later we get dressed up and as we are climbing into the car, she says "Oh my dear I have left my glasses in the Dog House, would you mind popping down to get them for me?" I am quite used to these little hiccups so say of course I don't mind and trot down the garden to the Doghouse.

It is getting dark, and it is very quiet down there. I put the key in the lock and as I open the door all the lights go on and music bursts forth. Aunt Lorna has organized a wonderful surprise party for me. There are about thirty people there from the horse world, the sailing club and friends from round about. They have all bought me presents and we have a cracking time. Aunt Lorna takes great delight in playing tricks on people and really enjoyed making the day as dull and quiet as possible! She has a very, special sense of humour and a great twinkle in her eye.

Many years later when visiting her in the winter she plays another trick on me, sadly then she is in a wheelchair but still has the same sense of fun. We are sitting in her bay window in the Doghouse overlooking the lake. Outside she has a complex contraption for feeding the birds and wild animals. She has made collars, similar to the ones worn by dogs to prevent them from licking wounds, but these are made from aluminium and attached to the trees to protect the feeders for the small birds from the squirrels, other animals and larger birds. They all have their own feeding areas and different food.

She points to a small bird high above the feeder, some minutes later she says she is worried that the little bird is still there, and she is afraid he has got caught in the wire. She asks me to go to the basement, bring up the stepladders and go into the freezing cold and climb up the tree to rescue the bird. Obediently off I go. It is half-light and very cold, so I don't inspect the little thing outside I disentangle its leg and carry it carefully back into the house wrapped in the cloth. It turned out to be an imitation bird beautifully made with beady eyes and feathers, but not real. She asked the gardener to put it up the tree to play one of her practical jokes on the next unsuspecting victim. Everyone hoots with laughter that just like old times I have fallen for Aunt Lorna's practical joke. One year I go in the winter, for a holiday, MAYBE looks like a bear even though in summer his coat is as fine as a thoroughbred's, all the horses grow tremendous coats in winter. We ride although it was 30 degrees below zero. There is a good meter of snow, but the arena is kept harrowed and with the horses' winter shoes it makes a good working surface. We also cross-country ski which is beautiful but jolly hard work. We ski with the dogs in the arboretum and Aunt Lorna gives me some bird food. I hold it in my mitten with my arm outstretched and the most beautiful little birds came and sit on my head and arm, happily feeding from my hand.

In North Hatley we ski across the frozen lake. We see the people drilling holes in the lake to fish. We lay on our backs in the virgin snow moving our arms and legs making snow angels. One day I go cross country skiing with the McTaggarts, who are both in their eighties; we make our way across the lake, climb a hill and ski downhill through some woods in and out of the trees. I find it really hard work and struggle to keep up with them!

We also go to a sugaring off party, out in the open they collect the maple syrup in buckets from the trees. It is boiled and then trickled over pans of snow, so it sets immediately and then we eat it. Maple syrup is a taste I soon acquire. We have it with everything on bacon, waffles, ice cream and pancakes or crepes it is truly, delicious.

MAYBE has far less work in the winter and gets a bit above himself, so by the time Spring comes nobody will ride him. The first spring I go back after our Olympic adventures he hasn't been ridden or loosed for some time. I get on him and he stands on his hind legs. He doesn't want to leave the stable. I just keep his head in the right direction and keep insisting. Twenty minutes later having trampled over Mrs Dillingham's vegetable garden and lawn we finally leave the stables at a rate of knots. He is like that cross country too if he spooks at a fence he will say "No…no…nooo…Okay!" then take off at full speed as if the devil is after him. It will take half a mile to get him back under control. However, there is nothing nasty in him it is just his nerves get the better of him. He gets over excited and he doesn't know where to put himself. We only have one session like that then butter won't melt in his mouth, he is just sweet, but every year Mrs Dillingham shakes her head and says, "Ah hell, are you two going to dig up my garden again?"

The next year I stay a little longer to compete in Mrs Dillingham's two-day event in Montreal. MAYBE and I are not very successful, there is one fence on the course which is a tiger trap over a fast-flowing stream which spooks Maybe and he refuses. When he does jump it, he jumps six foot in the air and takes off at ninety miles per hour. I just steer as I try to get him back under control, but we catch up with the competitor who has gone before us. They are a bit slow, and I have a hell of a job to keep behind them, we come over the finishing line neck and neck and thoroughly confused the judges, so I am not very, popular. He has done a good dressage test that morning but the show jumping which followed was just too much he was over excited, went too fast and flattened sending a few poles flying. It is a pity; he has the potential, but we just haven't quite got it together yet.

Back in Evenlode, dear MARY STUART comes up from her summer rest vastly overweight. The previous year she came back skinny, but I had no problem putting weight and muscle on her and getting her fit in time. This year George had changed her summer location to the other extreme. I confess I love feeding horses up but hate starving them. She puffs up the hills, I take her slowly and steadily and George asks me to take her cubbing which I do, and she is not her usual sparky self. George comes down the next weekend to take her and comes back very, concerned, he is tall and weighs twice as much as I do, and she finds it hard work. I have her heart checked by the vet but just with a stethoscope the routine and he detects nothing he just comments on her weight. He runs further tests and detects angina we are all devastated, and George decides to retire her, it is a sad day. I feel George thinks I have not spent long enough getting her fit, but she has had the same routine as other years and I am sure it is the weight causing her problem.

George wants me to look for another horse for him. I find the perfect horse, a seven-year-old bay gelding, half thoroughbred. He is a middle to heavyweight hunter, so he has more bone than MARY and is up to more weight. He has been show jumping for two years and is a grade C but not going to go further in that field. He is snaffle mouthed and very easy to jump, George could jump all the gates with no problem. George takes him out cubbing and I am riding an ex-racehorse I have to sell. She is a flighty chestnut mare and can only canter on one leg, I spend hours patiently trying to encourage her to canter on the other leg! We are in a group with George, his friend David, the Airds. Lady Aird's mother is riding a lovely ex eventer, almost 17th which jumps everything like a dream. She leaves the group and follows some others over a substantial post and rails with an uphill take off making it look even bigger. The mare is fidgety, so I follow suit and she jumps it in very flashy style. George falls in love with her, another chestnut mare with character. She is cheaper than the show jumping gentleman plus the fact red headed George is happier on a fidgety chestnut.

I am not happy about the choice; I don't like the fact she is so one sided and feel George is too heavy for her, but he is adamant. He goes gate shutting on her to try her, I am not hunting that day so just take her to the meet for him. George's mother, a very aristocratic lady, is there and her first comment is that the mare was too small, and George is underhorsed. I fully agree with her and tell her I had found a perfect horse for him, but he is in love with the mare. He duly buys her; I know she will be well cared for and at least will only hunt one day a week so just hope all will be well for them both.

I have the yard full of my regular clients and a waiting list. Jane Sumner is on the list; she is going on holiday and wants me to have her two horses while she is away as she doesn't want to go away and leave them where they are. I still haven't learned to say "No" firmly enough. I do try, but this lady is so insistent. As it is only temporary, I succumb and rent two more stables in the village, it is foolish with hindsight, I manage of course, and the basics are done, food, beds and exercise, but it is impossible to produce the horses to the high standard I like and have established my reputation on. For two weeks I do no clipping, I don't oil hooves for exercise or clean the tack to such a high standard. If I could turn the clock back I would, I hope to be much firmer in the future and not let people persuade me against my better judgement. Satisfaction comes from taking time to do things to a high standard, apart from which rushing with horses is a big mistake.

Furthermore, another problem has arisen, for some time Mr Egerton has not been keeping tabs on the books and it transpires the poor man has a brain tumour. I clean up at the end of the season make sure I have paid all the bills before I leave rather concerned and hoping things will be better for Mr Egerton when I come back from Canada.

MAYBE is much more settled and goes really, well, although he still plays up in the winter our initial discussions in the Spring are only a gesture on his behalf to say, "Don't you dare take me for granted!" not that I would ever dream of such a thing. I have such lovely times with Aunt Lorna and David. Aunt Lorna can't offer me a full-time job but takes me to see a friend who imports young horses and wants someone to break them. The stables are lovely with a large indoor school, a spacious flat and a generous salary. I have to go back to England, so they say keep it in mind and let them know if I am interested in the future. They are having difficulty finding someone responsible to take sole charge.

When I get back to England the situation has worsened considerably, we struggle through the season and Mr Egerton's health deteriorates. Problems never come alone, as I am finishing the season, my mother falls and breaks her hip. She has previously had a cancer operation and is in a bad way so I can hardly take off for Canada. I ring Aunt Lorna and explain, promising to send her someone reliable. Mr Egerton is entering the terminal phase of his illness very, sad to see such an intelligent person losing control completely. His wife asks me if I wanted to continue with the horse business, but it doesn't feel right. I am sure she will not want to stay in that huge rambling house alone and I am not sure it is fair for the boys either, plus the fact that my mother needs assistance, so I decide to close the business. This will also give my clients time to make alternative arrangements for the coming season, but it is a very, sad time. Poor Mr Egerton passes away and they sell up. Mrs Egerton moves into a cosy cottage in the village.

I have been loosely in touch with Wendy since we took our B.H.S exams together. I know that currently she is not happy where she is, but as so often happens she puts up with a lot for the sake of the horses. I ask her if she would be interested in going to Canada. She is happy to accept, and I feel totally confident she will do a super job which she does. Aunt Lorna says not to forget the job offer in Canada for when my mother is settled. So rather sadly I close the business, George buys the trailer and I sell most of the equipment, pay the bills, pay the Egertons the agreed rent for the stables which leaves me with just a few hundred pounds to tide me over until I see which way the wind is blowing.

I am sad, it has been a wonderful experience and given me the liberty to be my own boss, work my own way and allowed me to go to Canada for four months a year for the previous four years. I will never find another job that will give me such freedom. I feel deep gratitude towards the Egerton family together with profound sadness for what they are going through. I go home to help my father when my mother comes out of hospital. My father is charming and intelligent but totally undomesticated and I am, if anything, worse than he is. I haven't a clue about running a home or cooking etc. I survey the dead leaves and dust in the porch feeling rather disgruntled, the porch has never looked a mess. There are dead leaves everywhere from the poor neglected plants. My mother always keeps everything immaculate, and I have never stopped to appreciate how much work that involves! My mother comes home on crutches poor soul and Dad and I interview people to come and look after her. We are lucky as Vivienne comes into our lives, she is tiny and slim, she has a little girl and is a very caring person who is to become a lifelong friend to my mother and the whole family.

I have meanwhile applied for the job in Canada but am waiting for the paperwork to go through. This is taking forever, I have a firm job offer I have Canadians to vouch for me, I speak French, but I am English. Quebec is still very anti English, there have been more letter bombs. Eventually I receive a letter from the authorities stating that they are not convinced a Canadian cannot fill the position, even though my prospective employer has been looking for someone for two years without success! Viv takes over mother and the house and is much better at it than I am. So, I need to work even if it is only temporary. I look after four horses for two weeks while the owners are away, but there are no good horse jobs in the area. Apart from horses I think I would like to work with disabled children following my experience with Riding for the Disabled. I still have qualms about mental handicap. I have no qualifications whatever but send off a couple of applications and to my surprise am offered two interviews. One is too personally involved there are only five profoundly handicapped young children, I feel they needed stability in their little lives, and it wouldn't be fair to get close to them when I know it may only be temporary. The other interview is at a larger home for mentally handicapped with a considerable team of staff. When asked in the interview why I think I can do the job, I reply I have been caring for and training horses and have to find a way of communicating with them. Communication, patience and caring I consider must be key factors in this job too. I get the job as Assistant Housemother with in-house training. Although my comment in the interview came off the top of my head nothing could be closer to the truth. On my first day a group of the residents arrive home from the training centre and a Downs boy, who is fourteen but quite big, rolls his eyes and rubs his hands when he sees a new girl. He rushes at me knocking me over and falling on top of me, I am so taken aback and can't move. Luckily, Jane, a colleague, rescues me by firmly saying "Andre put her down will you, she won't come again if you do that!"

They have a field at the back of the house and already have chickens. Some of the residents work in the house or garden, some looked after the chickens whilst others go to special school or a day centre. They live in family groups and are encouraged to perform simple chores and help each other.

I am chosen to launch a campaign on Television inviting people to befriend a resident. Some lovely people came forward and form Friends of Sunny Mount, apart from raising funds for treats and holidays, not to mention the joy they bring to some of the residents. We are also offered a pony, PEGGY joins us, a smart little grey pony later to be joined by JOEY an elderly bay pony. The ponies reach the children in a way we fail to do, the results are both fascinating and moving.

Chapter 13
England

I am in a daze; I can scarcely believe that Aunt Lorna wants to give me MAYBE and pay for his air fare. There are surely lots of people in Canada who would love to have him and yet she prefers to pay £1,000 air fare for me to have him. She insists that she feels we have a special relationship. It makes no sense, but I am delighted beyond measure, I have to keep pinching myself, at last I am going to have my very own horse! I must organize transport, the money for the duty, which I calculate will be my entire savings, and somewhere to keep him. I speak to the riding school where we have the R.D.A group and they say there will be no problem. Initially he will be turned out with the geldings and I can give a few classes there to help towards his keep.

Round the corner from Sunny Mount there is a racing yard behind which there are some stables with horses belonging to the people who own the land and the farm. Jo the owner's wife competes in dressage and her friend Sue keeps her mare there too. Jo has won the regional dressage championship competing with Sue's mare, I have seen them in the local press. It is a small world, Sue and I went to the same junior school, I remember her well from when we were four years old. Sue and Jo have ridden at the same riding school as my junior school horsey friend and neighbour Hilary. Jo is one of these wonderfully down to earth and super generous people.

The two ponies live in the paddock behind Sunny Mount and the committee announces they are having a bonfire and firework display in the paddock on November 5th. I think they believe the ponies will enjoy the party. I have seen Jo when taking the ponies down the lane with the children although I don't know her beyond saying "Hello".

However, at this point I am desperate. I go round to her yard as soon as I am off duty and ask her if she has anywhere, I could possibly put two ponies for bonfire night. Immediately she says there is no problem, there is a front paddock which she only uses for turn-out during the day so it is empty at night, providing I can take them home in the morning we are welcome to use it. Perfect, I can lead them round in ten minutes and collect them first thing in the morning. There is a clean water trough and plenty of grass, a mini holiday for the ponies.

Now I have another favour to ask her, I wonder if she could recommend someone, good but not too expensive, who could collect MAYBE from Heathrow Airport for me and transport him home. Immediately she shows an interest, he is flying into Heathrow, she says she has never seen a horse get off a plane and offers to take me for the price of the fuel, I could hug her. Jo's husband Tony comes too, they are curious about the whole venture. What's more they have a super horsebox which will be much more comfortable for Maybe as he is bound to be tired when he arrives.

When we get to Heathrow we have to drive out onto the tarmac and are escorted to the appropriate plane. Wendy is there waiting for us with all the papers, she says they are fine, and he has travelled well. I am expecting to see a plane with horse partitions like the ones we used to transport the Swiss team round Europe. Instead, there is a huge cargo plane, the side is open, and it is full of crates which are being lowered one by one onto the tarmac by a huge crane. Wendy affirms that Maybe has travelled in a crate and to our astonishment the next crate to emerge contains Maybe, he has his head out and is peering down at us, I can't believe he is so calm and doesn't panic as the crane swings him round and lowers him gently onto the tarmac. What a relief, we rush over to him and simultaneously a group of officials bear down upon us and announce that he can't leave his crate until the paperwork has been approved. Wendy and Aunt Lorna have been meticulous about everything, so we are quite confident. The custom's officials study the abundant paperwork and tell me the customs fee would be three times my calculation, I am aghast. I tell them I simply don't have that amount of money and ask them how they have made their calculations. Aunt Lorna stated MAYBE's value at the minimum, half the cost of the flight, but the Customs man has added the cost of the flight to the value of the horse. He says if he is not worth that amount nobody would have spent that money to transport him. I painstakingly explain that he is a gift and never to be sold hence his monetary value is the minimum. As they say in the horse world "meat money," a horrible expression, but less than half the cost of the flight.

162

I look the man in the eye and ask him what he proposes to do. I ask him if he is considering paying £1,000 to send the horse back to Canada or would he rather accept my humble offering as there is no more. Fortunately, after a series of phone calls and further discussion he reluctantly agrees to my terms, which goes to show how easy it would have been to pay three times the amount. The story doesn't end here as they then find a discrepancy in the paperwork. The English document states that no horse in Canada had suffered from African Horse Sickness during the last two years, the document that comes with Maybe signed and stamped by vets and officials states that Maybe has not suffered from African Horse Sickness during the last two years. I have never heard of African Horse Sickness and for me a horse going from Canada to the UK requiring such a certificate seemed ludicrous. Another long discussion follows. At first, they say he can't leave the airport, so I ask them what they plan to do with him? Several more phone calls, obviously they don't deal with this every day, meanwhile poor Maybe is still in his crate, luckily Jo is giving him food and water. Finally, they announce he will have to go into quarantine, he will have to be in an isolation box, padlocked in, with disinfectant outside the door and there will be a daily inspection from the authorities. I will have to give them the address and an inspector will be there to meet us and set everything up. I ring Jean at the stables, she says they don't have an isolation box as it is not compulsory. Fortunately, Jo comes to the rescue yet again and says they have an isolation box behind their yard, and we can take him there.

Poor MAYBE what a nightmare, finally we rescue him from his crate and load him into the horsebox. Fortunately, the stable is large, we give him a generous bed and a good feed. The inspector padlocks his door and fills and old sink with Jeyes fluid. He places it outside his box telling us to dip our shoes every time we go in and to wear gloves. I have to climb over the locked door to muck him out feed water and groom him, poor boy by the third day he is trying to exercise himself walking round on his hind legs. I keep telling him how sorry I am, what a welcome to his new home!

After what seems like an eternity, they give him all clear. It is a red-letter day, I put on the caveson and lead him into the field to lunge him, he puts on quite a show. What a way to treat a horse when he has been given to me because he needs lots of work and entertainment! It is wonderful to be able to ride every day again. Sadly, we have to leave Jo's as the isolation box is mandatory for the racing yard so it cannot be permanently occupied, and Jo's stables are full, so, we go to the riding school. We are fine for a while but in the autumn the field becomes very wet and being out with a group MAYBE isn't getting enough hay. Although I am giving him extra feeds every day, I feel he is losing weight. Jane, one of my R.D.A helpers, tells me of a field in Knowle behind the church. It is nearer where I am living and has lots of fresh pasture, so I move him. He soon starts putting on weight and feeling his old self. The only disadvantage being we have to ride down a fairly busy road, but from there I can hack to the Riding Club which had indoor school, cross country and lots of competitions to keep MAYBE amused. He has a real sense of humour; a huge empty car carrier can fly past in close proximity making a terrible noise and he doesn't bat an eyelid. Then there is a lady with a push chair, or a man with an umbrella and we are leaping all over the road, I have the feeling he checks when there were no cars coming and he can have a good old jump around, then any excuse would do.

The physiotherapist for our RDA, Christine Jones, has a smallholding in a lovely spot near Packwood House with two fields. She keeps a few sheep and offers me one of her fields for Maybe. The location is perfect, and it is still possible to hack to the Riding Club from there. I jump at it as the church field is now nearly bare and very muddy in winter apart from being on a busy road. MAYBE is excited at first but soon settles and the riding is much more pleasant from there.

Christine also persuades me to do a Reflexology course, I have just completed a Chiropody course which added to the basic nursing for the care work, means I qualify as some medical knowledge is required in order to attend the course. She really wants to see the effects of Reflexology when working with the handicapped people. Later I take a course in Metamorphosis with an amazing French man, this course is also held at her home. I like this one best of all, he says the technique is very simple and anyone can use it, in fact he taught a boy with Downs Syndrome to do it. This boy treated someone who was bedridden in a vegetative state all his life who never made eye contact and had never uttered a sound. The results were staggering. After a few weeks, this person was looking for his friend and later began to make happy noises when he saw him, imagine if he had been treated from a baby when he had been abandoned on the steps of a mental hospital.

My father comes to Christine's one day to see MAYBE and rides him round the field, I have never seen my father ride before, only photographs from the war. He is no natural horseman but credit where credit is due, he has a go. I also became friends with Carlos and teach him to ride on MAYBE. He even gets up at six in the morning to accompany me to a show and looked after my little dog Fleur and MAYBE when I go away on holiday to Greece with friends. That is what you call a real friend, and I can't believe how well MAYBE behaves as Carlos is trotting round the field practicing his rising trot. I am praying a rabbit won't jump out of the hedge and startle MAYBE, fortunately it doesn't. There is a little pub on the way back from the riding club and sometimes we stop there with MAYBE for a drink and Carlos introduces him to beer, he loves it, he really is a party boy. I have a problem and go to the Doctor who sends me straight to hospital, it is awful when something like that happens and you have animals. Carlos has gone back to Spain. My mum kindly has Fleur and Jayne who helped me with the RDA says her daughter will ride MAYBE, she has a very, good looking but slightly nappy horse and we have competed together at the Riding Club and she rides beautifully, but they ring three days later and said MAYBE is too excited and she would rather not ride him.

Jo to the rescue yet again, I ring her in desperation, and she says as luck would have it, she has a spare stable as her friend had left and is happy to ride him but at her place, so she offers to go and pick him up. I am so grateful; Jo is a very competent dressage rider, and it will be very, good for MAYBE. Of course, he is as good as gold with her and happy at last, a perfect home for my dear boy. He has a large stable, is ridden every day and turned out in a large field for the afternoon, an ideal lifestyle for him. When I come out of hospital it is marvellous to have MAYBE around the corner from where I live and work not to mention his living in the five-star hotel which he deserves. Jo kindly lets us stay for a very modest sum. We hack out a lot with Sue which is good for both of us, with schooling, hacking, shows and his big paddock he is very well behaved. The only thing he doesn't like is the pig farm where he tries to whip round and run for home. I always get him past, but he snorts with disdain, maybe it is the smell, he is fine with sheep and cattle. Some horses are terrified of donkeys especially when they bray, well we all have our fears, phobias and weak points and pigs are MAYBE's.

Jo competes in Dressage, she kindly offers me free transport to the shows she is going to, of course we accept gratefully as MAYBE loves a party. Occasionally there is combined training, so we have the chance to jump. Jo's husband Tony drives the Horsebox, rolls up bandages, holds horses, fetches numbers and score sheets and prepares a Bar-B-Q, what service, talk about spoiled! We also take part in the riding club shows and a one-day event there, we don't cover ourselves with glory, we have a hiccup at the water but overall, I am thrilled with him. I find having my own horse so different from riding six horses a day belonging to other people, invariably when you are really beginning to understand each other the horses are taken away or ridden by their owners. I loved them all, inevitably some more than others, but could not spend enough time with them to feel that closeness and telepathy I feel with MAYBE. I enjoy every second I spend with him and develop a special bond which comes from living in each other's pockets. I have the feeling he reads my mind; he responds to the slightest touch. Horses are big but extremely sensitive. One of the Olympic Dressage riders once said that in order to change legs in canter, she only had to move her head slightly from side to side. This adjustment of weight was sufficient for her horse to get the message and change legs. That is my aim to reduce the aids to a minimum, after all they are signals, by bruising a horse's ribs you are not going to physically make him to go forward especially if he has no idea what you want him to do.

Jo is in a different league from me, her current horse is called COMEDY. COMEDY is a home bred hunter with some Welsh blood in him which gives him knee action not ideal for dressage, but it just shows what perseverance and training can do. She bought him from two ladies who are neighbouring farmers. They bred him themselves and desperately wanted Jo to have their young horse. She has lessons with Richard Davison, a leading light in the art of dressage, and she works jolly hard. She upgrades him through the levels, eventually qualifying for Goodwood. Competing at International level is a remarkable achievement, and it is an honour to tag along, observe and learn. One day she is booked for a lesson with Richard, and I think for some reason he has a spare slot, so she takes MAYBE as well, and it is a real treat to watch.

One weekend when I am working, my old friend Hilary, an extremely competent rider who has ridden round Burghley and team chased, asks if she can take MAYBE show jumping, which she does. She comes back saying they nearly killed themselves he jumped straight legged over the wall and they demolished it and nearly turned turtle. Luckily, the bricks flew but even so, they nearly came to grief. She is a brilliant rider but much more demanding than I am and MAYBE couldn't take the pressure. However, that is clearly why she has done so much better competing than I have. I can only suppose he was busy fighting her, being unused to such a strong rider and he didn't focus on the fence. He dropped his forelegs which can be very, dangerous as you can turn upside down. She doesn't want to ride him again and even though she is a better rider than me I am more than happy with that. I have become very selfish and really don't want anyone else to ride him, I enjoy him too much.

Meanwhile back at Sunny Mount the results with the ponies are heart-warming. There is one boy with Downes Syndrome, Gerald also has a hair lip and cleft palate which means it was very, difficult for him to communicate as his speech is unclear, consequently he is very frustrated. He is about twelve, he has shot up suddenly, is quite heavy and can be very stubborn. The day PEGGY arrives he is very, excited and spends half an hour stroking her and gazing at her with his head on one side making crooning sounds. At lunch time he is nowhere to be seen, which is unusual as he loves his food. We find him in the paddock with PEGGY. At every opportunity he escapes to see his friend, he loves to groom her clean her hooves, he spends hours brushing her, it is a joy to see him so happy not to mention PEGGY who basks in such attention. He becomes enthusiastic and co-operative just the mention of a ride on PEGGY and he will bend over backwards to please. He reminds me of myself as a child, I fear he too suffers from Equine fever.

PEGGY makes another hit and takes part in the Mini Olympics with a girl with Downes Syndrome. She looks very smart all shampooed and plaited, so does her rider in her black jacket and white stock and they win the Silver Medal. Jan is another girl who comes to ride, she is spastic so has great difficulty controlling her movements. However, she lives alone, works in a factory, and comes on the bus to ride PEGGY. She loves her riding; she is such a brave girl and we all become very fond of her. I can't believe my luck; my life has turned upside down but here I am with my very own horse and very rewarding times with the ponies and children. Plus, at work I am promoted to Deputy Matron which involves working with doctors, psychologists, physiotherapists, social workers, and special education. I attend a management course, become the resident chiropodist, and do a reflexology course. If anything, I learn even more from our residents and the animals, having time to observe the way they interact. The animals seem to help the children even more than the so-called professionals with all our studies and preparation. The behaviour of the ponies with these children is touching, animals are totally accepting and non-judgmental. PEGGY can be quite naughty with a competent adult, but she is gentle, quiet, and trustworthy when a handicapped child is on board.

MAYBE is so well and happy. I send regular reports to Aunt Lorna together with photographs and she seems well pleased. In return she sends me recordings of the lake, the paddles dipping in the water and the birdsongs. She has bought a little mare to replace MAYBE and is very happy with her. Wendy, who has been over several years running, has fitted in perfectly.

However, the winds of change were blowing again, Carlos has asked me to marry him and move to Spain. I say marry me marry my horse and my dog, to which he readily agrees. All this happens on the phone. The next day I am riding MAYBE round the field in a state of disbelief, wondering if I have dreamt it, and if not, how on earth it will all work out. Jo is leaning over the gate watching us, I ride over to her and blurt out rather incoherently what has happened. She grins and says not to worry about MAYBE, to go over to Spain and get settled. She says they will be only too happy to look after MAYBE until I decide what to do. Then she asks me if her husband can ride him in the meantime. Tony has done some racing in his heyday, but currently doesn't have a horse to ride. The following weekend he rides MAYBE, and they click, they obviously enjoy themselves. Satisfied that it is the best solution for MAYBE at least for the time being, I began to make plans. I have to work a month's notice. Fleur my little Jack Russell Terrier is getting old and has slight heart problem, so I am worried about the journey and change of climate for her. My mother won't hear of putting her through such a traumatic change and offers to look after her. Fleur adores my mother and she instantly becomes the centre of attention, ruling the household. She lives on to the age of fourteen thanks to my parent's tender loving care.

Maybe and Tony become firm friends, Tony rides him every lunch time and shares his sandwiches with him. They have dressage lessons and begin competing. Jo and Tony also compete quite successfully in pairs dressage to music, MAYBE and COMEDY are both dark bay and make a handsome pair. Tony really loves MAYBE and plays with him too; he pulls his blanket up behind his ears and calls him "Prance-a-lot". MAYBE peers, round at him as if to say, "What on earth are you doing?" he is so comical. My father kindly takes over as Chairman of the Riding for the Disabled and my dear friend Claire who had been faithful helper and secretary takes charge of the ponies PEGGY and JOEY.

So, I go to Spain, I fear I will be horseless, but Carlos has been riding regularly at a riding school owned by English people and takes me there almost straight away. I ride a few times and in no time am asked to give lessons. They have four large stables, but they are full, and the other boxes are very, small, pony size really. Plus, there is nowhere to turn out, it is on the side of a mountain with two arenas built up to be level, but they are constantly in use, I can't take MAYBE from his five-star accommodation and perfect lifestyle to these conditions plus the fact he was now eighteen years old.

I looked at other stables, but it is clear Carlos has found the best yard in the area. Most Spanish stables still keep their horses in standing stalls, permanently tied up. Furthermore, many of the Spanish horse are only taken out at weekends. They have wonderful temperaments, aided by the huge curb acting as a lever on the metal serrated lined nose band so they dare not misbehave. Many Spanish horses have scars on their noses. That is certainly not the appropriate environment for my dear MAYBE. I keep Aunt Lorna informed of the situation, I cannot and will not sell or give Maybe away even if I cannot be with him. I have also kept in touch with Stuart who bred him, sending him photographs and progress reports over the years, he expresses a desire to go to England to see him, so he visits MAYBE, and Jo says he is moved to tears to see how well, happy, and much-loved MAYBE is.

In Spain I continue to give classes at the Hipica International and compete in their shows which are run in a totally English fashion like any English Riding Club. I ride a 17hh Palomino called BARON in Dressage and YELNA a thoroughbred chestnut mare jumping.

I spent three long holidays a year in England when I ride MAYBE every day. We also meet Spanish people with Spanish horses, so I start riding at a Spanish stable too. It reminds me of the western riding in Canada. The owner of these stables rides beautifully. Spanish style well done, and it is a joy to watch him work, it is not what you do but the way you do it. He has assigned a mare for me to ride and teaches me to ride Spanish style. The mare is for sale, her owner just stopped riding and she hasn't been ridden for a long time. He asks me to ride her as often as I can. The mare is always very cross in the stable and handy with her teeth. I feel for her, I am sure she has had a hard time and just needs patience and lots of T.L.C. The first time I ride her back is arched and she feels as though she is going to explode. She gives an enormous buck when she feels my legs on her side, but her head never moves, which combined with the armchair Spanish saddle, makes it almost impossible to fall off. She settles and proves to be very well schooled. Carlos is on the point of buying her for me when I discover I am pregnant, and we decide it is not the right moment to invest in another horse. I go on to have two beautiful children and they both go to England and ride

169

MAYBE when they are three months old. Sadly, little Fleur dies two weeks before our daughter is born. Fleur was14 years old and my parents have looked after her so well, they have been wonderful with her and even have her buried. She is proof of what love can do. I loved that little dog but was working and hadn't dedicated as much time to her as my mother had, and after her hard start in life it was much needed. I attributed her slightly aggressive nature to her traumatic beginning. She tended to attack first and ask questions later. A lot of small dogs have the same trait, it is a form of self-defence. My uncle was terrified of her he used to call her "Fang". However, with my mother's tender loving care she mellowed. With one exception, she defended my mother with tooth and claw, if my mother was in the car, she wouldn't even let my father get in!

On one visit home there is a huge stubble field opposite the stables where Tony has been galloping MAYBE a reminder of his racing days. He says I must do the same because MAYBE loves it, it is great to just gallop free no limits no obstacles and under those circumstances I am surprised by his turn of speed he flattens out and flies, it must be his Arab blood.

Shortly afterwards we move to Iraq. When we arrive, Carlos breaks the news to me that MAYBE has died. He was 22years old and was fit and happy but following a bad colic he died within three days. Colic is one of the most common causes of death in a horse. The vet treated him, and they were up all night with him as when a horse has colic it is important to keep them on their feet and moving. They tend to want to lie down and roll, which is the worst thing they can do as in doing so they can twist their gut, and that is the end. The vet tried a stomach pump, walking and injecting muscle relaxant. Sadly, it did not help MAYBE, having suffered for two days he was getting worse, the vet decided it was kinder to put him to sleep and he was buried in the paddock. I feel dreadful I was not there for him although I know he has been in the best of hands and can never thank Jo and Tony enough for the way they cared for him. Jo had some professional photographs taken of him at the Royal Showground at Stoneleigh. In one he is standing like a prize hunter all plaited and smart and the other a lovely study of his head, wearing a double bridle, his beautiful head with his lovely white markings and cheeky expression, I shall always treasure them.

Chapter 14

Iraq

We move to Iraq for Carlos' work with the children then aged two and four, our son has his fifth birthday there. I reflect sadly, once more, that I will have to sacrifice my contact with horses but again miraculously fate is kind to me. In these third world countries the foreigners come together, and everyone knows everyone. As soon as horses are mentioned it transpires that a Spanish boy who works for the Embassy in the Commercial Office and who is also from Andalucía like Carlos, loves riding. Through his work he met a wealthy Iraqi who has a "country" house and land outside Baghdad where he has four or five beautiful Arab horses which he never rides, so he gives permission to Antonio to ride them whenever he likes. As you can imagine, we go riding with Antonio. It is all a bit wild, as are Antonio's methods, but just the smell, the touch, the feel and the gaze of a horse is nectar for me. I feel like a fish out of water without horses in my life and although it is not as often as I would have liked, it keeps me going.

A large group of us go to the horses for the first time, two or three want to ride but have little experience, so Antonio suggests that he and I should ride the horses first to settle them down. The tack is scant, a plain snaffle with no noseband and saddles that look as though they were left over from World War Two which they probably were. Strangely enough my father passed through this country with horses during the war. Later they left the poor horses in Palestine and went back through Europe with tanks. In Baghdad there is a huge English cemetery where many soldiers had been laid to rest. The Arab horses are lovely looking, quite tall for Arabs and all dark bay, but obviously totally unschooled and scarcely broken. We both mount with difficulty and much whirling around. Antonio shouts to me to follow him, he says they just need a good gallop. He takes off and I follow in a series of leaps and bounds. We have no brakes or steering, the only hope is to keep more or less behind the other horse. Having galloped up and down the drive half a dozen times Antonio deems it safe for the others to have a ride. Other times we go out into the desert past some very humble dwellings and ride alongside the River Tigris. These little horses are tough, but life is hard for them, as it is for the majority of the people there. I often wonder what became of these noble horses when our stay there was cut short by The Gulf War.

I leave Baghdad with the children in the middle of July as the temperatures are soaring up to 50 degrees, you can literally fry an egg on the car, and you need a glove or a cloth to open the door. Carlos is to join us in August for a summer holiday in Malaga. Fortunately, purely by chance, Carlos brings forward his holiday due to work commitments. He leaves on one of the last flights out of Baghdad before Sadam invades Kuwait, supposedly only for a summer holiday. I travelled with two children and two suitcases, one suitcase containing two lovely antique hand-made carpets, so we have one case of summer clothes for the three of us.

The children and I never return. About a year later we receive a trunk containing children's clothes, which they have outgrown, half of one of Carlos' suits, my riding hat and some old sheets and towels I have never seen before. Back in Spain, the children now three and five begin nursery school in the mornings and I waste no time in going up to the Hipica to ask if they have any horses that need riding. Iris greets me warmly and asks me to wait and speak to her partner Linda who lives in the house below. Linda has come from England with her husband to take up a partnership in the Riding School as Iris was finding it a bit much. Her husband is an eventer and brought his event mare with him.

Unfortunately, shortly after their arrival African Horse Sickness broke out in Spain, once again I come across this strange disease. As a result, all movement of livestock is banned, which means all Equestrian events have been cancelled. Linda's husband can't stand the inactivity and goes back to England but can't take his mare with him. Linda doesn't have the confidence to ride her, and they have no-one else to take her on, plus the fact that there has been heavy rain, so the arenas have flooded, consequently there is nowhere to lunge either. As a result, the mare hasn't been out of her stable for two weeks and presumably she is strong at the best of times. They tell me to put on the double bridle with a martingale and draw reins and to be very, careful. In England she had been tried by a girl on the British Team who deemed her far too strong, saying she was a man's ride.

I find LADY FARMER in one of the big boxes, I open the door and into her stable. She seems agitated, cross, probably frustrated. She is a lovely, big, scopey, chestnut mare with a big star and fine white blaze, I put on her head collar and tie her up. I take my time cleaning her and talking to her. She seems perfect to me, she is a warmblood, thoroughbred quality but with good bone, a slightly long back and a long, elegant neck. Her sire was HILL FARMER a grey thoroughbred, already with offspring winning at International level and her mother was a Welsh, thoroughbred cross, a great combination. Strangely she reminds me of my friends in England, Jo's COMEDY who has done so well in dressage is half Welsh and Sue's home bred mare THISTLE is also by HILL FARMER, an amazing coincidence. LADY FARMER already feels like one of the family.

I tack her up and lead her into the yard taking her to the mounting block, Linda comes to try to hold her still, but she feels like a hand grenade with the pin out about to explode at any moment. The stables are on a mountainside, so we walk out of the yard and up the mountain. I sit very still and just concentrate on keeping her in walk, I have to check her every other stride and when she spooks try to turn her to bring her back to walk. What a walk, she has a super long active stride and eats up the ground. She is divine, I love her from the moment I sit astride her. After an hour and a half, we come home, she is still walking very, fast, but she is a little less tense. So, I begin riding LADY every day, she is bold and responsive she gives me a huge amount of confidence. I trust her, she is headstrong and fast but clever too. We go for miles exploring the mountains and down to the beach, then when the arenas dry out, we begin working, her flat work is not easy, she runs with her head in the air giraffe style anything to avoid a steady contact. I have the feeling it is a defence mechanism. Linda says when Eventing in England her dressage scores were appalling. Only once had she done a decent test when it was pouring with rain and blowing a gale and she had lowered her head against the elements. She is so fast and has such a long stride the dressage arenas just feels too small to contain all that power and energy. It is difficult to maintain a contact with her mouth, her head shoots up when she feels any pressure on the reins, she hollows her back and runs. The same with her sides the smallest brush of the leg and she is off like a bullet. I use the method I had learned in Canada using ten-meter circles, opening the inside rein to lead her onto the circle and balancing her on the outside rein so avoiding a dead pull, then giving and taking with the inside rein. This slows the express train run and engages her hocks. At least then she accepts a contact on the outside rein relaxing her poll and back a little. So, on a small circle she is lovely but when we take a straight line, she is off again at ninety miles an hour. Then we work on transitions and half halts, but it is a long slow process. When I go to ride LADY one day Linda comes to the stable whilst I am preparing her. She tells me rather sheepishly that now LADY is being ridden she will have to sell her. She has promised to lend her to a German boy who show jumps, so she will be seen competing.

Oliver comes to try her; he puts up some jumps which she flies over but then he can't stop her, so he rams her into the railings to stop. The railings around the arena are over five-foot-high but LADY is more than capable of jumping them and the other side there is a rocky descent down the mountainside. We are all alarmed, but he seems unconcerned and simply says he will put a bigger curb on her and a tighter curb chain. I have my doubts but can do nothing as she isn't my horse, and he is an experienced show jumper with a good reputation. I go home distraught and blurt out to Carlos that they are going to sell LADY FARMER. I am surprised at the deep sadness I feel, I have a heavy lump in my chest. I realise I am being unreasonable, after all I have only been riding her for a few weeks.

We go to the Show in Fuengirola to watch her jump. She is tied down with a tight martingale and has a bigger curb but even so Oliver can't control her they are fighting each other. He manages to steer her round the course but fighting into every fence she hollows and drops her legs so has four fences down. Linda says she just isn't a show jumper and in that part of Spain there is very little cross country. Fortunately, they decide it isn't a good idea to continue jumping her, it is good for neither LADY nor Oliver. I feel a selfish pang of relief as it means I can continue riding her.

On my Birthday I have the best present I could have ever dreamed of, Carlos buys LADY FARMER. I can't believe it. I have two small children and without Carlos' total support it would be impossible to have a horse, let alone compete. I wouldn't have dreamed of even suggesting it. I have had years of nothing but horses, now I have two beautiful children and am well aware that you cannot have everything in life, you have to make choices, yet here is Carlos defying all logic and making my dream come true. We are all euphoric at the Hipica and

Linda generously throws in all her husband's elite gear. There is a German Stubben jumping saddle, there are three bridles (a Pelham, a snaffle and a double) martingale, breast-plate, rugs, travel boots, brushing boots, overreach boots, bandages, lunge gear and grooming kit etc. all top quality. What a birthday present, I hug a somewhat perplexed LADY FARMER.

I ride her every day and schooling on the flat improves slightly, although it is never good as neither of us have much time or patience for dressage, even though we know it is valuable for the jumping too. Jumping is another story she has such power, once lined up for a fence she flies, the problem being if you try to steady her, up comes her head and her back hollows. This means she isn't focused on the fence; she is intent on fighting her rider. I realise what a difficult ride Oliver must have had at the show. She is far too strong for me, so force is out of the question she is dynamite.

I walk her to line her up to the jump and then just follow her as best I can. Initially I use a placing pole a small cross pole one stride and then the jump. This allows me to line her up in walk and place her perfectly for take-off. On landing she takes off, so I just steer her onto a circle and use rein caress with the inside hand, talking to her until she slows down. I school alone so when she eventually stops, I get off, make a fuss of her, lead her over to the jump put it up a notch higher and climb back on. I walk her around until she relaxes then line her up and repeat the process. This way she is eventually jumping a big fence beautifully, but only one fence and out of a walk. After a while it takes only three circles after the jump to bring her down to walk instead of at least twenty which it took the first time.

Two weeks after Carlos buys her, they have a show at the Hipica and everyone says LADY and I should compete. I can't imagine jumping a course and there is no time to practice but she has proved to me she has terrific ability, so I decide to have a go and just steer round the course. In the collecting ring I walk into the practice fence and canter our circles to stop. When I walk the course, I am careful to note where I can circle at the end. She makes nothing of the fences and to my amazement wins both classes, one meter and one meter ten, it is a good start. The jumping is timed and although our turns were very wide due to her speed, she is still the fastest. At a later show she comes second in the Chase me Charley, a humble version of the Puissance. There are only two fences which are heightened, it is eliminatory, if you refuse or knock one down you are out. Before long, it is down to two of us and the other horse is an experienced show jumper, whereas I am on my cross-country LADY who everyone says will never make a show jumper. To everyone's surprise, especially mine, she clears one meter sixty with a two-meter spread. The next time she stands off a little too far and tips the back pole, but I am well pleased with her, she gives me such a magnificent feel over the fence, it is hard to put into words.

I am fortunate to have the support of my family, especially Carlos as he encourages me wholeheartedly. The family follow us round the shows with children and friends in tow. LADY and I have our own fan club who cheer our every clear round with embarrassing enthusiasm. However, our success also creates enemies, there is a Dutch rider from Fuengirola who we keep beating. He visibly hates us and is always complaining to the judges and trying to get us eliminated. We nearly make a mistake on one course, but I realise and correct being careful not to cover our tracks which would lead to elimination. I take longer but go clear and he has one down, he appeals, but the judges dismiss his claim.

Linda tells me as tactfully as possible that we shouldn't continue competing in the local and club shows. LADY has won at all of them, and it is time to give someone else a chance. It is true it has become too easy, and it is tantamount to pot hunting which cannot be further from my intentions. LADY and I just jump for joy. However, I understand the situation and it has become uncomfortable to go home with so many trophies. This implies we will have to compete at National Shows which are farther afield and last for three days, so I am resigned to just enjoying LADY and the family. LADY has become one of the family, at Christmas I dress up as Father Christmas and dress LADY up as a reindeer, then we come down the mountain with a sack full of toys for the children. She also takes part in the children's fancy dress ridden by Ana who is four years old and looks like a pea on a drum, she is on the leading rein of course. Ana will never forgive me, I dress her up as Mrs Mop, poor girl, she just longs to be a princess, I realise too late!

LADY loves our hacks out too, Carlos and I go miles, we have taken half livery on a lovely bay mare called ESPANOLA. In the winter we have long rides on the beach and in the summer up the mountains. Often on a Sunday morning we ride down to the village and have coffee and churros. Churros are made from a fried batter mixture poured into a huge pan of hot oil in a large coil which is then cut up into pieces the size of huge cigars and strung together with pampas grass. It is typical to dip them in hot chocolate. LADY is not keen on churros;

she prefers the sugar lumps. We also visit Carlos' father's cousin in the village, one of his sons rides too.

In the summer we all stay at my father in law's house just outside the village. By all, I mean twenty-two of us, nine children in the garden and six women in the kitchen. We get on amazingly well considering the difference in age, tastes and personality. I sometimes ride LADY down to the house and give rides to giggling members of the family. She is completely relaxed and happily accepting all the carrots and apples which were proffered in profusion from tiny hands.

LADY is so quiet to handle, the children love oiling her hooves and I can trust her not to move a muscle, she takes family life in her stride. We are invited, by the owner of a new Golf Course and Riding Club to jump at the Inauguration Show. In the light of Linda's comments, I decline saying I don't have transport. The owner tells me he will pick us up and take us home. He is so insistent I don't know what to say so we go but I insist on competing hors concours. We are collected by a swanky car and a single horse trailer which I hate, they are so narrow, and LADY is a big mare. She loads with no problem as she is very trusting, I feel she would follow me to the ends of the earth. The event is a huge success everything new, jumps, arena, stables, restaurant all very, nice. LADY jumps impeccably as usual and there are celebrations and congratulations all round.

LADY and I are waiting to be taken home, but the euphoric owner cannot drag himself away from the celebrations. When I finally persuade him to leave it is pitch dark and his car and trailer are parked round the back where there is absolutely no lighting. We get there and he has forgotten his car keys so goes back to retrieve them. LADY and I are fed up by this time, I lower the narrow ramp. I hold her on a long rope and go up the ramp to tie up the hay-net. To my surprise she follows me up and starts munching at the hay. I slip out of the trap door go round the back and put up the ramp. To load herself in a narrow trailer in the dark, you can't ask for more. I have known many horses refuse or hesitate to load in a single trailer in broad daylight! She never ceases to surprise me. One day Oliver comes up to the stables to encourage us to go to a National show. He says they are going to Antequera and have a space on the lorry. He says he will organize registration and entries for me. Everyone is excited, saying we should have a go. Carlos is the first to encourage me. I am doubtful as it means being away for three days, but he says he and the children will join us for the weekend, his family is wonderfully supportive too, always happy to babysit. Whenever I ask one of them to help me with the children, several others ring me asking why I haven't left the children with them instead, saying they have more time, or they have children the same age. I am so lucky to have married into a large Spanish family, although I am a strange creature for them, they tolerate me well. The girls of my age stay at home doing crochet and embroidery for their bottom draw. I do try, but I am useless at these things and I feel like a caged lion.

All is arranged and we are off to our first National Show. I am informed that in Spain there is betting on the show jumping, so I am warned that as an outsider, if we do well, we will be booed and jeered because people will have lost money as a result. We only enter the smaller classes, the equivalent to Newcomers and Grade C as there is little time to prepare, I don't have a white tie and no time to look for one, so I use a white serviette and make it into a stock! The stock with the stock pin is not normal in the show jumping world, a white tie was more appropriate. The stock with stock pin is typical out hunting where it serves as a bandage, sling, or tourniquet in case of an emergency. At the local shows I just wear a white shirt or short sleeved sweatshirt with no tie or jacket because of the heat.

It is swelteringly hot in Antequera and the stables are temporary, so we hose water onto the canvas rooves to cool them off. We all stay in the Parador, it is beautiful historic building converted into a hotel. I am relieved I know no-one, except Oliver, so I can focus on Lady. That evening I tack her up and we go for a long ride across the stubble fields there are magnificent views of the mountains and a glorious sunset. I pinch myself; I can't believe my luck, I am so happy I feel I will explode, and LADY seems to catch my mood, she shies at a rabbit and squeals with exuberance. The competition begins the next day in the evening, due to the heat. That morning I walk her out quietly and give her a cool shower, after lunch everyone goes to the pool or for a siesta, or both. I have a swim to cool off, change and go back to the stables. It is quiet and peaceful, and they have just completed the course for the first competition which is for us. I take advantage and walk the course. I still have very, little braking power with LADY and these jumps are more imposing than the ones at the local shows. I just need to choose a line which I can comfortably steer her through avoiding turns that are too tight and gauging the distance of the approach according to the type of fence to try to help her a little. I know we can't take any short cuts yet, so I just want us both to enjoy ourselves. I then spend time making her beautiful. I plait her and put check marks and shark teeth on her beautiful quarters, put in her studs and oiled her hooves. If we don't win the jumping, we will surely win something for presentation, she looks stunning. I could never have found a more perfect mare if I had combed the British Isles from top to bottom. Here we are, we have just been thrown together by chance or fate or whatever. Who am I to reason why, I am just extremely grateful.

The gang arrives from the Hipica, drool over Lady and take off to the stands saying we had better do well as they have put money on us, that doesn't do much to calm my nerves. Linda puts a cold lager in my hands and tempted because of the heat and the nerves I take a few grateful gulps. I think it relaxes me, although it is not planned as I want to have my wits about me. At least 80 percent of the competitors are military. I find that a little daunting, there are only two other female competitors who I don't know, and they all seem very serious. I warm LADY up around the stubble field, then walk around the collecting ring trot into the practice fences and bring her back to walk. We are about third to go out of a big class. We enter the ring, there are stands and masses of spectators it is more like a football match. I salute the judges and circle in walk. When the bell goes, I shorten my reins and Lady responds, what energy, I line her up for the first fence and we fly. The fences being bigger and more solid, she jumps them better than ever, she clears everything by a foot. There are three fences along the long side of the arena in front of the stand where our fans are seated, and I am sure I hear some squeals of delight. She jumps a spectacular clear, but as it is judged on time, I have no expectations, so I settle LADY and join my friends in the stands to watch the rest of the class. When I arrive, they are excited, so far, we are the only ones with a clear round. More clear rounds come of course, but our time isn't bad considering our wide turns, Iris says she has never seen LADY jump so well and I must say she gave me a wonderful feel. We come second to our surprise and delight. The next day Carlos and the children and friends arrived, it is like a mini holiday, as the jumping is in the evening, we spend the day together with frequent visits to LADY of course. She resumes her family role, Ana sitting on her back, Carlitos hosing LADY's legs and his parents, plus of course extra carrots and apples. I am sure the family help her to relax, they certainly help me. Over the three days Lady is placed in the first six in every class and there is prize money for all of them, so she pays all our expenses with her winnings. The prize giving is at the town hall on the last night with the press and champagne or rather Spanish Cava. The children help me carry the cups and rosettes. She wins one huge cup presented by Coca Cola which is so big my brother-in-law called "the bidet". It is late when we load the horses so Oliver says LADY can stay at his place. He has a spare stable and I still have food for her, so I can pick her up the next day.

I take all the gear back in the car and first thing in the morning Carlos drops me off at Oliver's place. It is at the foot of the mountain near the village. Lady only has her head collar and a rope; Carlos has taken her travelling gear in the car. I walk the first twenty yards up the steep hill and have a job to keep up with LADY. There is a low wall, so I tie the rope to the other side of her head collar to make a short rein and climb aboard. I haven't ridden bareback that way since I was a child and it is lovely to feel the warm, rippling, muscles although she does have a rather sharp wither. Let's face it, I don't have any real brakes with or without a bridle, so it makes no difference, and she is going home. We trot up the road and they all think I have gone raving mad. Linda says only once did her husband dare to get on her bareback and he was on the floor within two minutes.

Although the Nationals last three days there is only one a month on average which fits better with family life. We just enjoy our mini holidays and bless her LADY always wins enough to cover costs. So, LADY and I take to show jumping like a duck to water and thoroughly enjoy ourselves.

The following year at Antequera I realise that after each fence instead of rushing off Lady checks as if waiting for me to tell her where to go next. I also find in the warmup when I initiate a turn she immediately collects, this has evolved naturally from hours of patient schooling. It is a great feeling as I can now ride her and not be a total passenger. We can approach the course in a different way, and she has so much power we can turn in two strides off a fence cutting corners and jumping at angles and she just soars. The problem with such a brave and generous horse is you can ask too much and to my shame I fall into the trap. Sotogrande has a lovely show on the polo ground, jumping on green grass which is an unusual treat in the south of Spain. There is quite a ride up from the collecting ring to the arena. Two problems we have here, one being that now people know us they want to talk and take my concentration off LADY. I should politely ignore them until we have jumped, but I am English, and also a little chuffed at their comments, the dreaded ego! We get through to the jump off with no problem and there were two fences side by side meaning you have to make a U turn, there is another fence at right angles on the landing side. When we walk the course, I see other riders pacing to see if they can do the U turn inside the other fence instead of going round it, it is very tight. One of the riders achieves it but he is on a completely different kind of horse from LADY. That horse is not fast but very short striding, so it is not difficult for him and they go clear. Overconfident, I decide to try cutting on the inside too, Lady is a lot faster and has a longer stride. As I ask her for the U turn, I realise we have less than two strides and we are at a tricky angle, the fence is on top of us. Lady is so honest she stands off and jumps but clips a pole with her hind leg, impossible for her not to. We have four faults and came 3rd but I know I have really let her down. To add to my shame as we leave the arena, I hear somebody say, "That was the rider's fault".

Events are virtually non-existent in Andalucía, there is a tiny one in Algeciras, but they tell me LADY would trip up over the fences and it isn't worth the trip and expense. Then an English couple who have a farm in San Pedro de Alicante decide to build a decent course and hold a two-day event. They do a wonderful job, the only problem being there is nowhere to school, in order to prepare for cross country. At least Lady had done some Novice events before coming to Spain and we ride out in the country jumping every jumpable thing we come across, which she loves. The dressage and show jumping are to be on the first day and the cross country on the second. The cross country consists of four kilometres with 34 fences and some hills en route. LADY needs to be fit. It is good to begin serious fitness training again; we are ready for a new challenge. As chance has it, they are building a new road to bypass Malaga and Torremolinos. There are miles of level sand track laid between the stables and the coast. I go with the car to check the distances and we begin with 4km steady trot slowly increasing the pace and decreasing time then interspersed with canter work until she cantered 4km still with energy to spare, then lengthening to include short gallops. The show jumping will be very small for her now so that is no problem, but we have to work hard on our dressage.

We have some lessons from a local dressage rider who has been successful in the area. One day she asks me if she can ride LADY. After half an hour she hands her back to me, they are both in a lather of sweat. She shakes her head and tells me to just try not to get eliminated. To get some practice I go to a local dressage competition. We enter the arena and as we come down the centre line, I feel she is going to jump the judges sitting at their table at the far end. Fortunately, she doesn't. She is so excited when cantering a twenty-meter circle she changes legs eight times, we get a pathetic score and some very funny comments, needless to say we came near the bottom by a long way! To make matters worse spurs are compulsory and we must ride the test in a snaffle it isn't easy. Schooling at home with our ten-meter circles we sometimes manage some sort of collection and a steady rhythm and if she stays relaxed, we will manage to get through the test, even so I am not optimistic regarding our overall result. Cross country preparation is not easy either, I make a few makeshift fences in the country from brushwood and broken trees. By the new road there are some big ditches and banks which we negotiate from all angles and at all speeds, jumping open ditches, also jumping down a meter drop along a ditch and jumping out again like a sort of coffin. Carlos and I ride down to the beach once a week there we gallop 1km in the sand which is hard work for the horses. I struggle to get her into the sea she doesn't like the waves, but we jump all the upturned fishing boats which she finds easy enough and that is the sum of our preparation.

We stay in a little hotel right by the sea, I can hear the waves lapping from my bed which proves very soothing. LADY has a good stable and the venue is delightful, like being in a corner of England, the going is firm as everything is dry, but the fields are divided by hedges and stone walls and the jumps are superb.

Our dressage test is, as I anticipated, pathetic. Lady is so fit from mountain climbing and beach gallops that despite abundant warm up she is on her toes, added to which as we ride round the outside of the dressage arena, we come face to face with the last fence of the cross-country course, it is right in front of us and she eyes it up, so we enter the arena with a turbo charge. Miraculously we don't jump out of the arena or jump the judges and just manage not to get eliminated. That, for me, is a huge success although we come near the bottom of the table. The show jumping is in the afternoon and it is small, if anything too small, Lady rushes a bit but no problem we go clear and fast. Most of the competitors are the same horses and riders we have competed against show jumping, only a few real eventers have come from other areas. Jayne a teacher from the Hipica has come with our friend Vivienne's little mare "Quick" and they are competing in the smaller class, so we walk the course together. They have every obstacle imaginable, coffin, trakena, hay rack, water trough, drops, ditches in front behind and beneath the jumps. There is a road closed sign, a bridge, hedges, walls, tiger traps, steps, and a farmyard. There are jumps uphill and downhill and they have added spooky features like dummies of scarecrows, etc. They have used solid telegraph poles and planks; it is very well made. One of the other show jumpers asks me what I think. I say it is an excellent, if testing, course, the only thing that worries me is the fact that all the big fences are uphill towards the end of the course, so I hope we are fit enough. She is worried about the Trakehner, a wide, deep, ditch with a telegraph pole suspended above it. That is a riders' fence, when you walk the course and look down the deep gaping hole it seems like a yawning chasm waiting to gobble you up, and the impression is that the pole is much higher than it really is. I tell her that if you measure the height of the pole from ground level, as opposed to the bottom of the abyss, and the distance from take-off to landing it is not such a big deal. Psychologically it is off-putting as the ground line is not clear and imagination can get the better of you thinking what might happen if the horse misses his footing and you go down the hole. The course builder is in the collecting ring with his clip board, he is very nervous, I am way down the list, and he tells me that so far nobody had gone clear within the time.

LADY and I set off, the first fence is the road closed sign jumping downhill, then the steps, on the steps I can hear Linda screaming "Lean back". Then the bridge LADY hesitates, she hates narrow things, but my eye and my heart are already on the other side and she responds. The rest of the course which consists of bigger more solid fences she gives me a fantastic ride we fly round and thoroughly enjoyed ourselves. As we come over the last fence, she is still going strong, and we have to circle to pull up. The course builder comes up and hugs us both, we have gone clear within the time. Carlos is waiting too, and we nearly hug LADY to death it is an exhilarating experience, and the adrenaline is running high. Lady has the only clear round within the time everyone assumes we have won however I see one of our competitors who is highly competitive going into the secretary's tent, ten minutes later they announce she has won, and LADY is second. There is an uproar of protest and people telling me I should put in a complaint. The other girl fell off and had a refusal in the cross country, as well as having time penalties. It transpires she challenged the jump judge saying it happened outside the penalty zone. However, I decide not to challenge the decision, I thoroughly enjoyed my ride and I know our dressage was pathetic, so I don't really mind. There are some comments in the press later which praise and embellish Lady's performance, merely stating the winner had won due to a technical decision. Ironically the "winner" then wants us to compete with her in the pairs. I decline and decide to go home with my team very, very, happy. I am more than satisfied with the wonderful ride LADY has given me and Jayne wins the other class, so we leave together to celebrate in style.

Chapter 15
Malaga

Carlos is riding ESPANOLA; she is a comfortable ride with a lovely temperament. We have taken her on half livery from John her American owner who travels considerably. So, at weekends we have lovely long rides on the beach or in the mountains, when we aren't rushing off to shows. However, John buys a Finca, he builds super stables for his daughter who is keen on jumping, so he takes Espanola there too and it proves to be an idyllic home for her. She has acres of freedom and a posh new stable, so we are happy for her. Consequently, we decide to look for a horse for Carlos.

In my attempts to improve my dressage skills I go with my dressage trainer to watch a clinic given by a top German rider. The clinic is held in Mijas, the yard is private, and they have a full-size dressage arena and some lovely German dressage horses, mostly Hanoverians, really, big horses which are currently popular for dressage.

There is also a little grey Spanish horse which they tell me is for sale. He is finer than the typical Spanish horse and rather good looking, he is "toldo vinoso" grey with lovely roan, dappled quarters (strawberry roan, which is a lovely pink-brown mixed with white), he is called "CARAJILLO" which is the Spanish name for coffee with brandy. CARAJILLO was rescued. He was being beaten by a large drunken man when he was only three years old. His current owner, a kind man, bought him on the spot, gave him a long holiday, fed him well, then he was re-broken and has had careful schooling. After the clinic, his daughter rides him and gives us a good show. He has a lovely extended trot really popping his toe and elevating unlike most Spanish horses which tend to have a short stride and knee action finding this particular movement difficult. His lateral work is neat and rhythmic, his flying changes smooth and straight with good cadence. They assure me that Carlos could learn a lot and have fun with him. They know

Carlos doesn't have a lot of experience and they also know that we have two small children. Carlos and I return another day to try him. I ride him in the school, and he is very well schooled, and it is nice to be able to perform dressage movements with relative ease. It is a pleasure to do dressage with him, especially after my struggles with LADY. He naturally flows forward into a steady even contact giving you a good feel. Carlos rides him, then I ride one of the Hanoverians and we go out for a short hack. Mijas is on the side of a mountain so everywhere is rocky and steep meaning we can only walk, but he behaves well and as we have trotted and cantered in the school, we are not worried. Carlos rides him in front of, behind and alongside the other horses and he behaves impeccably. The story is he was re-trained for the owner's wife, but she has lost interest. The girl who accompanies us says that once she hacked him down to a local show and came second in the Novice dressage. We decide to go ahead, our vet goes to check him and gives him a clean bill of health, he is seven years old, a perfect age normally over the problems of youth and still young enough to be full of energy and enthusiasm a bit like us in our thirties.

I go to settle up and collect him. When I arrive, he is tied up in the yard? I observe he is tied up very, short but knowing some people do that as a rule I pay no attention. I bandage his legs and tail as LADY's travel boots are miles too big for him. He loads well and off we go. When we arrive, we settle him into a nice big stable and decide to start working with him the next day. The following morning is Saturday, and we are excited to get to know the new member of our family. Carlos decides to get him ready himself, he puts on his head-collar, ties him up and then proceeds to groom him. As he reaches his shoulder CARAJILLO lays back his pretty little ears, swings his head round and sinks his teeth into Carlos' arm. The ensuing pandemonium and shrieks are heard by all. I leap into the stable, remove the children, reprimand the horse and tie him up very short then examine Carlos's arm he has a full set of teeth marks on his upper arm, so much for a family horse. CARAJILLO is also handy with his heels, we have to hold up a front leg to brush his body and have a firm hold of his tail to bush his quarters or he kicks like a mule with both barrels. I can't believe he suddenly developed this behaviour when we acquired him although some people have the audacity to suggest such a thing.

I lunge him and then ride him before Carlos gets on for the first time. He mounts and is riding round the small arena whilst I go to fetch LADY. I mount and as I ride towards the arena, Carlos and CARAJILLO are at the far end and they come towards us at a flat-out gallop, bucking like a bronco. How Carlos stays on board I shall never know. CARAJILLO stops dead when he reaches the fence and Carlos ends up in front of the saddle, but he doesn't fall off, chapeau! We really should take him back especially having small children around, but Carlos likes a challenge, always has, and in this respect, they suit each other to a "T". Also, I am lucky enough to be able to dedicate every morning to the horses after taking the children to school. This means I can work him every day, so we decide to give him a chance. I now quite understand why the previous owner's wife was not keen on horses or riding, his behaviour is far from endearing. I fear he will never completely overcome the traumas of his early life. Handling him carefully but firmly every day he becomes manageable, he even lets me clean his sheath. Even so you can never take your eye off him, he is a cheeky little character. It is a joy to do dressage with him and Carlos quite enjoys learning dressage. They compete in a small show and come second with a score of nine for their extended trot. Carlos admits it is the most wonderful feeling, he collects him beautifully and they float across the diagonal. CARAJILLO has never jumped but nor has Carlos so they begin together, schooling goes well so we decide they can enter a small competition. With limited resources I have tried to make spooky jumps, hanging a rug over a pole, adding straw bales, buckets anything I can find as fillers. However, in the competition when he came to the planks he stops dead at the last minute. Carlos flies over his head and lands on his feet on the other side of the fence still holding the reins which earns him a round of applause, it was quite spectacular and very comical! This little horse is a bundle of surprises, there is never a dull moment. CARRIE as we call him settles down, although you always have to keep an eye on him.

I am busy getting LADY fit for an Event and there is an English ex jockey riding some horses up at the stables who is only too happy to come out with me on Carrie, Jockeys love a good gallop, he reminds me of Tommy in Ireland with his "tippety-tip" before schooling. We have great fun finding good places to gallop scrambling up and down banks to access stubble fields and race for our lives hoping the farmers won't catch us. No damage can be done galloping across a stubble field and I would never dream of riding across a planted field however some of the farmers are anti horse. I think it is a social issue they see horsey people as posh and rich. There are still very humble farmers in Spain and in general they are not as well respected and appreciated as they are in England. Some places LADY and I go even our jockey friend finds quite challenging, but

CARRIE had no problem he is game for anything and just loves it all. The beach and the preparations for the new road still prove the best options for distance and going, so CARRIE is getting as fit as LADY, but he so enjoys himself and totally overcomes his original spookiness, learning to go forward anywhere we ask him. Having failed to buck Carlos off one day CARRIE decides to try running away with him. Fortunately, it is uphill which gives Carlos the advantage to get him back under control, which he does and fortunately is not a bit perturbed. They really suit each other, and Carlos learns a lot from his naughty little horse, proving that he has a way with horses, he is very firm, but patient and quiet so they establish a mutual respect, and a quirky friendship emerges.

There is a good young dressage rider at the stables who has a lovely dressage mare. Her mare goes lame before a competition, and she asks us if she can take CARRIE. We are delighted, the more experience he has the better. She is experienced and knows she has to be careful handling him. We plait and polish him making check marks and sharks teeth on his quarters and he looks splendid. Unfortunately, as she is leading him towards the trailer her friend comes up behind them carrying buckets and grooming kit and he kicks out viciously, narrowly missing her head. He does this just in front of the bar and terrace, so everyone witnesses the exhibition. A somewhat shaken Iris reprimands me severely. At least it makes sure that everyone will be careful around him from now on. He does quite well in the competition, although he goes beautifully for Susana when she rides him, she is very wary about handling him on the ground and declines the offer to repeat the exercise. Fortunately, Carlos quickly masters the art of handling him and improves his equestrian skills too although he acquires a few bites and bruises in the process.

The children have been riding regularly, I borrow a rather elderly dun pony called DORADA (Spanish for golden) or DODDIE as we call her, and we have become very fond of her. Carlitos, aged five, rides her in gymkhanas and mini jumping and Ana now aged three in the leading rein classes and they begin winning their rosettes too. They spend ages brushing her and leading her around to munch the little bits of grass that grow round about, albeit sparsely. My father-in-law has a country house quite near the stables where the whole family stays most weekends, Christmas, Easter and for three months in the summer. The whole family consisting of Carlos, his three brothers with their wives and children, his parents and Aunt and Uncle, nine children in the garden and six women in the kitchen. It is a novel experience for me having been an only child.

I take all the children for walks in the country, lollipop hunting and those who are interested I take to the stables. My father-in-law noting the children's enthusiasm decides to buy DODDIE, Iris is delighted as she knows she will be well looked after in her old age. All the children and some of their friends ride her, fortunately some are keener than others if not she would be busy all day every day. Also, it varies as each holiday it seems a different child is keen on riding.

One summer one of the older cousins, Pablo, is enthusiastic and wants to learn to jump. It occurs to me to bandage DODDIE's front legs to give her a bit of support. I go to lead her out of the stable and she refuses to budge. I insist and she goes up on her hind legs lunging through the door with her forelegs together. We go to the arena in a series of lunges in the same manner, going on her hind legs and jumping with her forelegs together. Iris comes rushing out and solves the mystery "She must have been hobbled when she was young" she explains. Poor DODDIE thought I had put hobbles on her, and her front feet were tied together. I lead her once round the arena hoping she will realise her legs are not tied together but impossible she has developed this strange way of moving to a fine art. I remove the bandages and DODDIE goes back to normal. She is a good pony and Pablo is a gentle lad who rides her beautifully. Unfortunately, he lives in Madrid and by the time he comes down for the next holidays he has lost interest.

For Spain, the Hipica International is very English, logically as her owners are English. They establish a Pony Club with Pony Club tests and certificates. This encourages the children to learn about the care and preparation of their ponies, not only riding them, and it proves to be popular. They even get the adults involved, Carlos is naughty and cheats with "chuletas" (little notes hidden in his pockets), so he is in disgrace! Yet another cultural difference, cheating is frowned upon in England but is considered acceptable and even an art in the south of Spain. It takes me a long time to come to terms with this, but over the years observing the young people I come to understand and even approve. When acting as a vigilant for my brother-in-law for University exams, I am horrified by the blatant cheating and even more so by the unconcerned attitude of the professors. Later observing my own children and their friends I discover that the students share knowledge and help each other, and this surely shows other human qualities.

Two of our dear friends' children have grown up with our children and the whole family has followed LADY faithfully round all the shows. Their daughter competes in mini jumping with DODDIE and one Christmas their son, who is the youngest of the group, dresses up as Joseph and leads DODDIE ridden by Ana, who is dressed as Mary carrying a baby in the fancy dress. They are so cute they steal the show.

One day I was giving a lesson to a group of children and Ana was riding DODDIE. It is a windy autumn day and has been raining, the ponies are nervous, the wind often gets under their tails and makes them excited. There are also puddles which some ponies will shy at and others jump, so I shout to the children to be careful with the "Charcoles", to my indignation they fall about laughing. In Andalucía there is a tendency to eat the ends of the words, so I sometimes invent my own! A word like puddle is a word I have heard frequently but never seen written; in fact, it ends in "o" not "l" so the plural is "charcos" not "charcoles". My Spanish is embarrassing considering how long I have lived among Spanish people. Mercifully, Spanish people have a huge sense of humour and love teasing, having a double meaning for almost everything. Following my verbal "faux pas" a gust of wind blows a ball of loose brush across the arena and all the ponies take off. All the children fall off except for Ana. We sort out the ensuing chaos and get everyone back on board. As luck would have it, they are all fine and we continue with the class. The only one who is really frightened by the incident is Ana, which is really unfortunate as DODDIE looked after her so well that she was the only one not to bite the dust. Neither is Ana consoled by the old adage which states you have to fall off seven times before you can call yourself a rider. Strangely she is never nervous when I put her on LADY FARMER who is enormous for her, but of course I never let her off the leading rein.

Teaching one's own family is not easy, soon the children became overconfident and know better than mother. Carlitos enters the mini dressage which had no canter movements for children under 7. He is so indignant he enters, halts, salutes and proceeds to canter around the arena, cheeky monkey. I am also competing a lot, so Jayne takes over the children's lessons she is an ex police officer and stands no nonsense, but the children make notable progress under her eagle eye.

We have had some memorable years with LADY, CARRIE and DODDIE but all good things come to an end. Life is full of surprises, some good, some bad and some devastating. Following the boom leading up to the Olympics in Barcelona and the Expo in Sevilla there is an economic slump which hits Carlos' family's business hard. As a result, we lose our home and all our savings, fortunately Carlos has a job in Madrid so inevitably and sadly, change is in the air. I confess I cry buckets into LADY's mane. She helps me to keep a brave face in front of the children. A horse can help you through anger, frustration, fear and all the other negative emotions that crop up in life. Strange how when one thing goes wrong it is usually followed by a series of mishaps. LADY has won or been placed in every show for years and still loves her jumping. Maybe she is affected by my anxiety about our situation, together with strange circumstances. We go to a national show in Fuengirola where the organizers have entered her in the open class which is higher than we have been jumping. I know LADY is capable of jumping that height as we have jumped higher than that schooling, but over individual fences. We have never jumped a whole course at that height, and we haven't prepared. I go to see the secretary to protest and request that they put us back to the level where we have been doing so well. I meet opposition everywhere from the organizers of the show to fellow competitors and I don't know how this has come about. I certainly haven't made a mistake with my entries. I can only imagine that because they have fewer entries in the big class, they have pulled our name out of a hat. The options are made clear, to jump in the big class or go home. I should go home but overconfidence, ego and stupidity take precedence. Everyone says we will have no problem and I have become altogether too nonchalant. To cap it all I leave Lady's tack outside her stable whilst I walk the course when I get back the curb chain is missing. A complete mystery as was very tight on the offside, in order to avoid losing it I had tightened it with pliers. There is no time to borrow a curb chain or think of an alternative, foolishly I go into the ring. She jumps the first part of the course brilliantly but coming out of a tight turn in the corner of the arena there is a huge spread and for the first time ever we are on a completely wrong stride. My fault entirely, knowing it is a big spread I let her lengthen too much not allowing for the fact we had no curb chain and are already going too fast and flat, she stands off too far and we crash. We are both shaken, and it marks a tragic end to a successful career.

I am devastated as I feel I have betrayed her. I have really let her down and worse still she has hurt herself. I have a back specialist to check and treat her after which she seemed physically fine but is never quite the same. She jumps anything I ask her schooling but has totally lost her confidence in the ring. I tell her over and over how sorry I am and vow to take care of her although initially I have to go to Madrid without her as the children have a place in their new school there. I promise I will be back for her as soon as I have found somewhere to live, work and a suitable place to keep her.

Under the circumstances no way can we take three horses to Madrid. My dear friend Billie who has a nappy grey horse she adores, offers to take on DODDIE as she had two small boys, I promise to supply food etc., and take her over to her new home. It is perfect for her she is to be loose in a paddock in their back garden with Billie's horse they feed her veggies through the kitchen window. Also, we can go and ride her whenever we are down in Malaga, so she is on permanent loan and happy. It is a perfect solution as I could not entertain selling the faithful old pony.

CARRIE is another matter; he is still young but requires experienced handling. I know it will be far from easy to find someone to take him on. However, life is full of surprises when you when you least expect them. Iris has been wonderful saying not to worry about LADY they love her and will care for her until I can make arrangements.

I am in the bar talking to her one day when a Dutch lady comes in, she has been having lessons for some time and comes to tell Iris she would like to buy a horse. Iris tells her CARRIE is for sale but is not suitable for a novice rider. Anna has seen him and says she would like to try him. Iris and I try to dissuade her, but she is a very, determined lady. Eventually I agree that she can come with me and try him. We meet one morning, and I explain how to handle him and that he will bite and kick if you don't take care. Anna is a very stern sounding person with a strong voice, and I think CARRIE respects her from the start, although really, she proves to be a softie with a heart of gold. She comes every day for two weeks and we ride together, by the end of which she is preparing him by herself and riding him in the school and in the country. As happened with Carlos she can learn a lot with CARRIE, despite a few bruises, she is still enthusiastic insisting she wants to buy him. She enjoys riding him but isn't brave enough to get hold of his tail and brush his quarters so she stuffs a brush in her jacket pocket, mounts him and brushes his quarters as best she can from on top of him causing quite a spectacle. She is obviously a lady of resources who will never give up, she is the epitome of "where there is a will there is a way." There are people and horses I will miss terribly. There is Vivienne and QUICK her lovely little chestnut mare who lives up to her name. Jayne who has been teaching the children, rides QUICK in some competitions and has become a good friend, Kathy who also gives lessons and her lovely old mare Tiza, Kathy is down to earth, wonderful with horses and children but has an awful problem with time keeping which is a pity as it gets her into a lot of trouble. Once I challenged her about it with a view to helping her overcome her problem, but she was adamant there was no cure as she had inherited it from her father, what a character. Dear old Iris who is crippled with arthritis but loves the horse business, her husband Roger who adores sailing but gave it all up to support his wife with the horses. Linda, who sold us LADY FARMER and has encouraged and supported LADY and me and been one of our biggest fans. Ina, who bought Bonbon for her children. I rode Bonbon when I first arrived in Spain, Kristal who then owned the Hipica used to send me out to give him a good gallop before he went in a class to take the tickle out of his feet. He was a good little jumper and won quite a lot with Ina's two boys. Her daughter Sandra rides really well and is jumping with the American's daughter. His wife who is lovely lady, rescued an abandoned horse and spent a fortune on vet's fees, but the poor horse didn't make it despite all her efforts. Sandra later rode LADY before I took her to Madrid. Sandra's older sister Aranxa, whose mental age is similar to that of my children and often played with them.

I hate leaving LADY, but a place comes up for the children in the school in Madrid, the term has already started so we move immediately with no time to think. We move from a lovely house to a two-bedroom flat Carlos has already rented, it is crazy furniture and boxes stacked to the ceiling. I settle the children into their new school and start looking for a more suitable place to live, a job and a place for LADY.

I must have been to nearly all the stables in and around Madrid. I take the children for some lessons at some nice stables in Colmenar Viejo, but the lessons are hugely boring. They are given by a boy sunbathing in the corner of the arena, who just has them trotting round for half an hour occasionally telling them to change the rein.

There is a nice English girl who is the girlfriend of the owner's son and I also try a few horses there looking for a dressage horse for someone in Andalucía however somehow, I feel they are not totally transparent. I try one very good-looking horse, he is a nice mover and well-schooled, easy to ride with accurate if not spectacular movements I think he will be ideal, fortunately I decide to ride him out of the school. Once we get onto a hard surface the poor horse, his stride halves in length and he is obviously in discomfort poor thing. It seems more than likely he has the beginnings of ringbone, sidebone or even worse navicular, on closer inspection his conformation confirms my suspicions indicating that it is highly probable he will suffer one of these complaints at some stage in the future, such a pity.

Club de Campo has a good setup I meet an English girl there, she is a friend of a friend and has competition dressage horses. She rents the stables and pays the groom separately, the installations and arenas are first class so logically it is expensive. A great yard if you are competing and have financial backing but inappropriate given our current circumstances. Besides which you have to be a member or know someone and even so there is a waiting list. Las Ventas is another good place comprising of individual yards. I go to see the jumping eventing yard and make enquiries. Whilst I am in the office the jumping teacher comes in and gives in her notice. I go out to watch the trainer at work he is schooling a horse over some jumps, they have an arena and full set of show jumps including a bank and water jump. The horse he is riding bucks after every jump but he is clearly unphased and the horse has a powerful jump. He finishes schooling and rides over to talk to me, I explain I am looking for livery for my mare and also am B.H.S. qualified to teach. He dismounts and asks me if I would like to ride the horse to cool him off. I am not wearing riding gear but never say no to a ride. I mount and walk quietly round the arena, suddenly the horse takes off without warning making a series of gigantic bucks. I get him back under control and the man rushes over and says maybe I should get off. I tell him there is no problem, ride the horse for another twenty minutes and then put him away. They tell me if I stay around, I can help with classes in return for livery for LADY but it will only be sporadic to cover the classes when the trainer was away competing.

I visit another two stables beyond Colmenar Viejo smaller and okay but no decent paddocks plus a long way out of Madrid. Then I find a flat to rent for the family, it is near Arturo Soria a quieter area with lots of trees, the flat itself is old but what I love was the grounds. There are rambling old gardens well established with roses and vines and large shady trees. There are hidden corners with benches where it would be lovely to curl up with a book, not that I ever have time. There is a children's play area, a tennis court, a large swimming pool for the summer and parking for two cars. Sadly, it is too far from Las Ventas which is on the other side of the city, but I also have to consider Carlos' work and the children's school.

So, we move and soon after we go to Barcelona, our new home is near the National 2, the Barcelona road. As we leave Madrid, I notice some horses just past the airport and vow to investigate on my return. I see a couple of small establishments and then stumble on Coronado, it is new, in fact still incomplete but has large airy cage boxes with a good wide passage, all undercover and a new indoor school with outdoor arenas too, showers for horses, changing rooms and a bar. Paco is in charge; he seems charming and enthusiastic. Carlos and I go for a ride the following weekend and we decide to move LADY.

Meanwhile at the Hipica LADY has not been well. The vet thinks she has laminitis, fever of the feet, which is very painful, she is put on a drastic diet. When I see her, I am horrified, she has lost so much weight and all her muscle. She is pitiful, half her former self, my heart reaches out to her I have to get her to Madrid as soon as possible. Fortunately, there is an English family who drove from England to Malaga in an English horse-box as their daughter has her horse at the Hipica. They hear I am looking for transport to take LADY to Madrid. They tell me they are new to Spain and as they don't know Madrid so they offer to take LADY for the cost of the fuel if we can put them up for a few days and show them round. John is an experienced driver; he is also a course builder and a knowledgeable horseman. The offer is heaven sent I can't believe my luck.

LADY arrives safely and we settle her in. Paco says he will stay with her until she has finished her feed, which I really appreciate, as I take my weary guests home to entertain them and give them an introduction to Madrid, bearing in mind my limited knowledge as I too am new to the city. With LADY thankfully back near the family we embark on a new era.

Chapter 16
Madrid

Finally, the whole family is in Madrid, including LADY. We move into our new home, settle the children in their new school, (initially I ferry them to-and-fro) but soon they make friends gain confidence and dispense of my services. I find work teaching English fairly quickly, the applications in the capital mostly require qualifications which I don't possess, so finally I ring and beg for an interview based on my experience. In the interview they ask me to explain a few grammar points following which they invite me to start the next day. The timetable is perfect, early morning classes 8 a.m. to 11 a.m., then a gap until lunchtime and classes from 1 p.m. to 6 p.m. approximately, depending on the day. This allows me time to go to LADY every day and spend the evenings with the children, bearing in mind the Spanish timetables are quite different from the English.

LADY soon settles into her new home at Coronado. She is in a pitiful state, she had lost all her muscle, she is so thin her ribs show together with a dull coat and listless look in her eye, which I have never seen before, it is heart-breaking.

Paco seems caring and keeps an eye on her, making sure she is eating and is comfortable. The blacksmith comes and says LADY has bruised her foot and has never had laminitis. I am not surprised as she has never been overweight or greedy, which is the most common cause of laminitis causing inflammation in the feet.

She slowly puts on weight and the shine comes back to her coat. I begin walking her in the country gently increasing her work until her muscles and her spirit return. She is now 18, one day I take her into the school and jumped a few fences, she jumps willingly enough but without her former verve, so we do a little schooling for flexibility and explore the countryside.

It is pure luxury to live and work in a capital city and be able to ride in open country every day, no road work, just cart-tracks, hills, woods, and the river. This would be unthinkable in London or New York. Literally "A breath of fresh air" every day, which recharges our batteries.

At this stage I meet Annemarie, she comes for a hack with Paco, LADY and me. She is a bubbly, fun-loving, Irish girl who is to become a very dear friend. LADY loves having company after cantering together she will not settle and behaves like a racehorse going down to the start. Her "alegria" or "joie de vie" has returned in full force, for which I am grateful. Her enthusiasm for life is contagious and much appreciated following the traumatic upheaval of recent months.

Annemarie is also an English teacher. She works for Susan who owns a grey gelding called BALI and runs a language School in Torrejon, the village nearby. BALI is in the stable opposite to LADY, he is Spanish, about 15:3hh, grey with black legs, mane and tail and rather smart. He is a bit naughty sometimes and he has to be led out of his stable with a chain or he will run off and escape. Susan bought him as an unbroken youngster, she was only a novice rider, so it was a very brave or crazy thing to do. She has had several falls and BALI also has a habit of running away with her, but she perseveres. BALI is 7yrs old so should have settled by now, however, Susan's daughter starts having dressage lessons on him and soon he is going much better, even showing promise with some really nice movements for a Spanish horse.

There is a nice little mare at the stables whose owner doesn't have much time and often goes to her family's village at weekends, so she asks Annemarie to ride her. Annemarie is thrilled and devotes all her spare time and energy to the mare who blossoms under her care. It is lovely for me too as we coincide most days having similar work timetables, also we have a similar approach to horses, which some Spanish people find hard to understand. We love exchanging ideas regarding our equine friends, their behaviour, their problems and how best to overcome them. Sadly, as I know only too well from experience, when one becomes fond of someone else's horse there comes a time when they take them away from you. Such is the case with Annemarie and the little mare, her owner decides to move to a village and take the mare with her.

Susan suggests that Annemarie could ride BALI during the week. Miguel the dressage trainer is schooling him twice a week but is quite happy to let Annemarie ride him and instruct her, so she had double bubble a horse to ride and dressage lessons. Miguel is talented with young horses, he rides Spanish 'vaquero' but also trains and teaches classical dressage, he is firm and quiet. He encourages horses to go forward which is just what Bali needs as Spanish horses tend to have a short stride and go behind the bit. He has Annemarie flying round the school on a long rein much to my approval. Encouraging BALI to stretch down, use his back and activate his quarters he looks like a different horse.

Miguel is a gifted artist too he paints some beautiful horse studies. Maybe due to his artistic temperament he is rather unreliable and sometimes turns up late or not at all, nobody is perfect. He is also teaching Rosa's son who began riding a "Jaca", a small Spanish horse with a docked tail typically used for bullfighting. Sergio is a beautiful natural rider and soon he graduates to a lovely dark bay quality horse they buy from Germany. DANPECHO is not an easy ride, he can't take the pressure of intensive training and one day he takes off galloping wildly round the school being totally unstoppable. Miguel calmly tells Sergio to keep turning him and try to reduce the circle. Eventually they slow down, he is a beautiful horse and a lovely mover, but a dressage horse also needs a certain temperament and a cool head. I realise more and more that dressage is jolly hard work for both horse and rider. When it comes together it is a magic feeling, but I still far prefer the magic feeling of flying over a fence. I keep telling myself that when I retire from jumping, I will come to grips with dressage but the more I see the more I realise it will be no easy task.

GITANO, Spanish for "gypsy" is quite a character, he belongs to Bea who is half French, they also take dressage lessons with Miguel. Although he is no youngster, GITANO loves performing his dressage even well into his twenties he will do passage to the best of his abilities and has a great sense of "joie de vie".

ATARRA is a lovely flea-bitten, grey, mare belonging to Cristina who also has a Portuguese horse, she too has lessons with Miguel and is competing in dressage. Cristina, like Bea, is petite and they are both neat riders and close friends.

As often occurs in the horse world in Spain there is a fairly frequent turnover of staff and they are short of a teacher. The busy time is of course the weekend, however, our need is great at the time, so I began teaching the beginners. It is quite rewarding, and I enjoy being with the children. Gradually I take on more pupils and the added income helps towards LADY's keep.

A new client arrives, a young American girl with a mare, supposedly thoroughbred, called SUZIE. She wants to jump so I am invited to be the official jumping teacher. SUZIE, Diana's mare, is nervous and despite the Pelham and tight curb chain she has little or no control, no brakes and poor steering. This is going to be a challenge before we even think about jumping. Diana's father always comes to watch, he is American and has worked at the American base nearby but is not working at the moment.

At the beginning of the first lesson, I ask her to warm up in her usual way, they accelerate out of control and then she steers her into the boards to stop, lethal for both of them. We begin with flat work, lots of transitions and half halts, open rein turning and circles to slow her and avoid getting into a fight with her. Fortunately, they both respond well so we begin with trotting poles followed by a circle coming down to a halt, then a cross pole as a placing fence one stride and a fence we built up to a decent size, the same method I had used with LADY years ago. She has a neat clean jump when she isn't fighting her rider. She is also spooky, so we have to introduce all kinds of strange objects as jump fillers. The material we have is limited, the jump stands are very heavy, and I have to set them up before each class and then clear them away afterwards, so I am glad to have Diana's father to help me, it is hard work.

There are more and more curious spectators which leads to more jumping students. I organize a small show and work hard painting all the poles and stands, collecting barrels, panels, brush, plant pots and any material I can find to create new fences to complete a course. Diana's father helps me, and we complete it between the two of us. I am told there are no funds available for new material, but we manage to persuade them to pay for the paint if not the work of painting them. We make the numbers and the flags and even a few flowerpots it looks quite good and proves very popular, we have lots of entries. The riding-school teachers wants to enter some of her pupils in the baby class which we think is fine, but she uses some of the newly painted poles to practice and breaks two of them. I confess I am furious and attack her verbally in no uncertain terms. However, things calm down and the show is a great success with rosettes, cups, and a jolly presentation party in the bar. SUZIE jumps beautifully so we decide to register her and take her to the regional shows. I always accompany them and help them as much as I can. I charge just the same as for one class, even though it inevitably means half a day. I settle up with Paco at the end of each month and am now earning enough to cover LADY's expenses and have a little extra.

However, one day when I go to settle up, I see I haven't been paid for any of Diana's classes. Paco just shrugs and says they haven't paid him so he can't pay me. When I tackle Diana's father, he tells me Paco has increased the charges substantially based on the success rate and they can't afford it, so they haven't paid and are leaving. I can't believe it, so much for bending over backwards to help people, more fool me, it seems I will never learn. Diana meets a boy at one of the shows I take her to, and he becomes her new trainer, I suspect he also becomes her boyfriend. They come back to one of my little shows with SUZIE and the boy rides her. He is strong so doesn't lose control, but she is rushing, fighting and flattening so has a lot of fences down, such a pity. Diana does have the grace to thank me for all my help in the past, but they don't offer to pay for the last month of classes, not even at the old rate, as they say they are still angry with Paco, to my mind not very logical, "C'est la vie".

An Argentinian girl has been having jumping lessons on one of the school horses and her father decides he wants to buy her a horse. I am working full time and have a family so have limited time to go horse hunting plus the fact that, as yet, I don't know many people in in the horse world in Madrid. I find suitable candidates in Andalucía, but they don't want to go that far to try a horse. I accompany them to try a little mare in a small yard outside Madrid. She is sweet to handle and has good confirmation. The man who owns her first lunges her over a jump which he puts up little by little to about 4ft which is big on such a small circle. She has a lovely jump really using her head, neck and back, tucking her feet up neatly. Then he tacks her up and rides her, or rather tries to, she runs around with her head in the air and he clearly has difficulty steering let alone stopping and he never attempts to jump her. I don't let the girl get on as she was not a very strong rider, my son rides her and has the same experience as the owner. We take her back to the stable and I feel in her mouth and she has a huge wolf tooth. I tell them that if she has the tooth out and then is re-schooled with a rubber bit or a hackamore, she may overcome the problem but, at the moment she is traumatized. They have seen enough and are not keen. I mention it to the owner but doubt he will ever try to solve the problem, such a pity.

Paco buys horses from a dealer and asks him to send a couple for us to try for jumping, one is clearly not sound, the other is a tall quality horse and lovely looking. I am told he has a problem with his head, putting on the bridle is tricky,

I have to undo the cheek piece, slide the bit into his mouth and then do it up, this takes some doing as he runs round the box with his head in the air. Once tacked up he is lovely but obviously a novice jumper. Taking the bridle off is even worse he really panics, I manage to calm him down and remove it, but no way would the young girl ever manage to tack him up. The poor horse has obviously been traumatized by carelessness, ignorance, or an accident. Taking the bridle off a young horse carelessly and getting the bit hooked behind the teeth, banging on the bars of his mouth causes pain and creates a fear which is hard to overcome. Meanwhile Paco offers to lend me a big horse he has on trial for himself. The horse is being schooled by the dressage trainer, currently Carlos, but periodically he will nap and bolt for the stable. He asks me if I would like to try him for jumping. I pop down a placing pole and a fence and ask the dressage guy to put the fence up for me. He is lovely and balanced and rhythmic and seems to enjoy the exercise, he jumps really, nicely, and we build up to an oxer of about 3ft 6ins which he floats over with ease. His trainer says he goes better and seemed happier the next day. So, we try him with the girl, in training he jumps well with her even though she is nervous of him. Our next small show is coming up and her father and Paco wanted her to compete on him. I feel I should override them as I know she is nervous, and nerves are always accentuated in a competition environment. Her nerves together with the excitement of the show atmosphere make the horse nervous and it proves all too much for them, they jumped three fences and bolt for the stables where he whips round so fast, she falls off, she is not hurt but rather shaken and I could kick myself for not intervening to avoid the mishap.

She continues having lessons on the school horse and she and her father go to Club del Campo where she falls in love with a retired showjumper. He is old but steady and she can handle him with ease. She mounts and jumps 3ft 6ins with no problem, he is a perfect schoolmaster. Under the circumstances it is ideal for both of them, as he has obviously been somewhat abandoned to the riding school, he was rather thin and scruffy with a staring coat. However, the work expected of him, with a light girl, jumping maximum Newcomers will not be too taxing plus he will have care, attention and good food. YACABO joins us and soon he is noticeably happier, he fills out and his chestnut coat gleams in the spring sunshine, he looks like a different horse and he gives his young rider confidence which grows with every session until she proves to be not the shy little girl but an opinionated young lady.

Laura another teenage girl, who was having a difficult time as her parents are divorcing, is having lessons. Laura is very nervous and doesn't want to jump but she loves horses, and her mother offers to buy her a horse. She too falls in love with a retired show jumper at Club del Campo. A huge German horse, he is black with a white blaze and socks, so I accompany her to try him. He is a comfortable ride, maybe a little short striding for such a large horse on returning to the stable I take off his brushing boots and I see why, both his front tendons are like bananas, this is obviously why he is no longer competing and is for sale, poor horse. I explain he is not a sound horse, but she is totally besotted with him. We knock the price down accordingly and again it turns out to be a wonderful retirement for a lovely old horse. Laura spends more time brushing him and leading him out to eat grass than riding him. I treat his tendons and we walk him miles, as a result his legs improve beyond belief and his owner gains confidence, she calls him ISHTAR. He is a good-natured horse but before long he feels so much better, he can't resist the occasional buck, although strangely he always controls himself with his owner, horses have insight. I have known horses be angelic with children and turn into demons with adults, maybe we should all ride like little children.

Suddenly aged 16 our son expresses a desire to ride again, I am delighted, even more so when he wants to learn to jump. ISHTAR's owner agrees to allow us to share her horse as she is getting over her traumas and coming less. One day I am encouraging Carlitos to energize and collect ISHTAR, who promptly becomes over energized and bucks him off, luckily, he is not at all discouraged.

ISHTAR is a big horse, and his buck is equally enormous, he is obviously feeling well so we begin some gentle schooling over poles, and he seems to really enjoy himself. Taking it gently and looking after his legs, Carlitos jumps him in our little shows, and he jumps round the 3ft course like a dream, but I don't feel it is fair to ask him to jump much higher. A couple of new jumpers come to the yard and the owner allows Carlitos to jump her horse, a nice little grey and an experienced jumper, so at least he gets the feel of jumping a bigger fence.

Eli is from Finland and has two daughters, both having lessons on a dear old horse they have on half livery. Mum is as enthusiastic as her girls and buys a little chestnut horse called JORGE, he isn't young, but he was very nice looking, he is full of energy but light and responsive to ride and the girls make great progress with him. Eli is quite strict, so the girls look after JORGE really, well, keeping both horse and tack immaculately clean and they are a lovely family to teach. Eli has a few jumping lessons during the week while the girls are at school. She is a relaxed and natural rider maybe partly due to the fact she was brought up with horses as her father had trotters in Finland. From what she tells me, the trotting races in her country are very, hard on the horses. I imagine she has had a tough upbringing hence she is quite a tough lady herself, but very straight, she calls a spade a spade. Diplomacy however is not her forte, but I become very fond of her and admire her honesty and her energy.

At the stables there is a ripple discontent and jealousy not uncommon in the horse world. As a result, I am reprimanded for stealing dressage clients and given strict instructions that I can only teach jumping. The problem is I have several nervous students who want to stay with me, but not jump, probably because I am softer than the Spanish dressage trainers. As far as I am concerned horses are an expensive hobby and it is paramount that the clients should enjoy their riding, and not suffer physically and psychologically. We just have a different approach, I fully understand and agree that discipline and hard work are essential if you want to make progress, but if the rider is tense and uncomfortable then the horse will be too, thus hampering their performance, it is common sense.

Several students I have been teaching wished to continue with me at all costs. I confess we cheat, I include these students in a small novice jumping group at their request, but they only ever go over poles on the ground and focusing on their flat work, transitions, collection, bend etc and they seemed happy with that, and I introduce Prix Caprilli into my little shows, a dressage test including cavaletti and call it my pre-jumping class . Apart from which, although most horses are natural jumpers, there are a few which simply haven't got a clue and BALI is such a case. BALI has the most peculiar action when faced with the smallest obstacle he will thrust both forelegs out straight in front of him instead of tucking them up, this is lethal as he literally trips up. I try him on the lunge and Carlitos rides him in the mini jumping, but it is impossible. He is sweet and willing, he tries hard but definitely needs to stick to dressage, at which he is quite talented and much happier, as is his owner they just about cope with Prix Caprilli.

Tito is young boy who has a little 4yr old Arab has been working with the dressage trainer who also rides the little horse during the week, and they have some fair battles, he will rear and nap. They think if they try jumping maybe he will have more to think about, we try a couple of lessons, but it is all too much, he is rearing too high, and the boy is only about ten years old. I make him dismount and take over, about which the dressage teacher makes some very disparaging remarks. I agree with his principle, but I am not going to risk a young boy having a nasty fall. I tell them until the horse is going forward and understanding the basic aids, we can't entertain the idea of jumping. I suggest he take him hacking with a safe nanny as an escort to get him going forward and enjoying being ridden. I help him initially and it works well, soon they are riding out, galloping around the countryside with friends, jumping logs for fun and both thoroughly enjoying themselves. The boy goes on to be a competent rider in his own right.

Riding back towards the stables one day with Annemarie we cross paths with a young couple, both tall and dapper looking and riding two lovely Hanoverian horses. They are all over the place, one cantering sideways and the other leaping up and down the bank on the side of the cart track. They don't appear to be very experienced riders but greet us jovially and continue their way in a somewhat erratic manner. When we get back Paco tells us they were new clients and as I am putting on Lady's rug before leaving Pepe comes and introduces himself. He is utterly charming and a real gentleman, he tells me he has just bought the two horses, one for himself and one for his girlfriend. They are beautiful horses, both Hanovarians, big, quality bays, ICARO is slightly taller than FIDELO. Initially they have everything money can buy, all manner of boots, bandages, rugs, tack, gadgets and added vitamins and minerals.

Pepe looks after everything impeccably, he himself is always immaculate and very elegant. However, either he doesn't have a lot of equine experience or he has some strange ideas. He will gallop the horses like mad, bring them in in a lather of sweat, still breathing hard, give them a cold shower and put them straight in the stable without a sweat rug, even in winter. He also takes them hare hunting, it is well known that many horses are lamed for life, as a result of galloping wildly on very hard ground takes its toll, not to mention the Galgos, (greyhounds) which are indiscriminately bred and then abandoned or even hung from the trees at the end of the season. The girlfriend soon loses her nerve and stops riding FIDELO.

The horses became very stressed because of these outings, and before long, Pepe finds he can't stop ICARO. He asks advice from all and sundry, frequently changing the bit and getting different people to ride him which confuses the poor horse even more. He joins one of my jumping lessons with FIDELO, what a fabulous horse, but Pepe is inconsistent and not easy to teach. He asks me to teach him English, he is a wonderful communicator but a hopeless student.

Although his language skills are limited, he uses his charm and always makes himself understood, so why study! Eventually he asks me if we can continue the classes whilst riding the horses, I happily agree. So, I ride FIDELO, and we have some great rides. He has been dabbling with dressage and as we are galloping across a stubble field, he asked me if I can get FIDELO to do a flying change as he has been having difficulty. I suggest it might be easier for the horse in the school, from a collected canter and changing direction or using counter canter as opposed to racing across a field in a straight line. Pepe is a bit crazy but extremely generous and utterly charming, nobody is impartial to him they either love him or can't tolerate him. I fall into the former category, despite the fact that some of the things he does with the horses drive me to distraction.

Whilst I am giving lessons at the week-ends Carlos rides LADY in the country, he goes on long hacks with Maria and her little grey horse SARASATI. I am happy as they obviously have a lot of fun. Maria has also bought a 4yr old Stallion for her daughter, he is out of a half German half Spanish mare by a Spanish stallion. He is a bight bay with a shiny coat, a lovely nature and they call him ADONIS, he is beautiful but to name him after a youthful Greek God full of beauty and desire is a bit over the top. There are already two young horses from the same breeder at the stables, one belongs to a friend of Maria's daughter, and another BONBON to Esperanza a nice girl but a novice rider.

Miguel is breaking in both horses and one day he asks me to ride BONBON, he is recently broken but so easy to ride even does passage with minimum effort. Unfortunately, his owner, Esperanza, is a nervous rider and however good he is, he is still a stallion and green. She is riding him quietly one day, but on a loose rein giving him no direction or attempting to control him, when he jumps on top of another horse which passes a little too close, she screams and falls off, there could have been a very nasty accident. Later she asks me to help her as she can't get on or off without him taking off. I hold him for her and while she is dismounting and she bodges her spur into his flank, not surprising that he tries to take off. I persuade her to ride him without spurs as she has no control over the use of them. The same happens when mounting, her toe digs into his belly. Every day for a couple of weeks Annemarie and I take him into the indoor school and using a bale one of us holds him and the other repeatedly mounts and dismounts until he eventually relaxes and will stand still without being held. A Basque family have joined the ranks, the son and the daughter are having jumping lessons and they own an old cob, who is a treasure and appropriately called TANKE. They later buy a young horse from the same breeder and call him DUNCAN as they are of Scottish descent. The dressage trainer breaks him in but then falls out with the father, so Paco asks me if I will take him on, even though it is obviously not for jumping! He knows he will lose the client if someone doesn't take them on, so I oblige. I ride him during the week and give the boy lessons at the weekends. We also start taking him out into the country and when they are away Carlos sometimes rides him, with their permission of course. Carlos is good with young horses because he is quiet, firm, and confident. Usually if he is going to ride DUNCAN, I lunge him first and check his girth once Carlos is on board. One day I am exceptionally busy with classes and he says he can manage alone. I mean to go and check his girth anyway but am in the middle of a class when I see them going out of the gate. Twenty minutes later DUNCAN comes galloping back to the stables with his saddle on his side. Fortunately, there are no serious consequences, he is neither injured nor traumatized, nor is Carlos who soon appears in his wake, somewhat embarrassed and on foot. The horse shied suddenly, as young horses do, and the saddle slipped, impossible to stay on board, poor Carlos!

Everything has been good at the stables up to now, but sadly things get out of hand. Paco takes on regional dressage competitions without having the facilities. Hence, he has the grooms making new dressage arenas moving tons of sand by hand with little time to spare. As a result, the horses are not mucked out for three days! The horses I look after are big horses and they are almost down to the floor risking capping hocks and elbows, not to mention wet, dirty, beds and getting thrush. Having been promised the previous two days that the beds would be done later in the day, I am furious. Instead of riding I grab a wheelbarrow and begin mucking out, Paco storms down the yard asking me what the hell I think I am doing. I tell him in no uncertain terms that I cannot leave the horses in these conditions. He replies that his own horses are in the same state, so I tell him he may tolerate that, but I will not, furthermore we are paying to have the beds done every day. He is enraged and tells me he doesn't interfere in my business and I have no right to interfere in his. He then grudgingly sends one of the men to start cleaning the stables.

The grooms have changed several times mostly they are Moroccan or Rumanian, some barely speak Spanish and have little or no knowledge of horses. Consequently, there are unnecessary accidents. ICARO is tied up in the passage one day and the boy loses control of the dumper and drives right into the terrified horse. Paco pays for his veterinary treatment but ICARO never fully recovers. Pepe continues riding him but although he doesn't appear lame his quarters are over to one side, and he can no longer go straight.

ISHTAR is a big horse nearly 18hh and another boy leading him into the stable doesn't open the door wide enough and turns him too sharply, he bangs his hip, slips and falls in the doorway, he struggles and has difficulty getting up scraping his legs and hips and ribs in the process, this is carelessness or ignorance or both and does not inspire confidence.

The summers are hot, and the groom is so angry with Paco he doesn't feed or water the school horses for the duration of their holiday. Paco and most of us are away at the time, the poor creatures are skin and bone when we get back, the groom gets the sack and fortunately the horses recover.

Problems never come alone, Carlos has been having great fun with LADY and she is still keen. Sometimes the spirit is willing, but the flesh was weak, her body doesn't respond, she still wants to gallop and so does Carlos sadly they have a cracking fall, so I feel the time has come to retire her. She looks magnificent and there is a man who has rented part of the finca and breeds from two lovely German mares, he is always admiring LADY and telling me I should breed from her. I am concerned that if she is having problems with her hocks, it will be hard for her to carry a foal, but he assures me that nature is very, wise and if she isn't fit to carry a foal she will not take, and it will be impossible to get her in foal.

A lady is flying in from Barcelona to give horses acupuncture, so I ask her to treat LADY, then I go to see a lovely stallion and LADY duly goes on her honeymoon. When she comes back the tests say she is in foal but two months later she absorbs the foal. This is quite common and was probably for the best, but it means I need to find a suitable place to retire her.

Meanwhile poor Maria who used to ride out with Carlos develops cancer, circumstances allow me to drop in to see her most days, she is such a bright plucky lady, but it is hard to see her suffer. Her daughter is looking after her but is planning to go to London to study and Maria is worried about the horses. Her husband is not interested in the horses, poor Maria knows she is dying and wants to find a solution. She desperately wants us to buy ADONIS and offers him to us at a lower price than other people who are keen to buy him. If it wasn't for her husband, I think she would give him to us. We are not really, in a position to buy another horse, but Carlos comes up trumps once more and agrees to buy him.

I take the children to see him, with Maria's illness he has not been out very much except when Patricia a friend of Susana's finds time to ride him, so he is bored and cross. He lays back his ears when we go into the stable and Ana feels quite intimidated saying she doesn't want to ride a horse that wants to bite her. I start working with him a little every day and his happy nature is soon restored.

Carlitos starts riding him and having dressage lessons, Carlos hacks him, and we even jump him a little. He is a sweet horse he is quiet with Ana, fun with the boys and proves to be a perfect family horse. Another summer is approaching, and my father is ill so I will have to go to England. The grooms have all changed again and Paco isn't even leaving his own horses there for the summer. I can't risk leaving the horses in my care to the mercy of these poor grooms who apart from speaking no English or Spanish know nothing about horses. Meanwhile Rosa has opened her own stables, Pepe describes it to me he tells me there is a huge jumping arena and says Rosa will build a house and go to live there, although this proves to be mostly in his imagination! He says we should move there, Cristina and Bea have already gone. I go to see Las Bridas, Rosa's new stables, she has done a lovely job, they are well designed and solidly built, two passages of light airy loose boxes with tack room and showers in the middle, she is building an indoor school and later plans to install a horse walker, the same model as the one the Queen of England has at Windsor. There is a large working arena as Pepe has described, but no sign of jumps. There is a dressage arena, a nice bar with a terrace, changing rooms with showers, but no paddocks, as yet. I find Rosa and Bea in the bar and see Cristina riding her horse, beautifully turned out as always. I like it all, but it is quite a long way from where I am working and down a very, long bumpy cart track, so I will have to spend more time in the car and less time with the horses. I say I will think about it for September.

Meanwhile I read an article, in the "Equestre" magazine, written by a Dutch man. It is about the care of horses who are old or injured and don't deserve to be abandoned or put down. He says they give us everything, so they deserve a dignified and caring environment for retirement or convalescence. He has a finca about 50 kms outside Madrid, it would be too far to go every day, but I feel that I have to go there and investigate. I arrange to meet him in the village square. I arrive a little early, Chapineria is a delightful old village nestled in gently rolling hills of glorious countryside. The soft grey stone and historic corners give it an air of tranquillity after the buzz of the city. I am sitting in the car in the square breathing in the peace when I see Willem walking towards me. He has an open, round, friendly face with a warm smile and a twinkle in his eye. I instantly feel I can trust my beloved LADY to the care of this person and the more we talk the more certain I become. I follow him through the village to "Kurrito", the finca lies on the edge of the village. Huge fields with groups of horses sheltering under big old trees, the water tanks are kept spotlessly clean, the stables are rather old, but the horses only came in twice a day to feed and be checked.

The groom is a small, wiry man, with a weather-beaten complexion. Mariano is a little brusque, but the salt of the earth and very, knowledgeable with a lifetime of experience. Mariano had worked at Kurrito when it was previously home to the military who kept stallions and bred, trained, and competed. They also built a cross country course which although in need of repair is still evident. Mariano looks after the horses then, Willem tells me he is quick to spot lameness or colic and saves many a horse through his quick diagnosis and treatment. I decide this will be perfect for LADY. I now have to find somewhere suitable for ADONIS and Maria's elderly grey gelding SARASATI. ADONIS being a stallion I cannot not take him to Kurrito he would jump on the mares and fight the geldings, but I so want him to have a summer roaming free.

Carlos, the Dressage trainer has built his own yard and is in the process of moving. He tells me he has a paddock with a stable that might suit ADONIS for the summer. It is perfect, big enough for him to run round and with a huge old tree for shade, so SARASATI and ADONIS go to Carlos. I explain to my students I will be away for the summer and maybe longer. I arrange for another teacher to take them under her wing. However, in Spain many people go away for the entire month of August, YACABO's owner decides to send him with Lady, so does ISHTAR's. They are both old horses and will benefit from being turned out for the summer. Pepe also decides to send his two horses for a summer holiday and offers to transport all of them which is a great help. I haven't moved LADY since she has been in Madrid and as it transpires, I don't have the relevant paperwork for her, the regulations in Andalucía are different from those in Madrid and everything is happening very fast, Pepe wants to take them, so I ring the vet. He saves the day, he comes over and gives me a letter saying I have to move her for health reasons, and it is urgent with no time to apply for the papers, another hiccup fixed. Carlitos and Pepe go to load LADY and ISHTAR, I am going to go straight to Chapineria to meet them there when I finish work.

As I finish my last class I ring Carlitos to see where they are. They are still at the stables they haven't been able to load ISHTAR, they have tried putting LADY on first, then taken her off to open the partition and give him more space, no way, they have spent an hour and a half trying to load him. They have tried bribing him and getting cross, to no avail and are at their wits end. I hurry over and Pepe asks me if he should just take Lady, I reply vehemently that no way am I leaving ISHTAR there to his fate. I put LADY back in the trailer and get ISHTAR to the foot of the ramp, lifting one leg at a time and placing his fore feet on the ramp. I then hook the lunge rein on one side of the trailer, ran it behind Ishtar and threaded it through the other side using it as a pulley. Step by step, I literally haul him into the trailer, I keep telling him he is nuts, he is going to a lovely place and I don't know what will become of him if I leave him behind. He is almost eighteen hands and a big boy, but I use every ounce of strength I have and twenty minutes later he is on board. What a relief, he is such a dear old horse and I feel responsible for him. I hug him and stuff him with carrots, my dear LADY too who has the patience of a saint, and off we go. I inform Paco regarding these seven horses which will be going away for the summer, I tell him LADY will, definitely not come back as she is retiring, and I will confirm the others for September later. He knows Pepe is taking his horses to Rosa's after the summer and several have already gone there. All in all, twenty-two horses leave that summer, it marks a new chapter for us all.

In September I go to see Paco and tell him face to face I will not be returning to Coronado. He just shrugs and to my disappointment he doesn't even ask me why. I am happy to explain why twenty-two horses have left! Later I receive an irate phone call from his wife who tells me I am a wicked person and have stolen their clients. Nothing could be further from the truth. I have no interest in taking on more students and scarcely have time for my current commitments. Furthermore, I made provision for everyone to stay with them, it is not my fault if no-one is satisfied with the service they have to offer. Maria Jose is adamant she tells me I am such a bad person I will end up in hell. I tell her I am sorry she feels that way. I remind her that we have had some very, good times, but after careful consideration I feel I am at liberty to choose and entitled to make my own decisions, as are other people. Unfortunately like her husband she doesn't bother to ask me why. I hate finishing on bad terms with people, it is quite unnecessary, but there is nothing more I can do or say. They are angry but unable to see why the exodus has occurred, they just blame everyone else. Other clients have quite violent confrontations, so I get off lightly, but it confirms my conviction that I have made the right decision.

Sadly, Annemarie won't be coming with us, she has been riding the blacksmith's horses and he too has fallen out with Paco and moved to another yard, so she goes with him. He is a good blacksmith, but he really abuses her good nature and love of the animals. She cares for all his animals, dogs, birds of prey and horses, while he is away. He has illusions of grandeur but doesn't appreciate the jewel he has by his side. One of his horses, dies from a tumour in his head it is awful. I have seen him hit the horse over the head when it tried to rear in desperation to escape his iron fist hands. Annemarie nurses the poor horse to the end. The blacksmith loses interest in the horses and Annemarie finally comes to her senses and leaves him taking his other horse FRAILUCO with her. He has always had problems with sand cracks needs special care. What a lucky little horse but I am sure he appreciates her; you can see it in his eyes he is a happy sparky little horse. ADONIS has spent an idyllic summer in his paddock in Guadalajara. He is completely wild, happy, and excited when we return. He has rubbed the lower half of his mane on the big tree, so he is bald halfway up his neck from his withers and has this huge volume of thick, long, wavy hair on the top half of his neck and a great forelock covering most of his face, he looks, and behaves, like the Lion King. It takes three of us to tack him up. Carlos, who was strong, holds his head, he is whirling round from side to side and would have plastered us against the wall. I hold up a foreleg and Carlitos put on his saddle. I lunge him and ride him, he whinnies so much I think he will lose his voice, at first, he is tense, and he is obviously using all his self-control. Fortunately, he has a lovely temperament which is every bit as important as breeding and good movement. Carlos, the owner of the stables, offers to take ADONIS over to Las Bridas as he wants to see the installations and I think he is disappointed we aren't going to stay with him in Guadalajara. Distance wise his stables are similar to Las Bridas, also with a long rough track leading up to it with the added inconvenience of several gates to open and close on the way. The main reason for my choice being that many horses and people I am already involved with are either already at Las Bridas or planning to move there, together with the confidence I feel in the standard of care. Carlos is good, he does classical dressage too and his stables are new with decent loose boxes and a small school, but I don't know anyone there and most of his clients ride Spanish style, which well done is an art and can be fabulous to watch, but sadly is not always well done. They have saddles designed for the comfort and safety of the rider, but which deny you close contact with the horse. They use huge curbs and the zagetta, zig zag metal that digs into the horse's sensitive nose. You see many horses with scarred noses, and they wear and use huge rowel spurs, long spurs with a spiked wheel at the end. These gadgets in good hands are fine but they can be vicious in the wrong hands. We northern Europeans are considered rather soft and renowned for being over fussy about the care of our animals, we just have a completely different approach. Fortunately, Spain is changing radically and is to change even more in the coming years, at least now most of the stables have decent sized looseboxes with automatic water and are mucked out every day, but they still don't make the bed they just chuck in a pile of clean bedding. When the country suffered civil war followed by dictatorship her people had enough to worry about surviving themselves, so understandably consideration for animals was secondary.

In countries with a higher standard of living and fewer problems, where people's necessities are more than covered, they can afford the luxury of caring for such things as their surroundings, those less fortunate than themselves, animal welfare and the environment. The change in the South of Spain has been both rapid and radical. When I first lived there few people owned dogs and those who did kept them outside mainly chained up as guard dogs. Fortunately, these days many people have dogs as pets, in their homes, as part of the family. Horses were kept in standing stalls and often only taken out at weekends when they were ridden into the ground. Still today some horses collapse, and many go lame on the Romerias, non-stop fiestas, singing, dancing, eating and drinking, alcohol flows and the horses take the brunt. Of course, this probably applies to a minority but as always, the minority spoil things for everyone.

Bullfighting is another issue we northern Europeans have difficulty coming to terms with. Paco often buys cheap horses for the riding school from a dealer, one such horse was a little bay that had been gored by a bull, he had literally been stitched back together and the scars ran the length of his body and his flank, it must have been horrendous. Apart from the physical damage there is the psychological trauma, when approached unexpectedly from that side he flinches and quivers.

BALI and JORGE join the ranks at Las Bridas, and we resume our classes at the weekends. I ride BALI and ADONIS during the week, Susan also lets me use BALI for one of Eli's girls, which is good for the older girl helping her to get a feel for dressage and means the girls can ride together. The jumps never materialize as most of the clients are purely dressage riders and they seem to think we will upset the dressage horses if we start jumping! It is evident there was never any intention of having a jumping arena. I build a few little jumps outside the arenas which we are careful to pop over when no one is around.

The hacking from there is quite good, there is a short ride to the river which has several crossing places and on the other side there is a wood. The trees are tall, and it often floods in winter, so some trees fall each year. I build a little cross-country course with 14 fences and we take the horses there to jump and have picnics, letting them graze on the lush grass near the river. They are happy days; we find good places to have races especially after harvest there are vast stubble fields with wonderful going so, we let the horses really gallop which they love as much as we do. I also let Eli borrow ADONIS during the holidays so she can ride with her two girls. The only downside to that is that when her daughter rides him, she let him eat grass so he will be quiet and keep still. So, he develops the bad habit that if you are not concentrating, he will wrench the reins out of your hands and grab a bite of lush grass. ADONIS is jolly strong even a bit brutal at times, he nearly pulled Carlos' shoulder out of joint. He will do the same to sniff a dropping if you are not careful. Once he has achieved his objective, he is so absorbed by the delicious fresh grass or the scent of a gorgeous mare that he is oblivious to his frantic rider. He leaves you behaving like a Thelwell rider, flapping legs, and stick, if you have one, and tugging at the reins pony club style, all to no avail. However, it keeps one on one's toes, if you spot the temptation ahead and simple apply your legs, shorten your reins, and ride him forward then he is a perfect gentleman. We have a Gymkhana and to my surprise the Dressage trainer and some of his students joined in. ADONIS goes well he is neat and quick but Eli's elder daughter rides BALI bareback and is brilliant, they win the day.

Carlitos meanwhile is having dressage lessons on ADONIS with Pepe the new dressage trainer, (Miguel has moved on again). We call him Pepe Cubano as he was on the Cuban Olympic Dressage team, Pepe, and his partner Itzia are schooling horses and giving lessons. They work very, hard and are both conscientious and experienced. Carlitos' lessons are at eight o'clock on Sunday mornings. He gets up at 6:30 to get Adonis ready in time and much to my surprise and delight seems to enjoy it, they are going really, well. Pepe even gets them doing passage, mostly to activate ADONIS before doing other movements, but

Carlitos is beginning to get quite a good feel and some pleasing results. Sadly, they only manage to go to one competition where they come a commendable second in quite a strong class, following which he wins a scholarship and goes to study in the United States.

Ana enjoys riding but is not a fanatic like her mother or as keen as her brother and father. She is rather nervous of ADONIS, which is a pity, she was really, confident on LADY who was bigger and stronger but of course never rode her off the leading rein. ADONIS is well mannered, comfortable, and easy to ride. However, being a stallion, he is prone to whinnying and prancing, at the most he shakes his head with excitement and sometimes goes into passage, but he is always careful not to unseat his rider. He is a bit pushy in the stable which makes her nervous. Unfortunately, he runs off with her when some chickens get behind the kicking boards in the indoor school and spook all the horses. The same applies to BALI with Susan, they are going really, well in class and she just walks down the drive with another horse to cool off they come back at a flat-out gallop totally out of control. BALI periodically does this with Susan but rarely attempts it with other people. Horses never forget and they are creatures of habit, rather like us humans I suppose.

ATARRA is a lovely flea-bitten grey mare, just my cup of tea, she looks like a typical eventer 16:3hh, nice quality, although she has no thoroughbred ancestry, she has a trace of Arab blood which is evident from her pretty head with a very slightly dished face also her tireless energy. Cristina has done some eventing with her, but now wants to concentrate on dressage and ATARRA, like LADY, has little patience and concentration for dressage, so she has bought a Portuguese stallion with confirmation and temperament, rather like the Spanish horses, and easier to train for dressage.

ATARRA like LADY is fast and a good jumper but dressage is definitely her weak point. Cristina rescued her and although through good daily treatment all Cristina's horses are a delight to handle, she has never forgotten the bad experience of her youth. They try giving her intensive dressage training but one day, Itzia comes out of the school dripping blood. She has desperately been trying to get ATARRA on the bit, but the mare flipped throwing up her head so violently she broke Itzia's nose. There is blood everywhere including all down ATARRA's white neck and shoulder. I help Itzia to dismount, Pepe rushes her to hospital, and I clean up the mare. Following this incident Cristina gives up

214

trying to convert her into a dressage horse but she doesn't want to sell her so is delighted to let us have her on loan.

The son of a colleague of Carlos has been riding in the summer at their country house and they are considering taking a horse on half livery for him near Madrid so he can continue riding all year round. Miguel also wants to study to become a vet, so it is complementary to his possible future career. We decide to share the livery costs with the boy so Carlos and I can ride her too.

The first time I go to try her she is in the paddock and I have been warned she is difficult to catch. Forewarned is forearmed, thanks to my years catching ponies in fields I hang the rope round my neck, gave her a carrot and placed my hand on her shoulder, sliding the rope round her neck before attempting to approach her head, no problem. Once in the stable she rushes to the corner with her head in the air, eying me suspiciously when I go in with the bridle. However, she allows me to tack her up with no resistance. I love her she is my type; she is forward and active like LADY but much lighter and more obedient. Also, like LADY she is resistant to a steady contact, her reaction being to throw her head in the air. This is nothing new for me, so working in circles, taking a steady contact on the outside rein, and giving and taking with the inside rein, whilst gently pushing her forward, she relaxes and rounds her back giving me a lovely feel which we lose when we came out of the circle, but even so she is so much easier than LADY ever was. Miguel comes to try her; he isn't interested in schooling and is quite happy to hack out with us. He is a quiet boy, and she responds well to him; they are fine together. The only problem being he is so slow getting her ready, but in a way that is nice for her as he has a calming effect. Before long she comes to greet us instead of hiding in the corner.

I ride her out one day on a long ride with a large group. One member of the group is very nervous, Berta has a stallion and keeps him on a very tight rein which makes him nervous too. I feel responsible for them as I persuaded her to come on a long hack to gain confidence. The others want to take advantage of the beautiful rolling stubble fields for a good gallop, temptation indeed. Berta pales and says she will go home so I feel duty bound to stay with her, I tell her to keep behind ATARRA. The others take off and although excited to my surprise ATARRA is easy to control she canters sideways so blocking Berta's horse, even better, but remains light and obedient. When the others are out of sight over the brow of the first hill, I persuade Berta to trot and once settled in a steady trot to canter slowly. Again, ATARRA is perfectly behaved, and we eventually catch up with the others at a sedate collected canter. With LADY that would have been a nightmare!

Sandra, Ina's daughter from Malaga has moved to Madrid, her mother and sister come to help her settle in. Ina is concerned because Sandra has been show jumping and wants to ride, I take them to see ADONIS and explain there are no jumps there as all the clients are dressage fanatics. Ina is relieved she loves her children riding but hasn't enjoyed watching Sandra jump. Pepe is still having some problems with ICARO's brakes or rather lack thereof. He has let various people school his horses, FIDELO manages quite nice dressage with Itzia, although flying changes one way he still finds difficult. However, poor ICARO is physically and mentally at a disadvantage since his accident with the dumper. I suggest that Sandra might ride his horses she is more than capable of schooling them. She will be able to ride, and he won't have to pay for schooling. It proves to be an excellent arrangement and she does a really good job. We have some great times riding out together and Pepe begins to enjoy ICARO again. Sandra is a jumper and rides jumping style, but the basic training is the same for both disciplines. She is an effective rider soon gaining the respect of the dressage riders.

FARMER is a tall handsome Danish horse; he is black and must be nearly 18hh. Strange I have LADY FARMER, but she was bred in England by HILL FARMER, who has sired eventers in the U.K., FARMER on the other hand was bred in Denmark with equally good lineage but unconnected to my LADY. Merete, his owner is also tall and the nicest person, totally dedicated to her horse, but FARMER is young and has a mind of his own. The first time I see them she is trying to ride him down the drive and he is rearing, bucking, whipping round, and leaping all over the place. Merete perseveres, but he is naughty and sometimes gets the better of her. When leading him out in a head-collar he has developed the habit of escaping from her just by just taking off at great speed, there being no way she can stop him. She has had a succession of trainers and he has certainly improved albeit slowly. Despite his naughtiness she never gives up, she loves him and spoils him to death. On his fifth birthday she organizes a party in the bar and brings him into the bar to eat his goodies from the table. Itzia gives him a present of a face made from melon and apples and carrots which he wolfs down, he even has a cake with candles.

FARMER is going much better in his lessons but between lessons he is still giving her some headaches. Seeing Sandra's success with ICARO she asks her to have a go with FARMER. Sandra is a no-nonsense rider, quiet but very firm, she just rides forward in a business-like manner and FARMER responds to her like a dream. Merete's first local show is the same one that Carlitos goes to with ADONIS. They hack there together and apart from a gigantic buck in the warm-up FARMER goes really, well, he comes first and ADONIS second. Merete is so determined and although many people tell her she should get another horse; she is never put off and stands by her FARMER. She says it is ironic that a jump rider has sorted out her dressage horse.

When Sandra leaves at the end of her studies Merete allows me take FARMER out for a hack occasionally. He still gives the occasional buck, but I particularly remember one day doing the most magnificent extended trot down a stubble field, he has all the potential. It is like flying he has terrific power and activity and maintaining a steady contact he gave me a great feeling. Eventually Merete can take him anywhere and the two of them go to shows all over the country. She also takes him to Barcelona on holiday, chapeau to the pair of them. Later they move to Andalucía to a lovely house with stables, school and paddocks, lucky Farmer, few people would have had her tenacity and patience.

Meanwhile the boy who is sharing ATARRA with us isn't doing too well at school. He wants to be a vet so having the horse is complementary and there is a lot he can learn. However, his parents issue an ultimatum if he doesn't pass his exams goodbye ATARRA. I see the writing on the wall, he is a delightful boy but if he studies as slowly as he prepares the horse it meant ATARRA's future is on the line.

Willem's old horse BENGALI has gone lame. We have been looking at possible horses for him to buy, but he is getting desperate and says if he doesn't have a horse to ride soon, he will end up never riding again. I ask Cristina if he can come during the week and ride ATARRA with me, she agrees, so Willem comes to try her. ATARRA is rather tall for him compared with his little, long-distance champion, but the relationship with a horse is like chemistry with people, you never know. Willem is in his late seventies, has had heart surgery and suffers from diabetes so perhaps I have been looking for horses that are too quiet. I realise Willem likes a very, active, forward, horse and still loves to "run" as he says. With the aid of a mounting block ATARRA's height is not initially a problem.

I ride ADONIS and we ride out together, when they are settled, we have a long trot, then a steady canter. We cross the river, clamber up a steep bank and cross a little wooden footbridge. Willem and ATARRA go first as ADONIS is very wary it being so narrow. Willem is impressed and quite at home with her. Cristina says she will consider selling her to Willem as it would be a wonderful home for her. She knows he will care for her in her retirement too. Willem takes the plunge and buys her; I will miss her but at the same time am very, happy for her.

Eli is a strong character and calls a spade a spade, she never hesitates to complain loudly if she feels something is not 100%. If the feed is late or the manger dirty, she complains so she and Rosa have their confrontations which leaves me uncomfortably in the middle. The first time the blacksmith shoes JORGE there is a gap between the hoof and the shoe on the hind hooves, she goes mad and changes the blacksmith. She is right, but Spanish shoeing is different, in England for example the shoes are much lighter and made to fit the hoof exactly, so they are changed at least once a month. In Spain, the shoes are heavier and although they shoe hot, they have a tendency to make the shoes bigger to allow for growth of the hoof and the horses are only shod every two months. Now it is changing and has improved considerably since I came to Spain. Eli moves to a new house and decides to move JORGE to some stables near their new home. Susan also decides to move BALI to the yard where Annemarie is, as it was nearer her home and she has been riding very, little due to the distance. This frees me from giving classes at weekends meaning at last I can ride with Carlos and accompany him to ride with Willem. He has told me about the marvellous country where Willem rides.

Pepe also has less time for the horses and has gone from one extreme to the other, he previously lavished everything money could buy on them, but now they are back to basics. Heaven knows where they had spent their last holiday, it wasn't with Willem, and Pepe left them there until the winter set in. When he finally goes to see them poor ICARO doesn't make it he is in such poor condition he has to be put down. He brings FIDELO back in a lamentable state, his ribs and hips protruded, and his coat is matted and dull. Pepe is strange, I am mad with him for letting them get into such a state, but he doesn't take offence. In his usual generous manner shrugs and tells me I can take over his horses and do as I like with them, he will come and ride them occasionally. I set to work on FIDELO but it takes a few months and a lot of hard work to get him back into condition. He is a lovely ride in the school and out. I ride him in the school during the week and Carlos and I have some incredible rides at weekends. We go out for hours exploring, getting lost, racing across stubble fields, jumping logs, scrambling up and down banks and crisscrossing the river they are good times.

Rosa is an excellent cook and a group of her friends often stay for lunch at the weekend often lunch runs into the small hours of the morning! Pepe and Bea formed part of this group and the wine flows. Pepe has been known to get up to pranks like riding bareback by moonlight apparently one night, FIDELO dumped him rather unceremoniously, he wasn't hurt but it could have been nasty. I do not normally form part of this group as usually we rush off to eat with the children at home, but occasionally I stay to enjoy the company, lots of horse talk and the excellent cuisine. Rosa lived in Paris for a while and her dishes have a special touch, furthermore she is generous enough to share her culinary secrets, for example, for years I have been battling with aubergines, I love aubergines fried in batter and drizzled with honey, but mine always go soggy. I soak them, salt them, press them and fiddle around with them to no avail they still go soggy. So, when Rosa produces delicious crisp aubergines, I ask her how on earth she does it, she tells me she makes the batter with beer and no salting, soaking or pressing, just cut, dip and fry, the result is unfailing, wonderful, crispy, batter.

POTRI is the young chestnut gelding Pepe brings to Las Bridas, "potro" is Spanish for "colt" so his name is not too imaginative. He is home bred by a German horse out of a home bred hunter mare, a good looking four-year-old. Pepe has decided to break him in himself, he has ridden all his life and watched many good professionals at work but never schooled or trained a horse, let alone break one in. It is rather hit and miss, and it appears to be the blind leading the blind. I witness them having a few discussions where it is not clear where either of them intends to go, it is only evident that they are not in agreement. He has offered him to another friend to ride who politely declined. He then asks me to take him on. I begin work in earnest with POTRI, he is like a teenager whose limbs have suddenly grown and made him very clumsy, he is all over the place and totally unbalanced. I work him on the lunge to develop his muscle, balance, and obedience. Initially he is very spooky but improves with regular work. Before long I am riding him in the school, and he is beginning to go forward into a nice contact, and I am starting to enjoy him. Unfortunately, ADONIS pulls a tendon sheath in a hind leg and is off lame with rather lengthy treatment. So, Carlos takes to riding FIDELO and I start taking POTRI out with him. POTRI is rather hard work in the country, as so often happens with green horses he pulls like a train behind another horse and puts the brakes on when in front. Still, we enjoy ourselves although he still bucks when asked to canter. I rather feel he is uncomfortable in his back as Pepe was rather heavy to have ridden him so young, sadly Pepe refuses to allow me to call in a back specialist. I ride as lightly as I can and give him some gentle physio and massage, so he builds up muscle and gets fitter and stronger. Pepe hears he is going well and decides to ride him again but comes back saying he bucked a lot. There are several theories, one he is uncomfortable in his back Pepe is tall and a lot heavier than me, two, when he bucks, I always push him forward as opposed to stopping him to reprimand him, and finally he is now fit, previously half a mile at a spanking trot and he was too pooped to buck, but not now. Probably a combination, but he looks a picture and is a sweet horse to handle.

ADONIS is generally very well behaved during his convalescence. I don't know whether vets find it amusing but they tend to leave a horse shut in a stable for a month and then say ride him at a walk. One is tempted to say, "After you". I am riding ADONIS round the outside of the dressage arena one day in walk as instructed and Pepe the trainer and Itzia are schooling. Pepe sharply reprimands the horse he is riding with voice and whip, it is like an electric shock to Adonis, he leaps in the air all four feet off the ground, not the best thing to do when recovering from an injury. Itzia shouts for Pepe to stop but too late, it is no one's fault but it is nerve racking after lengthy treatment. One buck can undo all the good and put you back to square one, fortunately we are lucky and there are no repercussions.

On one occasion I stay to lunch at Las Bridas, after a lengthy "sobre mesa" or "after dinner chat" round the table, a delightful Spanish custom, one I like even more than the siesta, I take my leave and go to check the horses on my way out. As I walk down the passage towards Pepe's horses, I hear Pepe talking to POTRI. When I reach POTRI's stable, POTRI is lying down and Pepe is sitting in his manger chatting to his horse. He has his "sobre mesa" with his horse and a glass of whisky although he assures me it is camomile tea!

A little later he brings a new girlfriend who is later to become his wife. Isabel is attractive, but more normal than the barbie type girls who he has previously appeared with. She begins riding FIDELO and they go on long excursions and take picnics. I am so happy for them except for one day when both horses come home without them. Fortunately, the horses are unharmed, but the happy couple have a job living that one down.

There is currently a very hard-working groom, he is Rumanian and can turn his hand to anything. Apart from keeping the stables meticulously clean he is a mechanic, electrician, plumber, welder, decorator you name it, Florin would find a way. However, he is a bit playful both with the girls and the horses. FIDELO has a habit of rushing off when you lose him in the school or paddock. Florin instead of correcting him compounds the problem by flailing the rope at him making him run off even faster which Florin finds amusing. As a result, Angeles, who offers to help me one day, says she will turn him for me, I warn her he tends to rush off, but she forgets her gloves and ends up with a nasty rope burn on her hand. I always wear gloves and put the caveson, and the lunge rein on him so as he rushes off, I stop him in his tracks, approach him and give him a carrot repeatedly until he stands quietly with me allowing me to lose him in my own good time. However, he continues rushing off from Florin to Florin's delight. One day during this procedure he gallops flat out stops dead and throws himself down to roll but when he gets up, he is desperately lame pathetically waving a foreleg in the air. The vet happens to be in the yard and thinks it is his shoulder, he gives me some liniment to rub in and some danilon for the pain. The next day poor FIDELO has a tendon like a banana. He has treatment, one month's rest and then I walk him in hand every day for another month just as I did with ADONIS. I have just completed ADONIS' convalescent walking, so we are riding him again. I seem doomed to walking convalescent horses.

Pepe builds himself a new home in Estremadura and duly decides to take his horses there. I have painstakingly got FIDELO sound and fit again, I am glad he is sound and fit when he leaves as clearly, he will get no cosseting in his new home. However, I feel a profound sadness, almost a sense of bereavement to see FIDELO and POTRI leave. Why does one become so fond of these long-faced creatures, I miss those lovely faces and pricked ears welcoming me every morning and brightening my day, but sadly they are not my horses.

PUPEN is Cristina's new mount, a beautiful bay Oldenburg mare from Germany. She is in a different league, so good looking and she moves like a dream, she floats with perfect cadence even though she is green and only five years old, with natural movement like that the job is half done. The day she arrives, Sergio rides her in the indoor school, she is nervous and excited and a bit flighty, but she looks spectacular. PUNTAL, although he is from Portugal, is similar to a Spanish horse in terms of confirmation and action. They are shorter and more compact with a tendency to flex their knees so having a shorter stride, although I must say very, comfortable, and easy to ride. Cristina has done well with him and mastered a good deal of the art of dressage. She is a hard worker and a neat rider, but to go further she needs a different stamp of horse and PUPEN is the first of a series of lovely Oldenburg horses she acquires. The Oldenburg's are represented in Spain by Cristina, Rosa and Pepe who frequently go to auctions in Germany. They bring over Oldenburg horses for clients all over Spain and also German Dressage trainers to give clinics.

Cristina and Rosa both buy brood mares, so we have the joy of seeing foals again cavorting and playing as they do. However, good fortune does not smile upon them. The first foal from Rosa's mare proves to be an obsessive wind sucker, luckily for them all, Merete buys him, ostensibly for her husband who is English with a wry sense of humour and absolutely no interest in horses. So, he is lucky and goes to Andalucía with FARMER. The next one dies, when turned out on a farm as a yearling, through eating a poisonous plant, a real tragedy. I am lucky enough to arrive one day when the next one, a little filly, has just been born, she isn't feeding so I help her begin to suckle. That tiny muzzle that fits in the cup of your hand, those long wobbly legs and short body you can wrap your arms around, foals are just adorable. Unfortunately, that beautiful filly has an awful accident, as a youngster she tries to jump over the stable door when they take her mother out. She breaks her shoulder, poor ROXIE spends the best part of a year shut up in a stable, I visit her every day it hard to see.

Cristina is reluctant to sell PUNTAL, her Portuguese stallion, but agrees to allow Carlos and I to have him on livery so, with Adonis' fully recovered, once more Carlos and I can ride together. PUNTAL is a sweetie, he is easy to ride. He is a well-schooled horse, so I ride him in the school during the week and he enjoys his gallops in the country with Adonis at the weekends.

Change is on the horizon once more, Pepe and Itzia leave taking their clients with them, so we are considerably reduced in numbers. The groom is good but not an experienced horseman, Rosa does her best, she feeds the horses on the groom's day off and somehow, they manage. However, Rosa is not physically fit enough to handle horses if required and one very windy day one of the large doors at the end of the passage sweeps her off her feet and damages her hand, she fears will never recover full use of it. Beatrix has moved house to Fuente el Saz so living nearby is able to help Rosa whenever she can. She also helps Cristina and is allowed to ride some of her lovely new horses.

GITANO, Bea's dear old horse is now retired although she still gives him lots of tender loving care. When I go away, Bea rides ADONIS for me, she is a very competent rider. In return I take care of her old horse during the week when she is working, just cleaning his feet turning him out, brushing him and giving him apples. He still has great character even though his poor old body doesn't respond as it used to. He still spooks and gets excited; it is the same with people the spirit is willing even when the flesh is weak. There is something poignantly sad about old age in both animals and people, it must be so frustrating. GITANO keeps trying to tell us he is still that great old boy which he has always been, battling to the last.

ZAFIRO is a huge Portuguese horse with a roach back, his owner Angeles is a short girl but loves having a big horse. She looks like "a tomtit on a round of beef." She is a schoolteacher and credit where credit is due, she goes to the stables by bus from Madrid and then walks down the long track in all weathers. I give her a lift whenever I can, and she helps Ana with her Maths. Angeles was also in Coronado where she had dressage lessons with Miguel, she now has lessons with Pepe Cubano but ZAFIRO is lame on and off, his back troubles him. The way she mounts doesn't help, she insists on mounting from the ground and her whole weight hangs from his side, so he had to brace himself. I am a firm believer in mounting blocks to avoid pulling a horse's back. ZAFIRO is grey and he has a mass of growths on his chest the size of a cauliflower. The vet says it may have been aggravated, if not caused, by the rug being too tight round his chest although grey horses do tend to have this kind of tumour, especially as they get older.

ADONIS develops a problem with his ear. The vet comes and gives him a course of antibiotics but to no avail. It becomes more and more difficult to put on his head-collar and I have to dismantle his bridle to put it on. I remove the noseband and the brow-band slip the headpiece over his neck sliding it gently up his neck to behind his ears then slipping the bit into his mouth and do up the buckle on the near side. Once the bridle is in place when riding him, he seems quite happy, but even this procedure is becoming increasingly difficult. Following the antibiotics, he has anti-inflammatories, but he gets steadily worse. One day it is so bad I needed help to catch him I call the vet and we decided to take him to the Veterinary Teaching Hospital. There they x-ray and he has a huge egg-shaped lump filling his ear. He was so desperate with the discomfort in his ear that when trying to rub it he must have banged it resulting in a huge haematoma. They decide to operate, luckily, I am able to be present. They have a good little hospital, he has his pre-med in a padded room, once he is asleep, he is hoisted up by his feet to a pulley system in the ceiling and moved to the operating theatre and lowered onto a huge operating table tubed and monitored. They have all the same equipment as we have for humans, even plastic covers on ADONIS' feet. He is returned to the padded cell until he comes round and then spends a couple of days tied up on a drip. He behaves well but being in hospital is no fun for man or beast and there are some very, poor souls there. Once he is off the drip I am allowed to go and walk him in hand and finally take him home. ADONIS has his stitches out and for a while he seems perfectly normal, however, a few months later the problem recurs.

A new clinic has opened adjacent to a neighbouring stable and the vet suggests I should take him there. We take him over and they are very thorough. They take a swab from his ear, they do an eco-graph and take x-rays of his head in case he has a tumour. All the results came back negative, and they tell me it is psychological. I know him so well and even after the operation he was fine and had absolutely no hang-ups, he has let me touch his ear and put on his bridle in the normal way, however once again he is desperately uncomfortable.

I am researching into all manner of alternatives and have heard about people who talk to animals. I chase it up and there isn't anybody in Spain, but I contact a lady in France. I send her a photo of Adonis and we talk on skype. She tells me ADONIS has been psychologically hurt by a tall dark man, upon reflection the only tall dark man in his life is Miguel the trainer who broke him in at Coronado. Strangely since Pepe and Itzia left Miguel has come back to give classes he has to pass Adonis' stable on the way to and from the indoor school. This lady tells me that he hurt ADONIS' feelings terribly.

According to her, ADONIS, being very noble and generous, gave his all when Miguel was breaking him in. I vaguely recall, when Maria was so ill, Miguel was showing a client dressage horses with a view to buying. When they got to ADONIS, he told his client that he was for sale, but he wasn't good enough for them. According to the French lady ADONIS suffered from acute depression and his ears became super sensitive. It is true too that when we took him on, he was crotchety, Ana even said she didn't want a horse that laid back his ears, pulled faces and threatened to bite her. Strange because he soon became so sweet and affectionate, he is a stallion, but he is gentle. He never bites, he nuzzles you looking for titbits and sometimes blows down my neck when I oil his front hooves, I love that. Carlitos has taught him tricks, he will pull down the zip on his jacket, the tab on the zip is small and he gently takes it in his teeth and pulls it down. Maybe it is only coincidence, but even so I will be careful how I speak in front of any animal from now on, just in case. She also says ADONIS told her he has discomfort in a front foot, he is not lame but doesn't stride out on the hard ground, which proves to be due to the beginnings of bony formation and arthritis for which he can receive treatment. However, sweet words do not appear to be sufficient to relieve his suffering with his ears.

I read about a homeopathic vet from Segovia, I am willing to try anything. We make an appointment, and she comes over; she is surprisingly young and charming. As we walk down the passage before even going into ADONIS' stable, she says, "Poor horse has dermatitis in his ears and it is driving him mad, it itches and if he rubs it is painful." We have been struggling for two years with a string of vets, drugs, two hospitals and an operation and no-one has mentioned dermatitis. They have looked at all sorts of things from infection to a brain tumour. She instantly recognized it from the way he is carrying his head. She gives him some small injections round his ear and leaves me drops to put in his water and a cream to rub in his ear. ADONIS is wary to begin with he has been so uncomfortable for so long. I am as gentle as possible smearing the ointment abundantly inside his ear. After a couple of days, he relaxes and then actually comes towards me and put his head down proffering his poorly ear, psychological my foot! Within a couple of weeks, he is perfectly normal again until the following spring when he shows the first signs again putting his head in the air and moving away when I go to put on his bridle. I ring the homeopathic vet as I have run out of the ointment. She says before coming such a long way for a visit we should try Vaseline and let her know how it goes. I buy some plain Vaseline and smear it liberally inside his ear, the skin feels rough although not as scaly and scabby as it was before, in a few days he is back to normal, so by checking his ears and applying Vaseline maybe twice a week he has no more problems. When I think of the two years suffering, the masses of antibiotics and anti-inflammatories, plus an operation he underwent, not to mention the expense which totalled over 1,000 euros when an old-fashioned cheap tub of Vaseline would have sufficed.

I am riding in the dressage arena one morning when Rosa appears with a gentleman who recognizes ADONIS, he knows Antonio Paramo who bred him. Apart from the brand mark, ADONIS' mother being half German and his father

225

pure Spanish, the man had recognized the stamp of horse. Antonio is trying to breed Spanish horses more apt for classical dressage by introducing some German blood, he has in fact bred some big horses too, Pepe Cubana has been training a lovely big black stallion of the same line but much taller than Adonis. Rosa rents the one passage of boxes to this wealthy businessman who brings his own grooms and riders and a string of dressage horses, again the majority came from Germany and there are some very classy horses. The other passage is then rented by David, who trained in Holland at the same yard as Sergio, Rosa's son, and although young, he is competent and enthusiastic. He loves children and wants to start a riding school. He also takes over the liveries and teaches dressage, so he now looks after ADONIS. It is reassuring to have professionals permanently in the yard and David proves to be meticulous taking care of every detail. Even though he probably thinks I am an eccentric old English lady he follows my furtive instructions to the letter even adding suggestions and advice of his own. Unfortunately, there is tension between the two from the beginning. Gregorio, the businessman, comes to ride with his daughters at weekends when David is at his busiest involving a lot of children and their parents coming and going. David also likes holding birthday parties, having barbecues and summer camps. Gregorio does not approve and gets Rosa to restrict David's activities all very unsatisfactory for everyone. During this period ADONIS and I have fun hacking out with different people usually in the form of "Nanny". Although most people are dedicated to dressage, some want to ride out but have problems being unable or unwilling, to take their horses out alone. ADONIS is so reliable, in front he will go anywhere, behind he is strong but manageable and providing other horses don't come too close he is happy to go side by side. In fact, he comes to life in company and enjoys himself. He loves showing off, I think he was a little bored on his own, he is a bit lazy going away from home and keeps shouting to tell everyone where he is, then much more active going home as indeed many horses are. You would think they spend so much time in the stable they would be happy to go out, but I suppose they are herd animals and tend to want to stay with the group. The animosity grows between David and Gregorio, the latter finally makes Rosa an offer to rent the entire finca. Unfortunately, David is asked to leave, he is bitterly disappointed especially as she informs him by email, one of the hazards of mixing business with friendship. However, he rents stables in El Soto for his horses and the liveries and moves the riding school to another yard temporarily. He has looked after ADONIS very well and so we decide to go with him. Josif, who had previously been the groom at Rosa's for six years is working at El Soto, so knows ADONIS which is also reassuring. Carlos and I know the owners of El Soto, through mutual friends and we have even been to Jordon to a wedding and a holiday with them. Strangely just before we are due to leave Carlos is riding ADONIS down by the river and he loses a shoe. Carlos dismounts to retrieve the shoe and ADONIS gets nervous and escapes before Carlos can re-mount. He takes off at a gallop and we eventually find him at El Soto, he must have sensed there are some mares in season there because it is strange, he didn't head straight home as most horses do at the slightest opportunity. He could have caused havoc but fortunately the head groom hears him and catches him on the other side of the fence. Carlos calls me on the mobile and I go to rescue him in the car and then take him to collect a very excited ADONIS. We find him in a stable and when we bring him out, he puts on quite a show he is beside himself with excitement confirming the mares in season theory! At least his new home will not be altogether strange for him. Whilst there Bea continues to ride Adonis when I go to England, which is lovely as she gives him lots of T.L.C.

Chapter 17

Chapineria

KURRITO is a small horse Paradise situated on the outskirts of Chapineria, an old village nestled in the gently rolling hills in the direction of the enchanting mountain range of Gredos. Although it takes us almost an hour to get there it is always worthwhile. To live in a capital city and be able to spend the day in that glorious wild countryside is surely a luxury. Having driven through the quaint grey stone village, Kurrito is the last gateway on the right, iron gates set at an angle to the road opening on to a small, enclosed area with a little garden on the right, in summer it is full of margaritas. Later that year I buy a Christmas tree with a root hoping it will be happy on my balcony, sadly it is miserably shedding needles. So, with Willems's permission we plant it in Kurrito's little garden, where it flourishes. Willem is passionate about trees; he suffers during the summer droughts and waters every tree he can reach even though he has to pay for every drop of water. Out riding there is a young hawthorn which looks as though it is dying, every time we pass it Willem talks to it apologizing for the inclement climate. His joy when tiny green buds appear on its skinny branches in the spring is overwhelming.

We usually park in the top field beneath a shady tree where there are also some huge boulders and an enclosed lunging ring. We continue, on foot down a slope with a magnificent view across acres of lovely grazing spread out before us. The stable yard is on our right, the stables are old and the doors a bit rickety, but it serves its purpose as each horse knows his or her own stable. They come in twice daily, when they are called, they form a herd and come in loose each one going into their own stable. They have their feed and are checked over or groomed and tacked up for riding.

To the left there is a garage and a long building with a wide-open entrance and a fireplace, next to which there is a large stone bar-b-q with a dome roof.

Someone has made Willem a lovely long table with beautiful ceramic tiles inset on the surface, often they light a fire in winter and have a bar-b-q. It is lovely to huddle round the fire, gazing at that lovely view with the horses looking curiously over the fence in the hopes of stray titbits. This is all enclosed with a high post and rail fence forming a small paddock which is also used to introduce new horses to the tribe before letting them loose with the herd. A little farther on there is a mobile home complete with three bedrooms, living room, bathroom and kitchen where Regi and Willem often stay for the weekend. It must be beautiful to wake up there in the morning. There is a wide veranda running the length of the front complete with awnings where we have many a delightful lunch after a long ride, followed by a "sobremesa" with a lot of horse talk of course, Willem and Regi have many fascinating stories to tell. There are little wooden steps and a handrail leading up to the veranda and a small garden, it is also set in its own little paddock which a few horses are allowed into if they needed extra grazing or deserve a special treat and they stretch their necks over the fence to inspect the table. We have to be careful to shut the little gate too or the little rescue donkey will come up the steps right onto the veranda to join the party.

There are a lot of trees dotted around the property, the majority being holm-oak which have small thick leaves, to withstand the long dry summers, and long dark acorns which the horses adore. When the trees are laden with acorns the horses look like giraffes from a distance, with their heads up in the trees tucking in. They all put on weight as a result, of binging on acorns but they never seem to suffer from colic, nature is wise, and the extra calories set them up to face the cold winter months.

LADY FARMER has a happy retirement in Kurrito along with ISHTAR and YACABO, her first year there is perfect, it is a joy to see her head to tail with ISHTAR in the shade of a big old tree gently swishing the flies off each other's faces, scratching each other's withers with their top teeth, wandering free and grazing, always together One day Carlitos and I go to see them, Willem is about to ride so invites us to join him for a tour of the estate, there is only one spare saddle so Carlitos being a gentleman lets me have it for LADY and he rides ISHTAR bareback. We ride around the perimeter and explore a little for about three quarters of an hour only in walk, but LADY does feel strange behind, not lame but just uncomfortable, which for me confirms that we have taken the right decision to retire her. She runs around happily without a rider and is round and shiny. She has always known my car wherever we have been, and she comes rushing over. She behaves more like a dog than a horse and even with her new freedom she always seems happy to see us and follow us around bunting and nuzzling us, looking for goodies of course, I love that mare so much!

Whilst I am still giving lessons on Saturdays, Carlos often goes over to Kurrito to ride with Willem. He comes back ecstatic, enthusing about the glorious countryside saying he has never experienced anything like it. Carlos rides CHOCOLATE or CHOCCY, as he was known, who is a wide, strong, liver chestnut, gelding with terrific bone and feathers in his heels. He is steady as a rock and will go anywhere, even bulldoze through the undergrowth to find a way through. CHOCCY belongs to Regi but having ridden all her life she has had to give up following her last back operation. She kindly lets Carlos ride him, Carlos says CHOCCY knows more of his secrets than anyone on earth and he solves many a work problem whilst enjoying the magnificent countryside from CHOCCY's broad back. CHOCCY loves people especially Regi, who he follows round in a besotted fashion, and not only for the sugar lumps. However, he has been known to be aggressive towards his own kind, once he cornered and attacked Regi's lovely old mare, who was saved in the nick of time when Mariano arrived on the scene. Following that unfortunate incident Willem divided a section of the finca for CHOCCY and FARO who seems to be the only horse CHOCCY respects. FARO is a grey Portuguese horse, a little portly, he has a problem with his one ear, it suppurates continuously, it has been treated but recurs. The vet says providing it doesn't worry him it is better left alone, and he never showed signs of discomfort when putting on a head collar or bridle or cleaning it.

Willem rides his very dear BENGALI, they are perfect together, he is a little, compact, energetic, bay gelding who was a champion long-distance horse before Willem bought him. Willem rides on the buckle and completely trusts his little horse, if he gets lost, which happens periodically, he just loses the reins and tells Bengali to go home. This method invariable works, except BENGALI has a habit of taking the shortest possible route. The problem being he doesn't always take into account the fact that Willem is on top, hence poor Willem often loses his hat or glasses in the trees and comes home covered in scratches but laughing his head off. Willem also loves to "run", as he puts it, which means to gallop flat out. He rides in normal trousers, which invariable ride up to his knees, and slip-on shoes as he says he likes to feel his horse's sides. Riding behind Willem and

BENGALI when they take off at a gallop, you can see daylight between Willem and the saddle, this together with the ups and downs, twists and turns and low branches is perilous. It is a miracle they stay together, fortunately they invariably do and with apparent ease, I think Willem has a guardian angel!

Eli comes with me one day to Kurrito as I am still teaching her girls and they have ridden ISHTAR and know LADY, Carlitos comes too. We meet Willem and then walk across to the far side of the big field where the horses are grazing, blissfully unaware of our arrival. As always, they are happy to see us a nuzzle us to see if there are any goodies in our pockets, they look really, well and happy. Carlitos asks me to give him a leg up onto ISHTAR, who is a good 18hh, we don't even have a head collar, but Carlitos insists. He sits astride him for a while chatting and patting him then suddenly claps his legs on the old horse's sides and ISHTAR shakes his old head and takes off at a canter towards the stables, when we finally catch up with them, they both seem very chuffed with themselves, it has given the old boy a new lease of life. Laura also visits ISHTAR a couple of times and her mother Carmen continues paying for him to spend the rest of his days at Kurrito. This is a wonderful gesture considering she has never even ridden him, but she insists she is grateful to him because he helped Laura through a difficult time in her life. I wish there were more people with such a caring and generous attitude.

YACABO joins LADY and ISHTAR at Kurrito, he is a poor soul when he arrives, he was very ill towards the end in Coronado, it was touch and go, he was on a drip for some time. His owner the Argentinian dentist and his daughter do not follow me to Las Bridas as she only wants to jump, so they go to some stables run by a military guy where we have been to competitions. They visit YACABO a couple of times, he recovers amazingly as tends to happen in Kurrito, he puts on weight, his old coat shines and he even gets the twinkle back in his eye, but it would be unfair to jump him again. He has done a wonderful job giving his owner confidence and experience round the local shows, but he is old and has earned his retirement. They pay for about three months and then stop paying, they give no explanation and make no contact. I am very, concerned mainly for Willem's sake, I go to the stables where the girl has been riding but they are no longer there, I find out their address and go there several times, no reply, eventually I ask a neighbour who tells me they have moved, no forwarding address, probably gone back to Argentina. People have crisis in their lives and maybe they couldn't afford to pay any more, but why can't they do the right thing and discuss the options. They know Willem will care for the horse even if they abandon him, but I feel responsible as I introduced them to Willem. Willem continues to care for YACABO he has his feed, vaccines and feet trimmed together with love and extra carrots to make up for being abandoned by his family. About a year later YACABO doesn't appear for his breakfast and after an extensive search Mariano finds him under a tree, he died in the night, he just went to sleep.

LADY is having difficulty, she is not moving straight, her quarters are swinging to one side, so Willem calls the vet. After extensive examination, the vet diagnoses neurological problem, as a result of which she is losing control of her hind legs. On bad days he injects her, and she improves considerably, but he says there is no cure, and she will deteriorate little by little, it is sad to see. Although physically she is deteriorating her spirit and her enthusiasm remain intact, she gives her gentle wickers asking for carrots and head butts to protest about the slowness in producing them. The vet says I should put her to sleep, but when I go to see her, she still has a twinkle in her eye and the will to live so I just can't take that decision.

Unfortunately, my father is very ill, and I have to go to England. Willem is so supportive, on more than one occasion rings me to say that LADY is not well and asks permission to call the vet. I tell him I totally trust his judgement and to do whatever he feels necessary. He calls me again when the vet is there with a full report and sometimes again later in the day to tell me she is feeling better and lets me listen to her munching carrots over the phone. This sort of care and consideration means the world to me, especially at such a difficult time. LADY eventually becomes unable to walk in a straight line and progresses in a series of circles, this means she can't walk through a normal stable door. Willem clears out the building where he has his bar-b-q and puts down a bed for her. The entrance is wide and the building long so she can go in and out comfortably. As it is enclosed in the small post and rail paddock, she is free and can talk to her friends over the fence but eat and move uninterrupted, going in and out as she pleases.

However, one day following torrential rain Willem rings me to tell me that LADY has lain down outside and can't get up. They pack straw round her and tried to help her but in vain, so they call the vet. I am working at the time and as I finish my class, I see the message and ring the vet. He tells me that she cannot get up and her breathing is already laboured, he begs me to give him permission to put her to sleep. I am heartbroken and ask him to wait until I arrive. I cancel my next class and head off towards Chapineria. The rain is beating down relentlessly and there has been an accident on the M30 I am stuck on the motorway in stationary traffic for what seems like an eternity. The vet rings me back. He says the conditions are awful and Lady is suffering. He says it was cruel to prolong her suffering for my own selfish satisfaction of being present, especially when there is nothing I can do, only get upset and make things worse. My tears of despair and frustration more than compete with the pelting rain. I am still stuck in the traffic when the vet rings me back to say that she has gone peacefully to sleep. It is dark when I finally get off the motorway, Kurrito will be locked up and in the dark. Somehow in a daze I teach my last evening class and the next morning take off for Kurrito. When I get there Willem has beaten me to it and Lady has already been buried alongside Regi's dear old mare, he assures me that the operation was carried out with the utmost respect and dignity for a truly, wonderful mare. The following spring wild iris spring up above where she was buried, LADY will never to be forgotten.

Although LADY is no longer at Kurrito Willem still invites us to go and ride with him, as Eli and Susan leave Las Bridas I am liberated from giving lessons at the weekend which means I can ride with Carlos. We ride together at Las Bridas thanks to Pepe allowing me to ride his horses and with Carlos, riding ADONIS. On Saturdays we get up early, ride together at Las Bridas then drive an hour and a quarter to Chapineria to ride with Willem, as Carlos often says it is "una paliza" or "a beating" but we love it. On Sunday we have longer rides at Las Bridas especially after harvest racing across the stubble fields, followed by lunch at home with Ana, Carlitos is now studying in the United States. Ana is studying in Madrid; she usually goes out with her friends on Saturday night so is just surfacing when we get home from our ride.

The first horse I ride with Willem is FARO, CHOCCY'S companion. I think he hasn't been ridden for some time and his education must have been scant for there is a distinct lack of braking and steering plus he spooks at everything especially big rocks, of which there are many. I really don't mind it is good to have a challenge and better than a workout in the gym, you can't relax for a second.

Lucinda, the daughter of the couple who brought LADY to Madrid for me, has moved to Madrid and she takes her horse to Willem's. She is looking for land to start her own riding school so has time and Willem asks her if she can school Faro. She only ever rides him in the small, enclosed circle on her own and she insists he should wear a snaffle. He normally wears an egg-butt snaffle which is not at all severe but at least helps me to turn his head. Strangely she never rides out in the country with Willem, I am a snaffle fan too, but safety first and that rough wild country galloping with other horses is rather different from trotting him round a little ring on his own. Being less balanced he also stumbles quite a lot; it is hard to know whether it is due to physical failings or lack of concentration. One day coming home he comes right down when we are on level ground, we are alongside Willem at the time and it shakes him, so he decides to retire him for safety's sake.

So, I start riding GITANO a little black horse with some Arab blood which is especially evident in his perky little dished face. GITANO arrived with his stable mate who has since passed away. The owners were a couple who were expecting a baby, so the husband insisted on retiring the horses. They arrived with the very best of equipment, good quality saddles, bridles, boots, bandages etc. After a few months, the owners stopped paying and it has been impossible to contact them. Yet more people who have taken advantage of Willem's goodness of heart. The last payment being about a year ago, since when GITANO has lacked for nothing. He was very nervous when he first arrived but had settled by the time I met him. Willem suggests that as he has been abandoned and they owe Willem so much money the least we can do is to enjoy him, and he has some shoes put on him so I can ride him. A few months previously, Willem had allowed a boy to ride him unshod in Kurrito and he was fine but will need shoes to go out over the rough terrain on Willem's excursions. GITANO proves to be a joy to ride he is nimble, fast, and light footed yet easy to control with a lovely snaffle mouth. I enjoy our excursions so much more with this delightful little horse.

Willem and Regi have explored the countryside and created trails which they have named. There is the famous "Mariano Route" so named because Mariano has literally cut a trail through the bushes alongside a stream. Part of this route is like a roller coaster dipping down, climbing up, twisting, and turning interspersed with clearings of lush green grass and carpets of wildflowers in the Spring. There is one such clearing alongside a bubbling stream where Willem always allowed the horses to stop and graze for a while whilst we drink in the beauty of our surroundings, Willem refers to this magical place as "McDonalds". On this route we occasionally see deer and once a whole herd flew across the path in front of us. There are also signs of the presence of wild boar where they had been digging with their tusks, we rarely see them for they are shy creatures, but often a horse spook at a rustle in the bushes. Once on this trail an owl came flying directly towards us, it had an enormous wingspan and we looked straight into its eyes as it flew towards us and only a few feet above out heads, a thrilling experience and most unusual as they normally only come out at night. There are several places to cross the stream, the other side of the stream is more open and even more beautiful in its way with lush grass underfoot even in the driest of summers. This Willem called Regi's route, Regi says when she rode there years before she found links to other routes, we have great fun crashing through trees uphill and down dale looking for a way out. Another route Willem has kindly named the "Judith Route" he had been this way with Carlos many times always saying he wanted to take me there. This route begins at the end of Mariano's route there is a steep climb up a wide grass track, as the horses get older, we spare them this climb although the younger horses love it and the climb to the top was well worth the effort there is a 360-degree view of the most amazing countryside as far as you can see. On clear day you can even see the four big skyscrapers in Madrid some 50 kms away, but mostly it is rolling hills in all directions. There is an old stone obelisk on the summit denoting the highest point in the area. We always pause on the top to admire the view and let the horses recover, frequently there are eagles circling not far above our heads it is quite breath-taking.

There are so many varied and beautiful places to ride. There are also open rolling fields no fences occasionally we meet cattle roaming loose. We stumble on small lakes and ponds, then the rolling hills and valleys that eventually lead down to the big river. At one point on this river there is the remains of an old tower, this Willem always refers to as "The Tower of London". Willem however prefers to explore off the route and try to connect the routes cross country which means we come across interesting obstacles or even have to retrace our steps when we find ourselves entangled in a jungle or halfway up a mountain with simply no way forward.

Understandably Regi worries when Willem ventures off on his own, as he so loves to do. We have some tricky moments, luckily Willem is extremely pragmatic. One day he is trying to crash through the undergrowth up a very steep mountainside to the point where it is impossible to proceed. Willem's horse takes two steps backwards and the reins become entangled in a branch pulling them out of Willem's hands and over the horse's head. Willem doesn't panic, he merely holds the front of the saddle and calmly calls over his shoulder "I appear to have lost my reins, can you give me a hand?" I am further down the mountain behind him, I dismount put my horse's reins behind the stirrups hoping for the best and squeeze past Willem's horse to disentangle the reins and hand them back to Willem who waits patiently and thanks me politely. We have to reverse a good way down the mountain before there is room for the horses to turn round. He frequently loses his glasses, usually I find them but on one such occasion I just can't locate them, Mariano goes back to the spot but to no avail. Months later when riding past with his friend Pablo the pilot, Pablo spots them quite by chance, remarkable!

Regi supervises the preparation of the horses and helps Willem to mount, she walks up and opens the gates for us, then sees us safely across the road. While we are riding, she walks round Kurrito and checking all the horses. Regi has been riding all her life and is a fount of knowledge, Willem is very humble saying that he started late and being self-taught relies heavily on her judgement, they make a good team. Willem loves to explore and find new routes, he muses half to himself "If we can just cross this ravine surely over the next hill, we will reach the big river". Following which he points his horse in the said direction despite protests from Carlos and myself of "Willem it is very steep!" which he dismisses with "Don't worry I will ask the horse, he will know best", following which, his bold little Bengali sits on his hocks and slithers down the vertical bank, leaving Carlos and I to follow as best we can, never a dull moment with Willem. We have some wonderful rides usually followed by lunch, often vegetarian for my benefit, also prepared by Willem, on the veranda overlooking Kurrito and other times we go to a venta or the local restaurant, they are happy days.

Chapter 18
Farewell but Not Goodbye

BENGALI is left resting to recover from putting his foot down a rabbit hole. GITANO who is not so young either, shows signs of problems with his tendons too, the terrain is very demanding, we try treating and bandaging him, but he too needs rest. So, after some fruitless horse hunting Willem buys ATARRA from Cristina. ATARRA soon settles and is accepted by the herd, she is a lovely mare but the whole lifestyle is new to her and although she has crossed the river near Las Bridas with no problem whatsoever, some of Willem's stream crossings she finds a bit daunting. The combination of crashing through undergrowth, slithering down steep banks into the water or mud and negotiating tree trunks and roots on the way makes her nervous, she will always follow another horse, but Willem needed a bold horse to go out on his own or in the lead. She is comfortable and fast, which he loves, and he enjoys riding her, but Willem likes to be in front and doesn't want to have to push her. This means that I can ride her which was perfect for me as I already know and love her. ATARRA is easy to jump too, and Willem enjoys jumping a few of the remaining cross-country fences dotted around Kurrito, he even buys a few stands and show jumping poles.

ATARRA is a gentle mare, my dear friend Claire who took over the Riding for the Disabled for me when I moved to Spain comes to stay. She is a nervous rider and has not ridden for some time but feels perfectly at home on ATARRA and loves riding her. ATARRA gets braver out in the country but still needs time to adapt. She responds well to Willem's long rein style of riding, she fretted previously if riders wanted too firm a contact with a tendency to throw her head up in the air in defence. Riding out over rough terrain where she is allowed to stretch her head down to balance, to see where to put her feet and to scramble up and down hills. Her top line changes completely, she developed a beautiful neck with muscle on the top instead of underneath and lovely firm, muscled quarters. However, Willem is still looking for his lead horse to replace BENGALI.

Bea from Las Bridas has a friend with a horse to sell. He keeps him near San Martin de Valdeiglesias, which is in the same direction as Chapineria, so we go to see him. MAXIMO is so called because he is by far the largest horse in the yard, he is a tall, big boned and extremely wide chestnut gelding. The owners are keen on jumping and he has given them a good introduction but is not going to jump much over a meter, so they have bought a new horse with more jumping form. I try him first, he is very, comfortable but a little lazy and as many lazy horses do, when asked for more activity gives a little buck of protest. Willem rides him and seems fine, but not over enthusiastic, consequently I am surprised when he starts negotiating and closes the deal. MAXIMO duly arrives at Kurrito and is introduced into the growing herd, in the beginning he bangs the door when shut in the stable. Mariano and Willem neither being tall of stature have considerable difficulty putting on his bridle, he is tall to start with and has a tendency to put his head in the air. However, both of these hiccups are overcome with time and patience. MAXIMO is rather lazy and not Willem's type at all. He is stubborn in front and inclined to put in the odd buck, which understandably does not endear him to Willem. MAXI has always been ridden with stick and spurs, but no way will Willem even consider carrying a stick. He likes riding a horse that wants to go and hates having to push a horse along all the while, apart from which he finds it exhausting so it really isn't very successful! I must say I understand and agree with him, I also prefer to ride a forward going horse. On one occasion Willem is persevering with MAXIMO who is still new to the job, Carlos is in front on CHOCCY then me on ATARRA followed by Willem and MAXI. We are negotiating the descent of a very steep, almost vertical, bank. I wait to make sure MAXI is just behind us but once committed to the descent can't stop. MAXI balks on the top and when Willem encourages him, he gives an enormous buck landing halfway down the bank, they almost land on top of us and how Willem stays on board I shall never know. I shall never forget the sight of the huge MAXI in mid-air above our heads he crashes down right behind us skidding a full meter and how he stays on his feet is a miracle. Following this episode, we take it in turns to ride MAXI, there is another girl riding with Willem, so Gloria rides him too, with work he improves considerably but is still too lazy for Willem, especially in front, and an almost impossible for Willem on his own. About a year passes by and one day old

BENGALI comes trotting towards us completely sound, rest and nature have worked their miracle. Willem is so happy, he rides him round Kurrito to make sure he is okay, has him shod and starts to enjoy his riding again with more carefree adventures.

BALI left Las Bridas and went to Torrejon. Susan hoped that having him nearer home she would be able to ride him more often. Susan is a businesswoman, she works all hours and is a grandmother, she never has a minute to spare, hence she doesn't ride BALI very often. When she does manage to ride him, he is too fresh having had too little exercise and frequently runs off with her or nearly falls over, so it isn't working.

DUNCAN is in the same yard, Annemarie is there too, Annemarie helps Susan as much as she can, but there are no turnout facilities, so Annemarie has more than enough with work and her own dear FRAILUCO. Susan rings me to ask for Willem's number for DUNCAN's family as they are having problems, their old cob TANKE has sadly died and the mother who rode with her children is very, ill, so they are looking for somewhere to turn DUNCAN out. I give her Willem's number, but they find somewhere nearer home, so they can still go and see him. A week later Susan rings me again to ask if it is possible for BALI to go to Kurrito.

BALI arrives and soon settles into his new life in Kurrito, he loves his new-found freedom and falls in love with ATARRA. The first few times I ride him out he is excited but does not take long to adapt to his new role. In fact, he loves going in front, but Willem is back on his faithful BENGALI and insists, rightly enough, that BALI doesn't know the way and Susan is happy for me to ride BALI to get him used to his new environment. He rapidly comes into his own, he loves exploring and boldly tackles any challenge that comes up, he is in his element.

Eventually Susan comes to ride him, I am riding ATARRA, and Willem is out in front on his beloved BENGALI. I have been riding BALI in a snaffle but have put on the curb as Susan has never ridden him in a snaffle, plus the fact that he has run away with her on more than one occasion, so understandably she feels safer with a curb. We set off and BALI is very agitated, he follows ATARRA because he adores her, but he is getting more and more wound up, jigging sideways, stamping his feet and leaping about. I think he must have a horsefly biting him and driving him mad, I break a branch off a tree to try to brush off a horsefly I feel sure is under his belly. Willem glances over his shoulder at the commotion and just comments "Why doesn't she loosen her reins?" I grimace and pass the message on to Susan, she is dubious, but with encouragement little by little she lengthens her reins with which BALI relaxes, we are both impressed with Willems quick analysis of the situation. BALI feels Susan's understandable anxiety, plus the curb, the short reins impeding his forward movement and reminding him of past schooling battles, he became agitated and stressed. It proved a positive experience for both, but sadly Susan rarely comes to ride him, a pity as BALI is a wonderful addition to the team.

BALI and ATARRA have both been known to be difficult to catch and when they start running together all of the horses take off. Willem therefor decides to separate them from the herd, and they have a large field to themselves which means at least they can't disappear from sight and start everyone else running. They are still naughty sometimes, but I find if you can catch one of them the other will follow to the stables like a lamb. They are inseparable. One day ATARRA loses a front shoe so can't be ridden, I have to ride BALI out without her, he is completely wild and distraught for the first twenty minutes. When the situation is reversed and we try to ride ATARRA out without BALI, he crashes through the fence in his desperation to go out with his beloved. We put him in his stable but have to shut the top door or he will break out, it is love! As frequently happens when horses have been stabled for years and then experience freedom they don't ever want to be shut in a stable again and this is so in BALI's case. In the beginning to try to groom and tack him up in the stable is a nightmare, he keeps wheeling about, unwittingly plastering you against the wall and trying to make a dash through the door. Someone comes up with the idea of tying him up in the yard near ATARRA's stable and it works, there he is as quiet as a lamb.

Willem has signed us up for a sponsored ride to preserve the "Via Pecuaria" literally "Drover's Road" for practical purposes "Bridle Paths". We are going to start from a village some way away so are due to be picked up by Jesus with his horsebox, he agrees to pick us up at 10:00am sharp. Mariano and Willem say they will have the horses ready, and I go early to ride ADONIS and then drive over to arrive at 10:00am. I arrive at the same time as Jesus, he is a lovely man and excellent at transporting horses, he is quiet but firm and horses always load and travel well with him. Once he took Willem and Regi, together with car, furniture and horses to Sweden when Willem went there to work. Horses that travel with Jesus have no fear of travelling. I greet him and make my way to the stables while he is dropping the ramp. When I get there Willem and Mariano are chatting and the horses are still out in the field, far from being ready. I confess I am more than agitated, something one should never be around horses. I have been rushing like mad all week and then from 6 a.m. a Saturday day to make it on time and patience isn't my strong point, certainly not under these circumstances. I tell them the transport is already waiting and storm off down the field to catch ATARRA and BALI. I still need to learn the age-old lesson "more haste less speed", where horses are concerned this applies without exception. BALI has become so good and easy to handle I forget his tricky past and am rushing. He is tied up outside as usual and as I approach him with the saddle, Jesus came rushing down the slope to see what is going on, BALI is startled, he leaps in the air knocks me off my feet and lands squarely on my foot. Luckily, I am wearing good riding boots but there is a clear horseshoe shape imprinted in the leather and the pain is excruciating. I hop round the yard huffing and puffing and muttering the unspeakable under my breath. Then hobbling as best I can, continue with the preparations dismissing Regi's concern. Poor BALI is very, nervous and I know he will not be happy about the horse box, thank goodness Jesus is here, he is brilliant, firm and strong but quiet and patient. We load ATARRA first, she loads like a lamb and BALI is beside himself calling out to her, even so with him twirling around it is not an easy task to get him on board, finally in a series of leaps he charges up the ramp. To my dismay Jesus orders me to unload him and repeat the exercise, my foot is thumping and my heart sinks, but I know he is right. His methods work without fail and thankfully at the end of the day it only takes half the time to load BALI. The ride is fine, Jesus kindly helps me to mount and once in the saddle my foot is more comfortable.

Annemarie is there with FRAILUCO and a group from her stables, but FRAILUCO is so excited we can't really ride together or chat, she has her hands full! The owner of her stables recognises BALI and tells me I am mad to be riding him in a snaffle but thank goodness he behaves beautifully. The ride is long and too slow for Willem who loves to "run", also it pours with rain and we are all soaked to the skin despite rain jackets, the saddles squelch and we are a very bedraggled sight as we complete the ride. However, we enjoyed the outing despite the adversity and inclement weather conditions. When I get home, it takes a while to get my boot off and my sock is soaked in dried blood and stuck to my foot, I have to soak it to remove the sock, there is a sizeable cut and my whole foot is swollen and bruised, I can't wear my shoes, so I wear Carlos' shoes to work for about three weeks and lose my big toenail!

VIVACCI is not a happy or generous horse, maybe a difficult start in life or just his personality. His owner stopped riding him after she had her baby and bought herself a new horse, so she sent him to Kurrito. It is a pity as he is not old and could be fun for some young person but needs someone with experience. Initially Suzanna, his owner, had lessons with Juan an Olympic rider. I saw VIVACCI run off with him and he could neither turn nor stop him fortunately they were in an enclosed arena. She says we can ride him, but I know him as I rode him and looked after him at Las Bridas when she was pregnant. He could give some nasty fly bucks and would try to whip round and bolt for home. He never had me off, but he is strong and frankly I don't fancy battling with him on the rough terrain around Kurrito. Furthermore, if I ride him Willem will want to ride him too apart from which we already have plenty of lovely horses to ride, so VIVACCI joins the herd. I try to befriend him, but he is terribly jealous, if other horses come up to me, which they invariably do, he attacks them, he is just an unhappy horse. With a strange new environment, he is even more on the defensive, I feel rather sorry for him. After a few months he goes down with colic, Mariano injects him, but he gets worse, so they rush him off to the vet who operates and saves his life. Suzanna refuses to pay the vet's bill and said she can no longer afford to pay for his keep either, she says she will give him to Willem. They say don't look a gift horse in the mouth, but poor VIVACCI will only bring worry and expense to Willem. Suzanna rings me saying she is having financial problems, which is as may be. However, I tell her that from an outsider's point of view that is hard to understand when she has a house, her own business and another horse in training in an expensive stable with an Olympic rider, but she doesn't budge. She says she owes money at the other stable so can't leave. I fear it is yet another case taking advantage of Willem's kindness of heart. He of course pays the vet and continues to care for the horse. About a year later VIVACCI is very, ill again, he can hardly walk it is a kind of laminitis. Of course, Willem rings the vet and has him treated. We ring Suzanna to explain and see if she will share the vet's bill, she opts for putting him down, which is totally against Willem's principles. Once more miraculously he recovers and later befriends an old donkey also rescued by Willem. He settles down, seems more friendly and even lets me rub his face without laying back his ears, if food is not produced, he also lets me stroke the other horses and refrains from attacking them. This is a treat, I love to have a little chat with them all one by one, rub their heads, scratch their withers, check their legs and feet and now VIVACCI too.

BOMBA the old donkey mare is in a sorry state when she arrives, she has been at the riding school near where Willem lives and has been used for breeding but is now too old, she is skinny and her coat is awful, staring with clumps of hair and bald patches. The owners were going to put her down. Willem knows Regi loves donkeys and asks if he can have her. BOMBA, who everyone thinks has gone to Kurrito to end her days, soon recovers. She is also a Houdini and moves around Kurrito as she pleased regardless of electric fences. A year later she is unrecognizable round and shiny and happy, the horses accept her and at last VIVACCI has a buddy.

Cristina and Rosa have two lovely German Oldenburg brood mares, they have bred them for several years but have had bad luck and lost a couple of yearlings, another wind sucked badly, luckily Merete bought him. Rosa's last filly had an awful accident she tried to jump over the stable door and broke her shoulder following which the poor thing was confined to a box for almost a year. One brood mare came to Willem for a while but later was sent to Andalucía on loan for breeding. The injured filly ROXI is eventually allowed in a tiny paddock then one a little larger. However, when they trot her round the lunging ring, she isn't level, the vet says that possibly her one foreleg is shorter than the other after the break and of course she has no muscle. They can't even register her for breeding if she isn't sound, so decide to turn her out with Willem thinking she will either come sound or get worse and they will take it from there.

ROXI is young and ecstatic with her newfound freedom, she wants to run and play all day, the problem being most of her playmates are getting rather long in the tooth for her antics. Everyone loves her and after some time she seems to be moving better. She is so friendly and follows Regi everywhere even trying to get into the car with her when she wants to go home. Rosa decides she doesn't want to sell her but will give her, on permanent loan, to a good home. The blacksmith is also in love with her, but Willem says he wants to have her, but he is not sure whether to ride her or to breed from her, he is just convinced he wants her, and Rosa readily agrees. We decide to start working her to see if she will stay sound. I start her off but can only work with her once a week and then only a quick half hour after riding with Willem. She behaves well and soon she is wearing her saddle and bridle and lunging nicely, but she is a quality mare and to complete the job she will need working every day and so Willem decides to send her away to be properly, trained. I am hoping he will send her to David, where I have Adonis. David is particularly good with young horses I could continue working with her, but he sends her to his friend and neighbour in Boadilla. I understand as the stables are next to his house so he can follow her training closely and, Regi and his granddaughter can also visit her. After a month they invite me over to see her, she has lost weight, muscle, and her personality, she is so quiet. Javier is old school military style and although his wife is working with her, they obviously have her on rations of hay and water to keep her quiet, whereas at Kurrito she had good food and plenty of exercise and was fit, happy and full of herself. Before Willem can try her, she goes lame, so he takes her back to Kurrito and toys with the idea of breeding from her. Willem and Regi eventually decide that to have a foal at Kurrito would disrupt the peace that now reigns there, plus the fact they are both over eighty and to be realistic for Willem to start riding a four-year-old at the age of eighty-four is not practical, although knowing Willem he would be game to try. Meanwhile the blacksmith is very keen to have her for breeding, I consult Rosa who trusts our judgement, I have met Jose the blacksmith, who certainly has patience and loves horses. He has several horses at home and has bred them, they are all Arabs and as he is a fairly, tall man, so he is anxious to breed a bigger horse. Due to circumstances beyond our control, we are unable to go and inspect her new home before she leaves. She is unwilling to load in the trailer and so Jose decides to lead her home on foot, some 12 kilometres and two villages away. His daughters go with him, he says that way he will get to know her on the way, he certainly is not lacking in kindness and patience. When we go to see her, we are disappointed in the stabling. Fortunately, the horses are out most of the time and have lovely green fields, but the stables consist of standing stalls, admittedly wide and spacious, but the horses are tied up with a chain around their necks like cows.

Regi and I exchange glances and our hearts fall. I explain she was unused to that kind of situation and ask if he could close the bottom of her stall so she could be free or at least for her to wear a head collar instead of a chain. He neither understands nor agrees and argues the chain is much better for her as her head is free. I tell Rosa who offers similar suggestions to the ones I have already made. I try to visit ROXI from time to time, Jose rides her quietly mostly at walk as the first year he does not manage to get her in foal. The following year she is in foal, we are much happier about the situation as she looks wonderfully well, round, shiny and very relaxed and happy. On one visit he lunges her a little, to show us she is definitely irregular, when going round with her injured shoulder on the inside, all the more reason to be overjoyed that she is in foal to a French horse belonging to his neighbour.

Willem buys yet another horse. He tries a 12yr old stallion in a school and likes him but says he can't have a stallion turned out with the other horses, so the dealer has the horse castrated. The horse's owner had died, and the horse had been rather abandoned. Willem feels sorry for him, so he decides to buy him. Unfortunately, castration at that age doesn't always change the behaviour of the horse. This proves so in the case of POLEO, plus the fact that although he was a perfect gentleman in the school he is not used to hacking and less so alone, he rears and ran backwards when Willem tries to ride him out. Willem does not have the heart to send him back as POLEO had spent months shut in a stable after his previous owner died. As a result, POLEO has his own field and is on standby until one of us has the time to go and help Willem re school him.

During this time Willem goes back to the man who sold him his dear BENGALI and buys yet another horse, a younger horse with the same breeding and very, similar in looks to his dear BENGALI. This horse has also competed successfully in R.A.I.D.s (long distance riding competitions). Willem calls him HERMANO which means "brother" in Spanish, he is very forward going and quite sharp, but Willem is delighted because he can go anywhere on his own with him. Initially the horse just wants to go off at a gallop as soon Willem lands in the saddle as he had been trained that way. Apparently, they get fit on a horse walker and only ever ridden at a gallop. However, Willem is not deterred and with patience and miles of walking HERMANO calms down and adapts to his new role. With HERMANO comes MACARIO, they had been stable companions and the owner wants them to go together, saying he will be an ideal guest horse and offering Willem a good deal. While recovering from my operation I ride MACARIO out with Willem, he is well behaved except for the transition to canter when he had the disconcerting habit of thrusting his head to the floor. They both become stronger with the good life at Kurrito, so Willem is advised to reduce their hard feed which helps a little. The horses really don't need the amount of food Willem gives them, they are all a little too well, with a tendency to being overweight, but if I said anything to Willem, he always says he likes his horses like his ladies with curves!

For us change is on the horizon once more. I retire and as Carlos has a new job in Turkey, I plan to accompany him. Unfortunately, I have to have a heart operation before joining him, so for the first time in over sixty years, except for having the children, I am unable to ride for a while. Eventually David builds his own yard, but Bea decides she doesn't want to go there, she is still friendly with Rosa, and following the split between David and Rosa it was an uncomfortable situation for them both. Adonis is still with David who and amazing for his age and David has done a wonderful job creating excellent installations and a happy atmosphere.

Once recovered and having moved-house I go to Turkey which is another story and another experience. Sadly, I can only ride when I return to Spain. Strangely when you ride every day it seems effortless but when you haven't ridden for a month or so and then ride every day you really feel those riding muscles! On my return Willem kindly lets me ride HERMANO, Carlos rides MACARIO and Willem rides his old BENGALI but only goes gently. Willem insists Carlos and I gallop on ahead, we have the most amazing ride, his new little horse is fabulous really, forward going, and fast.

For us change is on the horizon once more. I retire and as Carlos has a new job in Turkey, I plan to accompany him. Unfortunately, I have to have a heart operation before joining him, so for the first time in over sixty years, except for having the children, I am unable to ride for a while. I have known and loved so many four-legged friends. They have taught me so much and I have loved them all in different ways. Our dear friend Willem sadly passes away, he was charming although we know he had been a bit of a lad. Poor Regi now eighty-four has two months to re home the ten horses still in Kurrito as the lease is up on the land. I support her as much as I can from a distance. I immediately email the owners of BALI and VIVACCI to inform them of the situation. VIVACCI's owner never replies, however Susan BALI's owner and her friend Eli set about looking for solutions, as does my dear friend Annemarie. David also says he will take a client over to see them which he does, sadly POLEO is too small, and MAXI is lame the day they go. Finally, they all find new homes, a friend of Regi's friend Javier takes BALI and BENGALI to Escorial to give rides to small children. The previous owner of HERMANO and MACARIO takes them back to Gredos and he also takes a shine to MAXI so takes him too. Worryingly this leaves the really, old ones CHOCCY, GITANO and BOMBA who is well over thirty, then there is poor misfit VIVACCI, however the man who buys POLEO says he has a lot of land and will take the other horses too, so they go to Galapagar. I just hope these old friends are well, safe, and happy in their new homes.

ADONIS stays with David who knows him and his little problems with his ears and his feet and has always cared for him exceptionally well. ADONIS goes out every day in his own paddock, he goes on the horse walker and is ridden once during the week, sometimes more. Bea goes at weekends to ride him and give him apples and T.L.C for which I am very, grateful. Eventually David builds his own yard, but Bea decides she doesn't want to go there, she is still friendly with Rosa, and following the split between David and Rosa it was an uncomfortable situation for them both. ADONIS, still with David, is amazing for his age, now twenty-six, and David has done a wonderful job creating excellent installations and a happy atmosphere in his own yard.

In Turkey we are living in Istanbul an enormous city with horrendous traffic. I visit two stables both in the city with the only place to ride being and overcrowded indoor school. Both are extremely expensive and competitive plus the fact it would take me two hours each way by car to get there. As Carlos needs the car for work it is impossible. I devote myself to the stray dogs and trying to learn the language.

Whilst in Turkey my mother has a fall and breaks her hip, at the age of ninety-three and so needs full-time care. So now I am in England and horseless except for my visits to Spain with intensive riding to compensate. However, I am also fortunate to have the occasional ride on Sue's friend's horses at Lee's stables, Gillie has kindly allowed me to ride her horses, Pat lets me ride her dear Jake a little coloured horse who is sweet, when you are sitting on him, he has one brown ear and one white. Occasionally I ride Elaine's FRED who is a character, also Lee's daughter Jo allows me to ride her daughter's super pony Mr DARCY and her lovely horse JOEY. I am so fortunate that horses find their way back into my life when all seems lost and so grateful to these lovely friends for allowing me to share their equine treasures.

My equine fever has not abated in the slightest. I still get butterflies in my tummy when I gaze into a horse's eyes. I still dream of a cottage in the country with a few stables and paddocks, with horses outside the back door, who knows? I would love to take care of ADONIS in his final years, and I am sure there will be more four legged friends sometime in the future. I cannot express my gratitude to each and every one of these noble friends or thank them enough for so many treasured memories.

I would like to thank friends and family for their encouragement and support and Annemarie without whom I would never have embarked on this journey of reminiscence. I am so grateful to all the wonderful people mentioned in this tale and apologise for any errors, as I have simply recounted from memory. Recalling all these varied and wonderful experiences I realise how fortunate I have been and send my heartfelt thanks to all those wonderful friends both four legged and two!